Mormons in Paris

SCÈNES FRANCOPHONES:

STUDIES IN FRENCH AND FRANCOPHONE THEATER

Series Editor
Logan J. Connors
University of Miami

Dedicated to scholarship on French-language theater, *Scènes francophones* publishes theoretically and historically informed research on dramatic texts and productions from medieval France to the contemporary French-speaking world. Linguistically focused but broad in scope, this series features monographs and multi-authored volumes on dramatic literatures, theories, and practices.

Scènes francophones, which publishes in English, welcomes new research on specific playwrights or actors as well as analysis of particular theaters, dramatic repertoires, and performance spaces. Research in which theater plays a leading role among other genres, themes, or institutions is also encouraged. This series supports research on the social, economic, and cultural history of theater across time periods, from hexagonal France to the reaches of the French-speaking world today.

Titles in the Series

Mormons in Paris: Polygamy on the French Stage, 1874–1892
Edited and translated by Corry Cropper and Christopher M. Flood

Playing the Martyr: Theater and Theology in Early Modern France
Christopher Semk

Acting Up: Staging the Subject in Enlightenment France
Jeffrey M. Leichman

Mormons in Paris

Polygamy on the French Stage, 1874–1892

Edited and translated by

CORRY CROPPER

AND CHRISTOPHER M. FLOOD

Bucknell University | University Press

LEWISBURG, PENNSYLVANIA

Library of Congress Cataloging-in-Publication Data

Names: Cropper, Corry, editor, translator. | Flood, Christopher M., 1975- editor, translator. | Leroy, Louis, 1812–1885. Mormons à Paris. English. | Mars, Antony, 1862–1915. Douze femmes de Japhet. English. | Bernède, Arthur, 1871–1937. Bijou de Stéphana. English.
Title: Mormons in Paris : polygamy on the French stage, 1874–1892 / edited and translated by Corry Cropper and Christopher M. Flood.
Other titles: Berthelier chez les mormonnes. English. | Scènes francophones.
Description: First edition. | Lewisberg, Pennsylvania : Bucknell University Press, [2020] | Series: Scènes francophones : studies in French and Francophone theater | Includes bibliographical references and index.
Identifiers: LCCN 2019059072 (print) | LCCN 2019059073 (ebook) | ISBN 9781684482368 (paperback) | ISBN 9781684482375 (hardcover) | ISBN 9781684482382 (epub) | ISBN 9781684482399 (mobi) | ISBN 9781684482405 (pdf)
Subjects: LCSH: French drama (Comedy)—Translations into English. | French drama—19th century—Translations into English. | Mormons in literature. | Polygamy in literature. | LCGFT: Drama.
Classification: LCC PQ1240.E7 M67 2020 (print) | LCC PQ1240.E7 (ebook) | DDC 842/.809382—dc23
LC record available at https://lccn.loc.gov/2019059072
LC ebook record available at https://lccn.loc.gov/2019059073

A British Cataloging-in-Publication record for this book is available from the British Library.
All images courtesy of Bibliothèque Nationale de France.

♾ The paper used in this publication meets the requirements of the American National Standard for Information Sciences—Permanence of Paper for Printed Library Materials, ANSI Z39.48-1992.

www.bucknelluniversitypress.org

Distributed worldwide by Rutgers University Press.

Manufactured in the United States of America.

CONTENTS

Mormons in Paris

INTRODUCTION

In 1883, the Parisian theater critic H. Moreno explained that *Carmen*, Bizet's famous opéra comique, initially suffered from sluggish ticket sales because its scandalous heroine offended bourgeois families: "Marriage interviews, representing 20% of the box-office, were significantly hampered; in their nuptial loges, young fiancées could not find enough fans to hide their blushes."[1] It is worth pausing on the statistic Moreno cites: a full 20 percent of the Opéra Comique's sales came from theatergoers attending so their marriage-eligible children could meet suitable spouses and so they could negotiate terms of their children's marriages.[2] Ludovic Halévy, the librettist who wrote *Carmen*, explained that the director of the Opéra Comique, Adolphe de Leuven, opposed staging Bizet's masterpiece in these terms: "Carmen! . . . Mérimée's Carmen! . . . Isn't she assassinated by her lover? . . . And this world of thieves, bohemians, and cigar-makers! . . . At the Opéra Comique! . . . the theater of families! . . . the theater for marriage interviews! . . . Every night we have five or six loges rented out for these interviews . . . You'll make our public flee . . . !"[3] The plays in this volume—*Mormons in Paris* (1874), *Berthelier Meets the Mormons* (1875), *Japheth's Twelve Wives* (1890), and *Stephana's Jewel* (1892)—filled with humor, intrigue, and marriage, are the very types of plays that Leuven wanted produced in his theater in order to keep his middle-class, marriage-obsessed public happy. Unlike *Carmen*, which was set in Europe and featured European characters, these plays all feature Mormons: members of a distant, exotic, American religion that at first glance seem strangely out of place in Parisian theaters.[4] But given Mormonism's experiments with religion, family, gender roles, and marriage—a lot of marriage—it became the ideal framework for examining at arm's length the key issues at the center of political and social life in Third Republic France. For French playwrights and authors, it was much easier to work out these complicated social issues by representing a community that, because of its otherness and sheer distance from Paris, could be depicted and laughed at without negative repercussions from ticket buyers or government censors.[5]

While the Catholic Church had long been the arbiter of marriage and family, secular republican values came to dominate the political and cultural landscape after the start of the Third Republic in 1870. In their essay about marriage in nineteenth-century France, Rachel Mesch and Masha Belenky explain: "The institution of marriage underwent radical transformations during this period. These changes were sparked by numerous revisions of inheritance and paternity legislation, the rise of companionate marriages in a new bourgeois society, the introduction of educational reforms that expanded women's roles both within and beyond the domestic sphere, and the emergence of modern medicine and the fields of psychiatry and sexology."[6] The National Assembly—and society as a whole—debated what the family should look like in the new republic. Divorce was legalized in 1884, and gender roles began to slowly evolve as French women petitioned for better education, more equitable laws, and more independence. In the late nineteenth century, the Parisian theater not only became a venue for matchmaking and marriage negotiations, but also largely replaced the Catholic Church as the social focal point where relationships and family norms could be explored and established. In her book *Legislating the French Family*, Jean Elisabeth Pedersen insists that debates about women's rights and the French Civil Code "occurred not only in parliament, in the periodical press . . . but also, especially, at the theater."[7] Given this historical context, Mormonism and its attendant polygamous families became a significant subject on the Parisian stage. As France was questioning its own definition of marriage and family, playwrights turned to an American religion where an experiment with marriage, divorce, and gender roles was playing out in real time.

In 1865, the social theorist Hippolyte Taine turned his attention and his pen to Mormons. After detailing their history and theology, he concluded:

> We can thank the Mormons for the perilous experiment they are conducting on themselves for our benefit. Nothing is more useful to history than grand projects tested out on thousands of people over many years, under our eyes, and in precise, well-defined par-

> ameters. This experiment, conducted in an isolated location, in what could be considered a closed community, will be both clear and instructive. We need to let the mixture ferment, and we will observe the outcome in a century. But one conclusion is already emerging. We have judged our century the way educated Romans judged the century of Augustus; we have found it prudent, intelligent, reasonable, and even skeptical; we told ourselves we had pacified, controlled, or calmed the all-powerful internal monster, the credulous and passionate imagination; we thought we had buried—beneath a mountain of reasons, of positivist documents, of science, of shared education, of the popular press—the fool that every man carries within himself. We were wrong. Now we can observe a civilization of businessmen, proud of their practical common sense, standing on the bedrock of three centuries of established scientific knowledge, whose freewheeling Protestantism has created a breach, and suddenly, through this breach, they have released the fool.[8]

Taine's assertion—that unrestrained religious belief, specifically Mormonism, had unleashed the radical monster squelched by Enlightenment rationality—implies the existence of a cultural unconscious, an atavistic impulse with the potential to undermine centuries of progress and sink modern civilization. The silver lining was that the experiment was being conducted in isolation, quarantined in the distant Rocky Mountains. But what may be most critical in Taine's stark analysis is his repeated use of a word describing what Mormonism had uncaged and what it represents: "the fool." In the French original, the word Taine uses is *le fou*. But in addition to "fool," the word *fou* can also mean a "jester," an oft-disguised eccentric character who uses humor to speak truth to power and to question the status quo. This second definition reveals how Mormons are portrayed in nineteenth-century French literature: superficially different from their French counterparts, often ridiculous, frequently disguised, but always revealing truth about French political, cultural, economic, and social issues. In the second half of the nineteenth century, the figure of the Mormon was used to reveal truth and explore hypocrisies in French perspectives on the subjects of social class, colonialism, the family, divorce, and gender roles.

By associating Mormonism with the fool or jester, Taine evokes the medieval Feast of Fools, a period during carnival where the poor and dispossessed ruled as sovereigns; where the fools were seen as wise and the wise as foolish; where high and low, sacred and profane came into contact in unexpected ways.[9] Mormonism—in these plays and in other French fictional works from the period that feature Mormons—opens a space for social classes to mix, women to command, and drunk Parisian coachmen to become apostles. But this is more than just a ritualistic reversal to provoke laughter. Seeing these shifts, even momentarily, promotes reimagining a world where social class is more fluid and where women play a role in the decision-making process of the body politic. Though the plays generally end in a conventional fashion with a traditional marriage on the horizon or with middle-class monogamy restored, the trip through Mormonism allows nineteenth-century audiences to see and experience a microcosm of the changing political and social landscape of their own country and to rethink conventional hierarchies and systems of power. In short, these plays release the *fou*.

Today in France, even with a Mormon temple in Paris and a concerted public-relations effort, Mormonism scarcely receives a mention. But in the nineteenth century, Mormons appeared frequently in French fictional works. At the conclusion of Paul Duplessis's 1859 five-volume novel *Les Mormons*, one character asks another: "What do you think of the renowned and mysterious Mormons who have captured our attention for the past several years?"[10] In the 1874 play *Mormons in Paris*, a character describes Mormons as "The . . . men newspapers speak of so often" (act I, scene 3, hereafter I.3). In nineteenth-century France, Mormons were, indeed, *often spoken of*: in plays, novels, comics, music, the press, political and sociological treatises, and travel narratives.

In nineteenth-century America, Mormons were largely depicted as everything that good Americans were not. Summing up the figure of the fictionalized Mormon, Terryl Givens writes, "What all such representations share is the function of throwing into stark relief the *un*-Christian, *un*-American, *un*-Western nature of the Mormon religion."[11] Spencer Fluhman shows how the negative portrayal of Mormons allowed a fractured country to unify: "Through public condemnation of what Mormonism was, Protestants defined just what American religion could be."[12] Paul Reeve demonstrates that Mormons were thought of as an inferior race, as a breed wholly separate from Americans at a time when "whiteness dominated the social, political, and economic life of the country."[13] Most pertinent to this volume is the work by Megan Sanborn Jones *Performing American Identity in Anti-Mormon Melodrama.* Jones analyzes "nineteenth-century anti-Mormon melodramas to expose how their representation of Mormon deviance was a foil against which American virtues and values were performed."[14] Jones continues: "In these melodramas, Mormons were portrayed as rapists, murderers, and Turks—all characters anathema to mainstream American culture."[15]

But in nineteenth-century French literature, including the four musical comedies in this collection, rather than standing in opposition, Mormons are represented as having a great deal in common with the French. Unlike American (and English) anti-Mormon melodrama, these plays are not really anti-Mormon at all.[16] They may inaccurately portray Mormons and frequently joke about them, and they all prominently feature polygamy, but they share none of the vitriol found in American representations of Mormons. The title of the 1874 play *Mormons in Paris* implies that Mormons are in France to begin with . . . they are in Paris and may be all around the theatergoers! In *Berthelier Meets the Mormons,* the key Mormons in Salt Lake City happen to all be French. In *Stephana's Jewel* Mormons are family. And in *Japheth's Twelve Wives,* Mormons come to Paris to stay. In these plays, the *fou* described by Hippolyte Taine leaves the isolation of its Rocky Mountain quarantine and comes to the heart of civilization. In France, Mormons were viewed as chameleons of sorts and as such could be seen as a perfect metaphor for early Third Republic France where wealth, class, political and cultural capital, and even marriage became fluid and negotiable.

MORMONISM, AMERICANISM, AND ORIENTALISM

Mormonism, founded in 1830 in the United States, was occasionally mentioned in the French press before 1850; but after 1856, it became a regular subject in news and literature. In a novel titled *Les Mormons,* published in 1859, Paul Duplessis's narrator writes, "Mormonism was much less popular in Europe in 1855 than it is today: it was only known through improbable stories, recounted in American papers, filled with grotesque and scandalous scenes; it had not yet raised the banner of revolt against its own country; it grew in silence, in the least explored solitudes of the New World."[17] The shift in perception of Mormons from 1855 to 1859 came about due to coverage in the press of the so-called Utah War (when U.S. troops were sent to take control of the Mormon territory); this attention would eventually coalesce in the publications of works about Mormons by well-known French social thinkers Jules Rémy, Elisée Reclus, and Hippolyte Taine. Mormonism was seen as a uniquely American religion. Consequently, the plays collected in this book provide insight into how the French viewed Americans in the late nineteenth century.

Japheth's Twelve Wives begins with this description of Japheth's home in Salt Lake City: "A large room with a wide bay window upstage that opens onto an exotic countryside. . . . Furniture is made of bamboo. Exotic plants can be seen." This fanciful description of Utah fed into the French imaginary of that time, that is, into the collective network of symbols, values, and beliefs that a culture accepts as real at a specific historical moment. In this case, it grew out of a misconception about warm climates that can be traced back to Diderot's eighteenth-century *Encyclopédie*: "In very hot climates, love was a blind and impetuous desire for both sexes, a corporeal function, an appetite, a cry of nature, *in furias ignesque ruunt*" (entry *climat, méd*).[18] In the nineteenth century, though he rejects the formulaic application of the principle, Alexis de Tocqueville nevertheless cites the same adage: "I do not deny that in certain climates the passions which are occasioned by the mutual attraction of the sexes are particularly intense."[19] Since polygamy was practiced in Salt Lake City, the assumption in France was that the climate there must of necessity be comparable to the climate in the "Orient," where polygamy was also practiced. Hence, the desert of the American West resembles the deserts of Persia or Africa. Even the architecture depicted in the set (visible in the cast photo, figure 1) exhibits a decidedly Middle Eastern style. What's more, when Japheth arrives on stage, he is dressed like and has the trappings of a colonial master: "Japheth follows behind [his wives] and a black child carries their parasols. Japheth is dressed entirely in white in a fanciful costume and carries a large umbrella" (I.5). When the characters in *Japheth's Twelve Wives* leave the climate of the American West and travel to Paris, they eventually conform to European cultural expectations and revert to monogamous marriages. *Climat oblige!*

FIGURE 1 Photo of cast members of *Japheth's Twelve Wives*. (BnF Gallica)

Americans are presented as both decidedly utilitarian and naively honest. The American Mormon in *Stephana's Jewel* visits France with the intention of marketing his new invention. This French conception of the frank, entrepreneurial American dates back to Tocqueville, who wrote in the 1830s: "Americans are at the same time a puritanical people and a commercial nation"[20] who direct a "prodigious commercial activity";[21] "What we should call cupidity, the Americans frequently term a laudable industry."[22] By playing up this stereotype in *Stephana's Jewel*, the playwrights contrast American and French attitudes toward romance and offer a humorous critique of French hypocrisy and the practice of marrying for wealth instead of love.

America is also a far-off desert where carnivalesque reversals can be set without directly contaminating Paris. Taine's quote above suggests that the French can take advantage of the Mormon experiment without succumbing to whatever nefarious maladies may be produced by it since Mormons are in a "closed community," isolated in the American West. Elisée Reclus, in his essay on America and Mormons, expressed a similar sentiment: "This republic is a large laboratory where religious, social, and political theories are tested. There one can experience both entire freedom and the worst slavery, the maceration of the body and the rehabilitation of the flesh, celibacy and polygamy, communism and unbridled capitalism."[23] This distance is reinforced by the sign on the stage in *Berthelier Meets the Mormons*: "Utah; Mormon capital; 35,000 kilometers to Nanterre." Salt Lake City, in *Berthelier*, as in *Japheth's Twelve Wives*, is filled with "lush vegetation" and surrounded by Native Americans. To underscore the otherness of the place, Berthelier is even attacked by members of a local tribe as he approaches Salt Lake City.

Despite the foreign locale, however, distance is consistently reduced throughout the plays. Jokes about Parisian construction, references to well-known Parisian actors and theaters, and even the mention of a specific Parisian crêpe stand remind the audience that the issues brought to the fore are uniquely French. In short, if the issues of family, marriage, divorce, and gender roles are at times hidden in American characters or in a far-off desert, the disguise is not a very good one. The America depicted in these plays grows more from the French imaginary of the late nineteenth century than from historical reality. The same can be said of Mormons in nineteenth-century French novels.

The first major fictional work in France about Mormons came in the form of two separate 1856 translations of Maria Ward's *Female Life among the Mormons*. The original English text was anonymously published in New York in 1855 and even brags a sequel: the much less successful 1863 novel, *Male Life among the Mormons*. It is one of the primary texts to codify Mormons as the great American religious Other. It paints Mormons as standing in opposition to monogamy, freedom, democracy, private property, and in favor of slavery, polygamy, monarchy, Catholicism, tyranny, and treason. When translated into French, however, Mormons are made to embody a different set of cultural values. B. H. Révoil titles his translation of *Female Life among the Mormons* as *Les Harems du nouveau monde: Vie des femmes chez les Mormons*. Translated back into English, Révoil's title is: *Harems of the New World: The Life of Women among the Mormons*. Not only does Révoil's translation bring Mormons into parallel with French perceptions of the Orient, thereby aligning Mormons with the most easily recognizable and most widely fictionalized Other in the nineteenth-century French imaginary, but Révoil also pluralizes the female experience, opting for "des femmes" instead of "la femme." Révoil's title places the reader's focus on the salacious, the erotic, and the multiple.

In his 1856 review of Révoil's translation, Victor Fournel writes: "For a time, Mormons and Mormonism captivated public attention from 2,000 miles away; today, they continue to arouse an enigma-like curiosity."[24] Fournel continues: "Révoil warns us himself that he often had to *interpret* rather than translate, out of respect for the chastity of French ears. We could not verify for ourselves the extent of the liberties he took; but judging by the title, they are fairly vast. The work is titled: *Female Life among the Mormons*; why add, as a first line, the pretentious title: *Harems of the New World*? It is undoubtedly less to spare French sensibilities than it is to pique our curiosity."[25] Fournel is certainly correct.

Révoil adds a translator's preface that draws more parallels between Mormons and French conceptions of the East. He declares polygamy to be Mormonism's founding principle, adding, "In Nauvoo they adopted a *diminutive Turkish culture*."[26] Révoil continues: "The Mormon sect was meant to attract the many people who love licentiousness and libertinage. And this is effectively what happened; the city of Nauvoo was soon filled with the worst of America's subjects (and the number is unfortunately large)."[27] In addition to painting Mormons as libertines, Révoil manages to characterize nearly all of America as a land teeming with bad apples, now concentrated with the Mormons. Révoil concludes the preface lamenting that his translation will not stop the new Mormon republic: "We will always find—even in the United States—people burning with passion that this dissolute life will seduce more than our more rigid European values."[28] One wonders whether there isn't a bit of wistful regret on Révoil's part in this sentence. But his declaration clearly posits an opposition between the hot-blooded passion of Mormons and the conservative, rigid morality of Europeans.

And, while the original text itself is blandly modest, Révoil declares: "I did not translate the volume titled *Female Life among the Mormons* word for word out of respect for the chaste ears of our French readers: I had to obscure many expressions that were too bold because often the *Mormon*, though dishonest in his actions, dares to be honest in speech."[29] Paradoxically, Révoil notes just a page later that Americans and Mormons "consider certain things *shocking* that would not even cause us to blush in France."[30] But these ironies are of little consequence and seem lost on the translator. The point is that Révoil sought to exoticize and eroticize Mormons, to make them into a type of Other his French readership would be drawn to.

In France, Orientalism became such a popular fad that Gérard de Nerval exclaimed in 1851, "Such oriental cafés can only be seen in Paris."[31] In other words, Orientalism became more French than foreign and the quest for the exotic became something of a cliché in France. For Edward Said, Orientalism is more "a sign of European-Atlantic power over the Orient than it is a veridic discourse about the Orient."[32] The similarities between polygamy and the harem made equating Mormonism and the "Orient" almost inevitable. However, despite this early comparison, Mormonism remained largely free from the gravity of violence and sexuality that accompanied depictions of the East in French literature. Stretching back to Montesquieu's 1721 novel *Persian Letters* and running through poetry by Victor Hugo and paintings by Eugène Delacroix, among many others, French representations of the Orient have a consistently dark underpinning of dangerous male desire and ruthless violence. In Montesquieu's *Persian Letters*, the harem devolves from tranquil paradise into a bloody, chaotic scene of revolt, murder, and suicide. Hugo's collection of poetry *Les Orientales* (1829) juxtaposes in poem after poem the harem and death, desire and violence. And Delacroix's famous paintings of languid Oriental eroticism—*The Odalisque* and *Women in Algiers*—must be viewed in the shadow of his paintings depicting violence, such as *Massacre at Chios* and *The Death of Sardanapalus*. Mormonism, on the other hand, remains unencumbered by the ominous weight of French depictions of the Orient. French authors could use Mormonism, as a new religion in a very distant but still Western locale, in a humorous rather than a tragic vein, and explore issues surrounding marriage and the family with laughter at a very safe distance.

POLYGAMY AND FRENCH DIVORCE LAWS

By the 1870s, unlike Africans, Asians, or Jews, who had a well-established set of stereotypes in French fiction, Mormons still represented something of a mixed bag, whose otherness could be harnessed in new and different ways. Theater audiences laughed at what they recognized as absurd about themselves in the Mormon characters, but at the end of the plays they could comfortably dismiss the absurdity as belonging to a distinctly different and very distant group. French dramatists in the late nineteenth century used Mormons and Mormon polygamy to work through two of the most pressing issues they faced: namely, gender roles and divorce.

But what do Mormons and polygamy have to do with divorce? In the United States, polygamy was viewed as the evil opposite of monogamy: one wife versus multiple wives. And it would be logical to conclude that polygamy is the opposite of divorce: subtracting a spouse versus adding several. But in France, divorce and polygamy were seen as synonymous. Alongside Elisée Reclus and Jules Guesde, Alfred Naquet proposed a radical rethinking of gender roles and pushed for the legalization of divorce. Even though his divorce law did not pass until 1884, Naquet began writing about reorganizing family structures as early as 1869. Naquet even turned his attention briefly to Mormons, describing their "mythology," their multiple types of family structures, and their many "forms" of marriage. He appreciated the mutability of the Mormon family, and admired the theological underpinnings of polygamy, going so far as to call Mormon beliefs "poetic."[33] After some time in prison and a brief exile in Spain, Naquet was elected to the National Assembly and proposed three different laws to legalize divorce in 1875.[34]

During the parliamentary debates on Naquet's divorce law, politicians on the right repeatedly equated divorce and polygamy. For example, Senator Chesnelong: "I maintain [what I said about divorce as] legal adultery. . . . If the law reestablished polygamy, do you think that would make it moral? Nor can it make moral this successive polygamy, and I might add, this successive polyandry that is another name for divorce."[35] Senator le vicomte de Lorgeril: "[If] this dissolute and dissoluble marriage that we are discussing leads to Saint-Simonianism, to Mormonism, polygamy first and promiscuity next, you should not be surprised or complain."[36] Senator Barthe: "Here, sirs, is what will happen, divorce . . . could become a veritable polygamy in the form of successive marriages."[37] Fearful of change, conservative lawmakers portrayed divorce as the first step on a path toward the collapse of the traditional family. If marriage could be tampered with, what would keep the French from falling into the depravity of promiscuity, or worse, of Mormonism? Not surprisingly, they were most afraid of women going from marriage to marriage, since the promiscuity of men was of less consequence, as subsequent examples will show.

The popular press likewise connected polygamy with divorce. In 1881, a satirical journal, *La Caricature*, mocking lawmakers' rhetoric, presented the debate in these terms: Hoping divorce would be legalized, a number of husbands sent letters to other women promising to divorce their wives and marry them once the law passed. "A good Republican woman . . . stood at the podium to declare that divorce was, in fact, impossible. She spread out, in front of all present, 792 signed and notarized promises from men to divorce their wives and marry her. In this case, the magistrate declared, divorce is of little help. There is only one law that can make everything right: it is the law of the Mormons; let us adopt it! A formidable cheer went up in the crowd . . . and the meeting ended with cheers of 'Down with Naquet! Long live the Mormons!'" The article continues with this addendum: "At the same time, on the other side of the ocean, the most incandescent Mormons were holding a meeting of their own in hopes of revising laws on marriage. A speaker stands at the podium and begins. . . . 'How long, O Mormons, will we be condemned to haul around seventeen wives or more everywhere we go. This state of affairs cannot continue! Must find something else! So many wives. . . . Drat!' The assembly, absolutely convinced, unanimously decides that . . . Mormons will have only one wife and that divorce be abolished."[38] This sardonic description of the debates around marriage underscores the hypocrisy of conservatives who were against divorce but fine with mistresses. But it further points to our central thesis, namely that many French writers saw Mormonism as a religion that was analogous to their own state of affairs. Mormons represented a sort of microcosm of possibilities and impossibilities for the French as they studied their own ideas of marriage, divorce, and gender roles.

This anecdote further points to a crisis of masculinity surrounding the French divorce debate. Following defeat in the Franco-Prussian War of 1870, anxiety about emasculated, weak Frenchmen had become an affair of state, with major educational reforms undertaken to toughen up young men. Divorce would further undermine virility, giving women power to leave husbands and to choose new ones. In 1886, the satirical paper *Le Tintamarre* considers the possibility of polygamous Mormons coming to Paris: "I have a hard time imagining Mormons in Paris," writes journalist G. Rémi. "It would be strange to see one man with several women in the city best known for its women having several men."[39] This quip points to a general sense (among conservative men, at least) that women now had the upper hand in relationships and were free to dictate terms to their husbands or lovers. Polygamy, in the French imaginary, repositions men at the center of the marriage relationship and elevates them as undisputed heads of their households.

The plot of *Mormons in Paris*, an 1874 musical by Louis Leroy and Alfred Delacour and the first play in this collection, hinges on the fact that the main character, Albert Savarin, married five wives while living briefly in Salt Lake City and now, back in France, finds himself afoul of the law—and of his new mother-in-law. Albert has returned to collect an inheritance and, as the play opens, has just concluded a traditional and ostensibly monogamous marriage to Mathilde Chamboran. During the opening act, a hard-drinking Mormon apostle named Jonathan arrives in France and recognizes Albert from his time in Utah, accuses him of desertion, and explains that while he has taken in three of Albert's abandoned wives himself, Albert's other two wives have come to France looking for him. Albert explains his Mormon marriages in these terms: "I was told that in order to stay I had to adopt the local customs. The next thing I know I'm stuck with three wives. . . . Later they offered me two more, contending that my wealth authorized this addition. They were nice, so, naturally, I accepted them. I made them happy for six months. What more could anyone want?" (I.6).

Albert manages to evade one of his Mormon wives, Eva, but later that night, he discovers that the other wife, Nadeje, has been hired as his maid. She ends up exposing Albert's past and inciting the ire of his new mother-in-law, who thunders, "Get behind me, criminal. It's no longer a misdemeanor trial that awaits you, it's a felony trial!" (III.10). With divorce illegal and the police searching his house looking for evidence of bigamy, he is forced into hiding in the suburbs.

The play's most important scenes take the form of a mock trial where characters dress as attorneys and a magistrate to debate Albert's legal standing. Albert begins by asking, "Of what crimes do we stand accused?" Albert's mother-in-law, in the role of the prosecuting attorney, replies, "Your five marriages!" Albert: "I deny them! Introduce the witnesses" (IV.4). Albert first questions Jonathan, the apostle, who arrives dressed as a coachman, because—it turns out—that is what he really is: Salt Lake City has cut off his funding, so he denounces Mormons as frauds and admits that he is really a Parisian named Isidore Plâtreux. He testifies that getting married in Salt Lake City "is about as serious as drinking a pint of ale here!" "Gentlemen of the jury," Albert explains, "the accusations of bigamy, of trigamy . . . of quadrigamy are fabrications made up by opposing counsel!" (IV.5). Albert then calls to the witness stand the two wives who followed him from America. They are introduced with husbands they have recently wed in Paris, leading Albert to conclude, "The presence of these two young maidens, arm-in-arm with their tender husbands, in their wedding gowns, with an abundance of orange blossoms in their hair, should suffice, I hope, to enlighten the court." Dubouloy, Albert's uncle who is dressed as the judge, declares, "Say no more, your case has been made. I order the prosecution to submit a retraction to the court" (IV.7).

Even though blissful monogamy is restored before the final curtain, *Mormons in Paris* sheds light on the legal issue of marriage and divorce. The costume changes and changing roles of the characters (from uncle to judge, from mother-in-law to prosecutor, from abandoned wife to newlywed, from apostle to coachman, etc.) underscore the fluidity of relationships and the shifting social hierarchies in 1870s Paris. And the question of divorce, even though not raised explicitly in the dialogue, nevertheless lurks as the major legal and social question that drives the entire play.

Not long after divorce was legalized in France, *Japheth's Twelve Wives* opened at the Théâtre de la Renaissance in Paris. The premise of this play is similar to that of *Mormons in Paris*: the Frenchman Beaujolais moves to Salt Lake City, where he becomes a Mormon and inherits Japheth Paterson's canned food empire. To close the deal, Beaujolais must take Paterson's name and marry his widow. He subsequently adds eleven more wives, bringing his total nuptials up to an even dozen.

From the very beginning of the play, comparisons between French and Mormon sexual mores abound. Beaujolais/Paterson's Parisian friend Des Toupettes arrives, explaining that he was forced to leave France to seek fortune in America after he had spent all his money on mistresses. Briquet, Des Toupettes's former servant now in the service of Paterson, reminisces about his time with Des Toupettes in Paris: "That's where I was happy. You had your friends, I had mine. Never more than one woman to serve at a time, even though they changed often" (I.2). Des Toupettes asks Briquet whether he remembers Ernestine, an actress who had left her husband to be with Des Toupettes and the only woman he regrets losing. We soon learn that Ernestine has changed her name to Arabella and is Paterson's newest wife. We later discover that she had been married twice before to characters the audience will meet when the action goes to Paris in acts II and III. What is striking about the beginning of this play is how it mirrors the French parliamentary debates about divorce. Naquet wrote that outlawing divorce had led to "cohabitation and clandestine unions" and to the "debauchery of society," in other words, to characters like Des Toupettes who frequently changed mistresses.[40] Opponents of divorce argued that legalizing it would amount to serial polygamy, as women would be free to go from one husband to another, just as Ernestine/Arabella does in the play. But she goes one step further: from marriage, to "serial polygamy," to actual polygamy.

Arabella goes on to perform a song that functions as a mise en abyme of the entire play. The song tells the story of an actress who receives one lover after another throughout the night:

When [the] old nobleman took flight,
A young investor took his place
And spent a good part of the night
Till a senator upped the pace.
And an entire dozen came
Of every age, every estate.
On such a good roll, the fair dame
Never tired though it was late.
These customs are all our own!
She welcomed each, one by one,
With neither murmur nor moan—
Oh my!—till the work was done. . . . (I.6)

All twelve of the lovers end up hiding in the same closet and, having been locked in by a debt collector, must pay off the woman's debts in order to be let out.

It is certainly not happenstance that the number of lovers—twelve—is identical to the number of Japheth's wives and that Arabella, an actress herself, has accumulated husbands and lovers throughout the play just like the woman in the song. Notably, the poem underscores that having multiple lovers is a French custom: "Ah! que ces mœurs sont bien les nôtres!" ("These customs are all our own!"). *Mœurs* are morals or customs, values that form a cultural identity. In this case, the value in question is the practice of taking multiple lovers. The song brings into focus the similarities between polygamy and a well-accepted French tradition, suggesting that there are not many steps between Mormon polygamy, taking multiple lovers, and serial polygamy/divorce.

Unlike Albert in *Mormons in Paris*, when Japheth and his wives arrive in Paris, he faces no legal trouble himself. His wives are arrested but only because they are staying in a disreputable hotel and mistaken for prostitutes. Instead of facing charges of bigamy, Japheth must divorce his wives so he can inherit from his uncle, Baliveau. This uncle, it turns out, was Arabella's first husband. Their divorce left Baliveau so heartbroken and cynical that he imposes a life of bachelorhood on Beaujolais/Japheth should he wish to remain his heir. Baliveau, a police commissioner, eventually discovers the truth about his nephew's marriages. In an effort to regain his uncle's favor, Japheth divorces his wives and, with the help of a marriage agency run by Arabella's second husband, manages to marry them off to lonely French bachelors. But unfortunately for him, his uncle is one of those lonely French bachelors. Since Baliveau has now remarried and hopes to have children of his own, he definitively cuts Japheth out of his will.

The play ends rather abruptly with Japheth declaring: "Well, I'm finally single . . . there's always that!" (III.15). Even though divorce is now legal, single women are unacceptable both in society and on the stage, and divorced women (more on this below) are particularly dangerous. But men, like Japheth, can always fall back on bachelorhood and remain perfectly respectable. In *Mormons in Paris* and *Japheth's Twelve Wives* (and in *Stephana's Jewel*, which we will analyze shortly), Mormonism is a vehicle that makes it acceptable to discuss, and even laugh at, divorce. Mormonism also allows the plays to raise questions about traditional marriage, about marital fidelity, and about bachelorhood and to imply that certain hypocrisies remain in the French familial ideology.

STAGING HYPOCRISY

While the translation of *Female Life among the Mormons* brought fictionalized Mormons to the attention of many French readers, the first work of French literature to focus on Mormons at length was Paul Duplessis's 1859 novel, *The Mormons*. Duplessis wrote popular adventure fiction, largely set in Mexico and the American West, in the middle part of the nineteenth century. In *The Mormons*, a sprawling novel of over 1,600 pages, Duplessis presents the adventures of the young French aristocrat Georges d'Hédouville, his fiancée Hélène de Rosne, the Spanish nobleman turned American adventurer Joaquin Dick, and the Mormon medium and leader Hiram-Harris. It offers a portrayal of Mormonism's origins and theology, along with descriptions of Mormon pioneers, Deseret (the nineteenth-century territorial name of Utah), and Salt Lake City.

The novel begins by lamenting the breakdown of traditional power structures in France and by noting that the abolition of the right of inheritance by the firstborn (the *droit d'aînesse*) has led to the creation of an alternate form of identity formation through the establishment of clubs frequented by men of the same social and economic standing. The club in question in the opening pages of *The Mormons* is named the Cercle des Pauvres (The Club of the Poor), a club reserved for aristocratic men of the Faubourg Saint-Germain and limited to those who could prove their nobility dating back to the Crusades. However, in a significant paragraph the narrator explains that the latter requirement was easily met since "for just over 200 francs—two gold coins less than the cost of a simple black suit—anyone can receive genealogies featuring illustrious ancestors from the twelfth century."[41] The narrator goes on to explain that all club members had an annual pension of at least 10,000 livres, "if not in cash, at least in a future inheritance."[42] This incipit sets the tone for the entire work: following the end of legitimist monarchical rule in 1830 (a year mentioned repeatedly in the novel as a watershed moment), the narrator contends that French social structures have become fractured and inauthentic and more particularly that young members of the aristocracy have become passive and feckless.[43]

Duplessis's novel is noteworthy for its description of America, for its portrayal of "mediumism" and its connections to the nineteenth-century Spiritualism movement, and for its depiction of racial prejudices. Most important for our argument, however, is the novel's focus on the encounter between the French and Mormons, particularly the way Duplessis uses Mormons to expose the very issues confronting France after the fall of the Bourbons, denigrating some of the posers from the Cercle des Pauvres while demonstrating the superiority of the authentic characters, primarily the secular Mormon medium Hiram-Harris. As with the plays translated in this collection, *The Mormons* tells us more about the shifting fortunes and emergent culture wars in Paris than about Mormonism in the American West, and the reader is left with the uneasy feeling that the novel's denouement has put off, rather than resolved, the narrative's deep economic, social, racial, theological, and political conflicts.

The novel is organized around two coming marriages: one between the young Georges d'Hédouville and his fiancée Hélène de Rosne and the other between Hiram-Harris and Hélène's sister, Martha. The narration underscores the frivolity and superficiality of the first couple, as Georges and Hélene repeatedly imitate the tropes and clichés of courtly love and Romanticism. Hiram-Harris, on the other hand, demonstrates sincere affection for Martha and, despite their dramatic deaths in the novel's final pages, the relationship involving the Mormon medium comes across as the most authentic.

The hypocrisy of the French view of marriage is more explicitly pointed out in Daniel Darc's 1886 novel, *Joyous Life: Parisian Polygamy.* The main character, Lionel, responds to criticisms that he keeps mistresses and remains unwed in the following way: "And doesn't our friend Raff—the handsome Raff!—have three parallel households, only one legitimate, that all function with the regularity of a bread-slicer?"[44] He continues: "Polygamy, whether we like it or not, is a law of nature, a hygienic, economic and philanthropic law that is as old as the world and that will last as long as it does; . . . a whole host of stupid or egotistical scruples have pretended to modify this . . . state of affairs. What has been the result? . . . What was once a charming and sacred duty has become a discreet but sterile pleasure. . . . There are just as many embraces exchanged but far fewer children acknowledged. A fine result that moralists can be proud of!"[45]

Lionel concludes his exposé of French polygamy—that is, adultery—with a reference to Mormons: "But look at the Mormons and tell me if polygamy hasn't been successful for them? Their neighbors are furious seeing them so strong and want to annihilate them, not to defend virtue as they say but quite simply out of jealousy!"[46] In short, Darc's novel makes it clear that polygamy, though it remains unacknowledged and may be called by another name, is widespread in French society. Moral causes have only appeared to modify the hypocritical state of affairs. Mormons at least have the advantage of being forthright about their relationships.

This idea is underscored in the writing of Henri Rochefort, who published an account of his trip through Salt Lake City and its environs in 1877. He describes a certain type of Utah polygamist who would travel regularly in order keep his families apart. Rochefort concludes with this telling observation: "Similarly, in Europe there are politicians who, though probably ardently hostile to Mormon theology, not unlike the traveling polygamists, have well-established stops between their districts and the capital."[47] Again, instead of depicting Mormons as repulsively Other, Rochefort compares Europeans to Mormons and implies that the latter are at least publicly honest about their multiple partners. Naquet himself, writing the same year as Rochefort published his account, makes a similar parallel argument about divorce: "Rejecting divorce . . . amounts to introducing or keeping hypocrisy in society."[48]

In 1891 *Le Journal amusant* published an article titled "Le Surménage." *Surménage* is a play on words: it is typically translated as "overworked," but it literally means a surplus in a household. The article explains: "[*Surménage*] is the compulsion . . . of some to have several women to care for. Several women at the same time, and not successively, because it goes without saying that polygamy, understood in the latter sense, is allowed and practiced all over and by everyone."[49] The article quips that many from the refined cultures of the U.S. East Coast and Europe denounce Mormonism while "carefully hiding their own corruption behind hypocrisy."[50] The article closes with this astonishing remark: "We conclude that Paris is the true capital of *surménage*."[51] According to *Le Journal amusant*, in the nineteenth century, Paris, not Salt Lake City, holds the distinction of being the world leader in polygamy. The Mormons really are in Paris!

Though operating in a slightly different register, the plays similarly use Mormons to highlight hypocrisy in French opinion and practice regarding marital fidelity. The most telling example of this can be found in *Stephana's Jewel*, a play that premiered just two years after *Japheth's Twelve Wives*. It, too, features a polygamist, Sir Gaveston. Of the four plays, this is the only one to feature an American polygamist husband, but his first name is French—Napoleon (a name that will be put to humorous use in the play)—and one of his wives is French and a sister of Madame Rubineau. Gaveston hopes to accomplish three things while in France: (1) find his seventh wife, (2) marry off his six daughters (who are accompanying him on his trip to France), and (3) find a market for his invention—a *bijou* or a small buzzer that rings when someone's declaration of love is sincere. He explains that women in America are always honest, so there is not a market for his device there. But, in a not-so-subtle criticism of French hypocrisy, he hopes to make a fortune in France, where lovers' duplicitousness is legend.

Gaveston's sister-in-law and her husband, Madame and Monsieur Rubineau, have two children: Charlotte and Auguste. As the play begins, we learn that Charlotte is engaged to Oscar de Pompignac, who was formerly with Stephana. But he left her, and Stephana is now Monsieur Rubineau's lover; to further complicate matters, the Rubineaus' son, Auguste, is in love with Stephana. Stephana manages to insert herself into the Rubineau family by pretending to be their American niece, and comedic chaos ensues.

It is notable that divorce is hinted at in this play and there is discussion of the legality of Oscar marrying without formally alerting Stephana of his plans. Stephana complains that he is attempting to marry "without my consent" and without providing "the customary notice" (I.2). She threatens to appeal to a judge if Oscar doesn't pay her a reasonable amount (I.3). And when Gaveston mistakes Stephana for Rubineau's daughter, she quips, "And now I'm marrying Oscar! Wouldn't be the first time!" (I.6). When Madame Rubineau suspects her husband of cheating on her, she declares: "I'm divorcing you! I'll go become someone's mistress" (II.16). Ironically, this is what Stephana has already done: left a former lover or husband to become Rubineau's mistress! But more significantly, most characters have multiple love interests and, despite monogamy laws in France, some form of polyandry, or successive polygamy, is practiced by most characters in the play. In *Mormons in Paris*, Albert was the center of the plot. Here it is Stephana: The single woman is a desirable and destabilizing force, and every male character in one way or another lays claim to her.

After many twists and turns, Gaveston and Stephana are engaged, and she agrees to become his seventh wife. This clears the path for Oscar to marry Charlotte. What's more, Auguste plans to go with the new couple back to Salt Lake City where he will become a polygamist and marry all six of Gaveston's daughters. Thanks to Mormon polygamy, Stephana, the disruptive single woman, returns to the safe confines of domesticity, and Auguste is able to satisfy his libido in the bonds of marriage. It is worth pointing out that *Stephana's Jewel* ends quite differently from the other plays: instead of dismantling or escaping polygamy to pave the way to a return to middle-class respectability, characters *turn to polygamy* in order to maintain the status quo. This reversal underscores the hypocrisy of a system that allows divorce but cannot tolerate single women, of a system that tolerates husbands—but not wives—taking lovers. The divorced man can remarry, but the divorced woman must take a lover who can support her or flee to Utah in order to have standing.

In all of these plays, Mormonism, divorce, and the "liberty" of women are enmeshed to humorous effect. The plays do not take a clear position for or against divorce or in favor of or against a reversal of traditional gender roles—doing so would have undoubtedly jeopardized ticket sales. But they do tap into the anxiety surrounding these issues in Third Republic France. What's more, they expose hypocrisy. In this case, the plays point to the hypocrisy of men who act like they are entitled to rule over women with military rigor, the hypocrisy of a system that criticizes divorce as serial polygamy but where people change lovers with regularity, the hypocrisy of a society that eventually allows divorce but shuns divorced women, and the hypocrisy of a culture that tolerates single men but not single women.

MORMONS AND GENDER ROLES

The hypocrisy surrounding marriage had been on full display in France in the two years prior to the 1874 premier of the play *Mormons in Paris*. A legal cause célèbre brought the double standard of gender roles to the fore in 1872 when Arthur Leroy Du Bourg killed his wife and her lover in a fit of jealous rage. The event consumed the press and the public debated and discussed it extensively. The historian Odile Krakovitch called the debates about the Du Bourg murder and trial "the most formidable quarrel over women's rights that has ever taken place in France."[52] Karen Offen explains the crux of the issue as follows:

> Had Du Bourg murdered [his wife] under his own roof, he would not have been prosecuted, according to Article 324 of the French Penal Code. . . . In the French Penal Code, a man convicted for keeping a concubine under the same roof as his wife was subject only to a stiff fine; if he kept the concubine next door—or across the street—the man could not be prosecuted. What was more, a husband who discovered his wife in *flagrante delicto* in their home and killed her would not be brought to justice; he was within his "right." If he killed her under the roof of another man, he would be tried but more than likely be acquitted. . . . A woman convicted of adultery could be imprisoned; not so the man.[53]

Offen continues: "The sensational trial of Monsieur Du Bourg . . . generated a new outburst of debate on the woman question, focused on the double standard of sexual morality."[54] *Mormons in Paris* and the subsequent French Mormon plays premiered in the wake of the Du Bourg affaire: they question and explore the role of women, the nature of marriage, the necessity of fidelity, the consequences of adultery, and the double standard imposed on women by a number of social norms.

In the late 1860s and early 1870s, French women began to organize and push for meaningful changes to the Civil Code. In 1869, the feminist journal *Le Droit des femmes* published a manifesto signed by a handful of women, including the authors Maria Deraismes and André Léo (born Victoire Léodile Béra). "Its objective [was] to mobilize public opinion in favor of the 'civil rights of women,' access to a secondary and university education, the right to work and equality of salaries."[55] During the Third Republic, these same women and others took up the cause again and argued in favor of divorce and the right to organize without needing the authorization of men.

In 1870, Léon Richer founded the Association pour le Droit des Femmes; in 1871, the Union des Femmes was founded; and in 1871, Richer organized the Association pour l'Emancipation Progressive de la Femme—all associations dedicated to promoting women's rights. The first women's rights banquet was held in Paris in June 1872. Richer claimed that if France were to be regenerated (following the Commune and the Franco-Prussian War), "we must begin with the women."[56] In other words, for many republicans and progressives, the foundational issue for a new republic was increasing the rights and role of women. Maria Deraismes, who was an integral part of this movement and present at the 1872 women's rights banquet, had complained in 1870 that "when a woman wants to speak publicly, she must first seek authorization from a man. If this man determines that this authorization might trouble the economy of his ego, he refuses."[57] Deraismes continues: "Now women unanimously and valiantly begin a movement of awareness and action. Their partial, local, and individual support for this movement has become general, universal, and collective. What do they call for? . . . They demand a broader application of liberty."[58] In a letter read at the banquet, Victor Hugo opined: "Man has put all the rights on his side and all the obligations on woman's side. Because of this, there is a profound problem. Because of this, woman is in servitude. Under our present legislation, she cannot vote, she does not count, she does not exist. There are *citoyens* but no *citoyennes*. This is a violent situation and it must cease."[59]

This transition toward increased independence for women plays out in *Berthelier Meets the Mormons*, a one-act sketch meant to showcase the well-known actor Jean-François Berthelier. This play, like *Mormons in Paris*, premiered at the Théâtre des Variétés during the 1874–1875 season. Berthelier plays himself, an actor traveling with his troupe in America. He is separated from his fellow thespians after being attacked by a Native American tribe and wanders into Salt Lake City. He soon meets Oscar, another Frenchman who had arrived two years earlier and who is now the Mormon prophet, because, as his confidant explains, he is a "superior man" (I.3). As with *Mormons in Paris*, polygamy features prominently. But rather than hinging on the legality of divorce, what is most important in this play is the challenge of traditional gender roles and the growing influence of women's associations.

Upon his arrival in Utah, Berthelier is forced to become Mormon by the prophet Oscar. Tiring of his many wives, Oscar offers a number of them to the new convert, Berthelier, who is initially delighted with them. But the wives, led by the Parisian Pichenette, have had enough of being treated like second-class citizens, so they organize themselves into an association and write up their demands in the form of a constitution-like code:

ARTICLE 1:

Given that women
Are delicate creatures
And love is the liniment
That enhances their features,
This judgment we render:
Husbands must be knightly
And constantly tender,
Treating us politely.
. . . .

ARTICLE 2:

Women are a bit coquettish
And no one will deny
That to bejewel and embellish
Must be done both far and nigh.
To have a calm domestic life,
We require you to know
That men get all the toil and strife
And women all the dough.
. . . .

ARTICLE 3:

Women are all very wise.
They're never known to fail.
And since some men we must advise,
Here's how we will prevail:
Should we disagree or fight,
We'll sing this little song,
"The wife is always right
And the husband always wrong!" (I.7)

Exasperated by his wives' demands, Berthelier asks them to leave him in peace. Instead of retreating, they surround Berthelier and, armed with riding crops, sing as they beat him:

We must avenge our sex;
We must do so right away!
For too long we've been vexed,
Forced to constantly obey.
So arm ourselves with riding crops!
We'll strike at the same time.
And if our cowardly husband drops
We'll repeat this little rhyme:
"Whip, whip, whip, whip!
This is how we right the ship!" . . . (I.9)

Berthelier extricates himself from the drubbing by claiming that he is, in fact, a woman masquerading as a man. He plays this role so well that the women give him a leadership position in their women's revolt and the prophet Oscar falls in love with him, mistaking him for an Italian named Barbarini. This gender bending and the rebellious pact point to a broad reversal of the gender hierarchy, a theme that runs from the opening scene to the final curtain.

The women then organize a larger protest, complete with music and banners, and in military fashion they march on the prophet Oscar and his advisers. Armed and with a drummer leading them, they issue this ultimatum:

We maintain,
Yes, we claim
The total end of your reign.
La-oo-la-la!
That here and now
Old man, and how!
Our reign you must avow . . . (I.12)

Oscar acquiesces and, thanks to some subterfuge from Berthelier, agrees to allow all of his twenty-seven wives to go free. The play ends as Oscar,

Berthelier, and Pichenette plan to leave Utah and return to Paris, their hometown.

When the women in *Berthelier* organize their revolt, French theatergoers would have immediately seen the connection to the state of affairs in their own country and would have sympathized with or rejected the women's cause according to their political persuasion. The play, however, points to the impossibility of treating women as less than equal partners in marriage or in politics and, as much as is possible in a comedy of this sort, suggests that men who seek to control women are ultimately weak and foolish. It also highlights the growing influence women held in the public sphere.

What's more, by setting *Berthelier Meets the Mormons* in Salt Lake City, the authors evoked contemporary issues that astute audience members may have picked up on. Women in Utah gained suffrage in 1870, a fact covered in the French press at the time. An 1870 article in the journal *La Science sociale* announces, "The emancipation of women is a *fait accompli* in a state of the American Union: on February 12, Utah proclaimed that the right to vote would be granted to women."[60] While the article decries Mormon husbands as "all-powerful masters," it nevertheless goes on to describe Mormon women as follows: "[They] enjoy complete financial freedom. They travel alone when and how they like, and their beliefs are only limited in the domain of religion."[61] Also in 1870, the *Journal amusant* published an image of armed Mormon women ready for combat, with their husband standing feebly by armed only with a broom (figure 2). In 1870s France, Mormons were seen—at times with derision and at times with praise—as leading the way in the emancipation of women.

Berthelier thematizes France's changing attitudes toward women by portraying Mormon women resisting and dissolving the patriarchal power structure, organizing themselves militaristically, and freeing themselves from the chains of marriage. Given the distance from Paris, the polygamous gender dynamics, and the otherness of Mormons, Utah provided an ideal setting in which French audiences could explore issues of gender roles, the rise of feminist projects, and the challenge to male hegemony emerging from the secular state of the Third Republic.

FIGURE 2 Albert Robida, "News from the Great Salt Lake." (BnF Gallica)

MORMONS AND THE MERCANTILE MARRIAGE

Jules Verne's famous novel *Around the World in 80 Days* (1873) includes a short anecdote set in Utah. Verne's characters arrive by train in Ogden and then visit Salt Lake City for several hours. The narrator focuses very little on the city or its inhabitants and instead emphasizes Passepartout's anxiety about marriage and his fear that some Mormon women may seek him as a husband. As their train pulls out of the station, a late-arriving passenger jumps on the last car and sits down out of breath. Passepartout learns that this passenger is a Mormon "escaping a domestic disturbance. When the Mormon man composed himself, Passepartout dared to politely ask him how many wives he had—and given his haste, he supposed he must have at least twenty. 'One, sir!' answered the Mormon raising his arms to the heavens, 'one, and it's enough!'"[62] The encounter with Mormons in Verne's novel focuses entirely on the French valet's fear of marriage and commitment. This encounter with the Other does little more than provide confirmation to the French character (and readers) of the correctness of his assumptions about Mormonism, women, and marriage.

A pastiche of Verne's novel, Albert Robida's *The Extraordinary Travels of Saturnin Farandoul in the 5 or 6 Parts of the World and in All the Lands Known and Even Unknown to Mr. Jules Verne* (1879), is much more expansive when it comes to its description of Mormons and marriage. In a section titled "Around the World in More Than 80 Days," the protagonist and his band of merry men travel through North and South America seeking adventure, fortune, and love. After taking over Australia with an army of monkeys and earning a fortune selling snakeskin boots, Farandoul and his men decide to seek wives in Utah. They enthusiastically set off for Salt Lake City, and while shouting "Hurrah for Mormonism!"[63] they telegraph messages ahead to Brigham Young to inform him of their conversion and imminent arrival and to negotiate for wives:

BRIGHAM YOUNG: Excellent deal. Senator has just divorced. Sixteen assorted wives, would give seventeenth as a bonus. Interested? There are a number of suitors, but you will have first dibs.

FARANDOUL: I accept! Thank you. Lieutenant Mandibul asks if there isn't a similar deal for him.

BRIGHAM YOUNG: Six negroes and one Chinese are a possibility. Don't speak French. Should I make a deal?

FARANDOUL: Mandibul also requests half dozen whites for sweet-talk.

BRIGHAM YOUNG: Found! Before making the deal must know if Lieutenant Mandibul is blond.

FARANDOUL: Light blond. Another request. Tournesol, 33 yrs., volcanic disposition. Would like Mexican wives?

BRIGHAM YOUNG: Mandibul's marriage done deal. Bulk of Mexicans for Tournesol. I will be at the station.[64]

Robida's characters focus here on the consumer nature of marriage: "excellent deal," "assorted wives," "negotiate," "half dozen," "done deal." In Robida's view, marriage, even polygamy—or perhaps especially polygamy—has become one more field of bourgeois exchange.

In Robida's subsequent novel, *The Twentieth Century* (1883), the narrator imagines a future where matrimonial agencies have completely

FIGURE 3 Albert Robida, "Matrimonial Curtain." (BnF Gallica)

taken over French nuptial arrangements and have thoroughly commercialized every aspect of marriage. "In Paris, the curtains at the Opera, the Opéra-Comique, and Molière Palace, where young women frequent, are intentionally covered with portraits of male bachelors; while the curtains at the Variétés, the Palais-Royal and other comic theaters are used to advertise young women to be married."[65] Robida includes his own illustration depicting the Théâtre des Variétés (the theater that premiered both *Mormons in Paris* and *Berthelier Meets the Mormons*; see figure 3).

The whole advertisement is titled "Affluent Marriages," and foregrounds the commercial aspect of marriage. Some women are displayed with their age; others with the label of "widow" or "orphan"; and still others with their profession, such as "medical doctor," while all include the amount of their dowry. Robida is here parodying the excesses of marriage agencies that by some estimates arranged up to 25 percent of the weddings that took place in Paris.[66] According to Dominique Kalifa, marriage agencies in nineteenth-century Paris usually received payment based on the dowry, typically earning between 5 and 10 percent of the promised amount.[67]

Significantly, the entire third act of *Japheth's Twelve Wives* is set in a marriage agency called "The Family Union." The act begins with men singing the following number:

We hope and pray—
And we will pay—
For wives from your agency.
We're of an age
To be engaged,
We'll love them faithfully . . . (III.1)

We soon learn, however, that the marriage agent, Cassoulet (who also happens to be Arabella's second husband), has run out of women to offer his clients. "I always seem to have at least four men for every woman, and I can't marry her to all four" (III.2). As a result, he begins a side business taking bets on horses. The obligatory conflation of horses and women follows where both are discussed based on lineage, weight, height, leg quality, and nature (jumpy, skittish, etc.). Even when women are not confused with horses, they are still discussed as consumer objects. Japheth, who is looking to divorce his wives and regain both his uncle's trust and his inheritance, comes to the agency to put his wives on the market. Cassoulet explains: "Do you know my terms? It's one hundred francs to register and one hundred francs once the item is delivered. I'll give you a discount given the quantity of the stock." As if describing race horses, Japheth responds: "Perfect. Here's the list of my wives with their age, hair color, and distinctive characteristics" (III.4). Cassoulet is quick to tout the soon-to-be delivered merchandise to his customers, telling Des Toupettes, "You've come at the right time, I'm expecting a delivery of a nice stock of beautiful women" (III.7). For their part, the men are attracted partly for companionship but mostly because they are looking for a deal. One client tells Cassoulet, "I'm a widower, and I'd like to remarry as soon as possible. I saw your ad in *Le Petit Journal* right below the ad for American suspenders where you advertise an heiress worth three million. That would suit me" (III.1). Des Toupettes puts it bluntly, "[Getting married is] still the best way to make a fortune" (III.6).

In the context of this play, Mormonism's difference from the dominant French economic perspective regarding marriage is ironically reduced. In fact, fictional Mormons simply take the French model to its logical extreme. Since marriage is purely commercial and wives can be negotiated for, then having more wives would be viewed in the same way as having more property, more art, or more wealth on display. As we will examine in the next section, just as the French markets, thanks in large part to colonialism, received goods from all over the world, so authors imagined Mormons and their polygamous wives as being shipped in from the world over.

MORMONS AND COLONIALISM

In *The Twentieth Century*, Robida imagines that Mormons regularly receive shipments of wives, sketching a delivery made to a port in England—a country Robida foresees as being under Mormon control (see figures 4 and 5). Beyond the commercial nature of these deliveries, Robida focuses a great deal on the nationalities of the women that form part of the exchange. When Saturnin Farandoul's group arrives at the Salt Lake City train station, the narrator describes the scene like this: "Dressed in white, crowned with flowers, the new wives waited, with bated breath, for the arrival of their husbands. There were women of all colors and all nationalities."[68] When Farandoul does a full roll call for his seventeen new brides, he finds that three are French, one Polish, five American, one Mexican, one Irish, one Chinese, one British, one Peruvian, one German, and one African of unknown birthplace. This cultural diversity is mirrored in the polygamist families in the plays. In *Berthelier Meets the Mormons*, wives are from France, Italy, Poland, Spain, England, and Switzerland; in *Stephana's Jewel*, wives hail from Russia, China, England, Switzerland, France, and the Auvergne region (considered something of a foreign country in nineteenth-century France); and in *Mormons in Paris*, Nadeje hails from Mozambique. Polygamy brings all these nationalities together under a single roof.

Robida's concern here is less about historical accuracy (Mormons in nineteenth-century Utah were nearly all white and European) and more, we would argue, about offering another perspective on the French colonial situation. Mormons, without any military presence whatsoever, managed to bring people from all around the globe to Salt Lake City. On one level, Robida's depiction of Mormonism mirrors the analysis of Collège de France professor Alfred Maury, who wrote in the *Revue des*

FIGURE 4 Albert Robida, "Arrival of the Spouses at the Docks." (BnF Gallica)

Deux Mondes in 1853 that this polygamist sect of the American West had "infiltrated" Protestant America and expanded throughout the West with such "perseverance" and unprecedented "colonizing energy" that it made France's own colonial enterprise look weak by comparison.[69] Farandoul gives the following discourse—reminiscent of the diatribe in Darc's novel quoted above—to a group of Mormons that welcome him to Utah:

> In my opinion, monogamous nations are destined to a quick decadence and degeneracy, and the time has come, unless we want to see this degeneracy accelerate, for them to throw themselves into

FIGURE 5 Albert Robida, "Marriage Docks." (BnF Gallica)

> our arms! Polygamous nations will begin to play an important role. We must be and we will be the initiating nation! . . .
>
> The renovation of the old world will come through the Mormon nation and I am ready to contribute what my few means allow to the triumph of our great pacifist and humanitarian ideal!!![70]

For Farandoul, polygamous *nations*—like Utah—will expand and cause the whole world to flourish. Instead of attributing a racial difference to Mormons because of their religion, as some American authors did, Robida viewed them as racially unique because they openly welcomed all races and integrated them into polygamous families.[71]

Farandoul implies that it is an inverted colonialist practice of inclusion, of bringing the colonies to the center of the Empire, that will strengthen Mormonism and eventually make it a world power. Robida may have been inspired by Jules Rémy's 1860 description of Salt Lake City, where "English, Scots, Canadians, Americans, Danes, Swedes, Norwegians, Germans, Swiss, Poles, Russians, Italians, French, Negros, Hindus, Australians, [and] Chinese" can be found.[72] Rémy continues: "All these people, born with different, even opposing beliefs . . . all these

Coupe d'une maison mormone, d'après un croquis du lieutenant Mandibul.

FIGURE 6 Albert Robida, "Cross-Section of a Mormon House." (BnF Gallica)

people differing by climate, language, culture, laws, nationality, taste, have come together, and continue to come together every day like brothers in perfect harmony in the middle of the American continent where they form a new independent and compact nation. . . . Seeing them, it is possible to believe in a universal fusion, in the future unity of all peoples in a single republic."[73] Rémy, Robida, and the authors of the plays in this volume all view Mormonism through a colonialist lens, presenting a vision or a model that contrasts with the exploitative colonialism practiced by the French state.

Of course, even Farandoul's idyllic polygamous colonial families prove extremely complicated and messy, as figure 6, Robida's image of a Mormon household, demonstrates.

Additionally, in Robida's narrative, Mormon polygamy is hampered by internecine political maneuvering: Brigham Young, fearful that Farandoul will prove more popular and take over the church, kidnaps Farandoul and turns him over to the Apache, proving that utopias are always undermined by petty human pride.

Where Verne's *Around the World in 80 Days* reflects French superiority and colonial ambitions, Robida's text undermines them and posits the impossibility of making any ideology global. But Robida's text also underscores the similarities between Mormons and the French: both have universalist intentions, both share a bourgeois economic model of exchange, both have a "polygamous" republic, and both are subject to political infighting. Robida's novel, as other French texts of the period, dresses French as Mormons. In short, French writers around 1880 create an image of Mormonism allowing French readers to confront their own cultural tensions. For both French and American writers of the period, defining Mormons is about identity formation. But where Americans define themselves *against* Mormons, French authors identify *with* Mormons and thereby invite questions about what it means to be French.

CARNIVAL

As mentioned briefly above, each of the plays in this volume can be understood as a staging of the carnivalesque. Mikhail Bakhtin explains, "All the symbols of the carnival idiom are filled with . . . the peculiar logic of the 'inside out' (*à l'envers*), of the 'turnabout,' of a continual shifting from travesties, humiliations, profanations, comic crownings and uncrownings."[74] Edward Muir sums up Bakhtin's carnivalesque neatly: "Carnival opens up the underworld of festive laughter and market-place language. This underworld [emphasizes the] duality of the body, the distinction between, on the one hand, the material bodily lower stratum of ingestion and secretions and, on the other, the ascetic upper stratum of reason and piety."[75] While most theater is carnivalesque, these plays, with their hierarchical reversals, festive laughter, transgressive marriages, and multiplicity of amorous relationships embody in an exponential fashion the topsy-turvy world of the carnival and ultimately call into question the duality between bawdy humor and religious piety.

In *Berthelier Meets the Mormons*, the women, usually powerless and at the bottom of the social and political ladder, take control and dictate terms to the Mormon leader Oscar, himself suddenly a prophet, rising precipitously from the streets of Paris to become Utah's ruler. The women defy the established order and assert a new order where the crinoline dress replaces pants and reigns supreme. Berthelier, a man, becomes a woman and leads their merry band as a new kind of ruler. The play ends, however, with Pichenette's discovery that Berthelier is, in fact, a man; order will be restored when they return to Paris where they will be married and become a traditional husband-and-wife couple. The return to Paris means a return to conventional gender hierarchies and middle-class monogamy, but along the way the play evokes other significant works of French literature that challenge or reverse similar hierarchies, such as Balzac's *Sarrasine*, Gautier's *Mademoiselle de Maupin*, or Rachilde's *Monsieur Vénus*.

In *Mormons in Paris*, the owner of the costume shop explicitly evokes carnival, indicating that while most of his business is based on renting robes to lawyers, he "also rents out costumes for carnival" (IV.1). But more importantly, a Mormon Festival is held during the play, and it is quite literally a carnival, a feast of fools, where hierarchies are explicitly reversed. Mormons roam the Parisian suburbs vandalizing homes, destroying gardens, uprooting plants, and generally upending middle-class tranquility. As they celebrate the anniversary of their leader's one-hundredth marriage, the Mormons sing:

Let's dance in France,
Lay waste and devastate!
This is how we celebrate
Our annual Mormon festival.

. . . .

Let's get revenge while having fun
And pillage till the day is done.
Make lovely garlands for our heads,
By tearing up the flowerbeds.
So now let's cut, steal, crush, and break,
Trample anything you can't take! (III.6)

At the end of the play, we learn that the Mormon leader, Jonathan, is a French coachman who had risen far above his station in Utah, but with his funding now gone, he returns to his lowly position in the social hierarchy. Polygamy gives way to monogamy. The separated couple (Albert and Mathilde) is reunited. Criminal charges against Albert are dropped. Being Mormon allows characters to test the limits of social and familial structures. And though the social fabric appears to be repaired by the end of the play, the immutable nature of French social institutions has momentarily been called into question.

Japheth's world, too, is upended when he rises to prominence in Salt Lake City. He goes from Parisian bachelor to authoritarian polygamist and back again. His return to conventional normalcy is thanks to both French law—in the form of the police commissioner in act II—and French commercialism—in the form of the marriage agency in act III. What's more, back in Paris all twelve of his wives rebel and refuse to obey (III.4). The influence of place and local culture is notable in this operetta, but as with the earlier productions in the Théâtre des Variétés, *Japheth's Twelve Wives* is organized around Bakhtin's principle: the values of the carnival dominate in Mormondom, where Japheth is wealthy, successful, and polygamous; back in Paris, the situation is reversed, and he ends up penniless and alone.

In his analysis of ritual in Europe, Muir remarks that violence is also part and parcel with carnival. "Even fights, blows, curses, and insults bring the adversary down either literally to the ground or figuratively in public esteem."[76] Unsurprisingly, violence peppers the plays in this volume. We have already discussed the beatings suffered by Berthelier and the Mormon Festival, a day of destruction that takes place in *Mormons in Paris*. Here is another example, a depiction of the moment of conversion, in *Berthelier Meets the Mormons*:

OSCAR

Pay attention! This is your initiation. Turn around.

BERTHELIER, *worried.*

What's he doing?

OSCAR, *kicking him in the pants.*

Pow! You're a Mormon.

BERTHELIER, *rubbing his backside.*

I'm touched . . . (I.5)

Of course, physical humor is as old as comedy and was an important part of French comedy dating back at least to Molière's farces in the seventeenth century. But this passage and others like it in French Mormon plays point to a certain amount of injustice and cruelty inherent in religious systems and in marriage. Where the medieval carnival was built in part around the contrast between religion and the material body, Mormonism embodies both: it is a religion (upper stratum) that promotes polygamy (lower stratum). At a time when the Catholic Church was losing its influence and when indissoluble marriage was being questioned, staging Mormons allowed audiences to question the power both these institutions exercised, often violently, in the distant and recent past.

MÉNAGE À . . . VINGT?

The four plays translated in this volume grow out of a specific style of French theater known as vaudeville (not to be confused with American vaudeville). Popularized in the early nineteenth century, French vaudevilles are comedies built primarily on quid pro quo and ménages à trois designed to appeal to French middle-class theatergoers. The best-known practitioners of the style from this period include Georges Feydeau, Eugène Labiche, Eugène Scribe, and Edmond Rostand.[77] The Mormon plays are all musicals and owe a great deal to the opéra bouffe, a genre popularized by Jacques Offenbach who premiered a number of his works on the same stages as the first two plays in this collection. These Mormon-centric musicals all feature polygamy and expand the conventional husband-wife-mistress triangles at the center of most vaudeville plays to ridiculous extremes.

Where comedies traditionally end with a marriage, many of these plays begin with one or several marriages and move toward their dissolution. These Mormon productions are all dotted with marriages and separations. And the resolution tends to be a return to either monogamy or celibacy. In this sense, by staging Mormons, playwrights subvert the conventional comedic arc—instead of moving from a young couple separated and overcoming difficulties to be together, they move from married couples overcoming marriage itself and returning to monogamy or bachelorhood, while at the same time questioning the conventions of monogamous-indissoluble marriage.

What we see in all these works is an exaggeration of the conventional husband-wife-mistress triangle. The Mormon apostle/coachman Jonathan puts it this way: "In France, marriage is a petty, narrow thing. People look for happiness in a union of two people . . . sometimes three . . . rarely four. It's unfortunate. Overseas, in the land of new horizons, the union of souls is more complex. There . . . your sisters aren't afraid to join with ten, twenty, or even one hundred others to make one man happy" (I.4). However, instead of seeking to add a lover to increase drama and passion to their lives, husbands are looking to escape the chaos of multiple partners and retreat into tranquil monogamy. This is the case for Albert in *Mormons in Paris*: instead of hiding his mistresses from his wife, he is hiding his wives from his fiancée! And in *Japheth's Twelve Wives*, Japheth escapes his wives to go to Paris—not to carouse with a mistress but to visit his uncle and to rest; "I shock my uncle with my moral purity" (I.10). As *Berthelier Meets the Mormons* begins, the prophet Oscar is married to over two dozen wives. But when he meets the lovely Barbarini (Berthelier in drag), he immediately pursues her. Instead of sneaking around on his wife or hiding his intentions to seek a mistress, Oscar openly tells his wives that they no longer satisfy him and that he is seeking a twenty-eighth wife to brighten his days. Where conventional vaudeville theater features the wife seeking to undermine or avenge a philandering husband, setting the play in Salt Lake City allows for the staging of a full-scale uprising; the domestic dispute becomes a public manifestation calling into question male privilege on a large scale.

Stephana's Jewel plays on the same vaudevillian tropes and features two husband-wife-mistress trios, both with the same mistress: Monsieur Rubineau, Madame Rubineau, and Stephana; Oscar, Charlotte, and Stephana. But in a key difference, Mormonism is the antidote to marital problems and stands in quiet contrast to the chaos of a traditional ménage à trois. Act II ends in turmoil when it is revealed that Rubineau has been cheating on his wife with Stephana. In act III, Gaveston flirts with Stephana and they are caught in an embrace by Gaveston's wife. Stephana stammers: "His wife! She'll claw my eyes out!" (III.12). But Gaveston's wife, Corpulencia, instead greets her warmly and exclaims, "We'll get along great!" (III.12). The contrast between a French ménage à trois and American polygamy could not be more stark and the play underscores the tumult caused by what had become commonplace in French theater, if not in French culture. This scene echoes what Alexandre Dumas *fils* wrote about Mormons in 1880: "For Mormons, where polygamy is practiced, the man cannot marry a second wife without the consent of the first; a third without the consent of the two others, and so on."[78] He goes on to attribute a number of benefits to polygamy, including that for women "it would be a much better solution than sterility or prostitution."[79] In the other plays, polygamy is something to get out of; in *Stephana's Jewel*, polygamy is ironically the solution that leads to a happy denouement and the restoration of domestic bliss; it is an answer to the deception, prostitution, and domestic chaos that Dumas and the playwrights see as the consequence of the time-honored ménage à trois.

CONCLUSION

From the time they settled in Salt Lake City, Mormons themselves were a theater-going people. In 1874, the well-known French journal *Le Tour du Monde* published an article about Mormons and the American West that includes this description of the theater scene in Salt Lake City: "Theater attendance has become part of daily life for Mormons, and the Church sees no harm in it. The pope [Brigham Young] even insisted that the theater should be completed before the Tabernacle because, he said, "Those who have fun, pray." He has a loge for himself and often attends plays, accompanied by several of his wives. The people cheer him and he applauds well-acted scenes with as much grace as the best-educated spectators."[80] One can only imagine that Brigham Young occasionally watched French plays in the Salt Lake City theater; but he was probably completely unaware that plays about Mormons were being staged back in Paris.

In his description of Utah, Henri Rochefort marvels that Mormons could be so successful in a desert, and he praises their devotion and hard work. He determines that at the heart of Mormonism there must be "a serious question, one worthy of attention."[81] He then adds the following lament: "This may be true, but the French won't trouble themselves to examine Mormonism. For in this nation [France] where ignorance flourishes, Mormons are clowns, created and put on the earth only to provide material for the playwrights who write vaudeville comedies in Paris."[82] This volume owes its existence to the very impulse Rochefort criticizes: Mormons do provide material for vaudeville comedies. But a careful reading of these comedies tells us a great deal about French anxieties in the face of the dramatic social changes of the Third Republic.

For centuries, French authors displaced their own culture wars onto the Other: the Spain of Corneille's *Le Cid* and of Beaumarchais's *Marriage of Figaro*, the Orient of Montesquieu's *Persian Letters*, the England of Voltaire's *Philosophical Letters*, to name only a few. What is unique about the Mormon Other in these vaudevilles is the very focused scope of social issues the plays address over a twenty-year period: marriage, divorce, family, and gender roles. These four plays open a unique window into how a popular art form grappled with the tension between remaining relevant and keeping its core public happy. They reflect the construction of a specific Other, fine-tuned to a narrow historical moment. And they offer a close look at how nineteenth-century satire operated to expose hypocrisy, to both question and reinforce the status quo, and, perhaps most importantly, to make people laugh.

NOTE ON THE ORIGINAL TEXTS, PLAYWRIGHTS, ACTORS, TRANSLATIONS, AND MUSIC

The four plays in this collection are organized chronologically: *Mormons in Paris* (*Les Mormons à Paris*) premiered in 1874, *Berthelier Meets the Mormons* (*Berthelier chez les Mormonnes*) in 1875, *Japheth's Twelve Wives* (*Les Douze femmes de Japhet*) in 1890, and *Stephana's Jewel* (*Le Bijou de Stéphana*) in 1892. Notes throughout provide context, mention significant handwritten changes in the manuscripts of *Mormons in Paris* and *Berthelier Meets the Mormons*, and occasionally explain translation decisions. *Mormons in Paris* and *Berthelier Meets the Mormons* have never been published and are part of an extensive holding of French theatrical scripts collected by nineteenth-century government censors who dutifully assessed the morality of the plays. These are now housed in a catalog titled *Censure des répertoires des grands théâtres parisiens (1835–1906)* in the Archives Nationales in Pierrefitte, France. *Japheth's Twelve Wives* was published by Librairies-Imprimeries Réunies in Paris in 1891. And *Stephana's Jewel* was published by Paul Ollendorff in Paris in 1892.

Each of the four works collected here—as is typical for plays staged during the period—had two authors. The playwrights largely spent their careers writing comedies and libretti for various theaters in Paris. The one exception to this is Albert Dubarry, a co-author of *Stéphana's Jewel*, who appears to have had only this single foray into theater. Arthur Bernède, Dubarry's co-author, was in his early twenties when he wrote

Stephana's Jewel and went on to write many more plays, screenplays for cinema, and over 150 popular novels of all sorts: historical novels, spy novels, detective novels, romance novels, and more.

As for the actors and actresses, some of them, like Aline Duval, Baron, and Berthelier, were monuments of the Parisian stage. Several actors who created roles in the two plays from the 1890s had careers that bridged from the stage into cinema. Anthony Gildès, who directed *Japheth's Twelve Wives* and created the role of Des Toupettes, appeared in well over one hundred films between 1916 and 1941. Two cast members from *Stephana's Jewel*, Andrée Canti who played Corpulencia Gaveston and Gustave Hamilton who played Auguste Rubineau, also acted in numerous films. They appeared together in Jacques Feyder's *Pension Mimosas* in 1934, and Hamilton lived long enough to play a small role in Marcel Carné's masterpiece, *Les Enfants du paradis* (1945). Following the convention of the period, the scripts grouped cast members by gender when listing the cast. We have reproduced that here. The last two plays include the names of the actors and actresses who created roles in the published script. For the first two, we found the names in the contemporary press.

All of these plays have musical passages.[83] In fact, *Mormons in Paris* begins at a ball and there are references to the orchestra in the characters' dialogue in the opening scene. The complete orchestral score for *Mormons in Paris* is in the Bibliothèque Nationale de France (BNF) at the Richelieu site, but it contains lyrics for only three of the chorus numbers (and unfortunately, not all of the lyrics are in the script). It was composed for a full strings section, flutes, oboes, clarinet, bassoon, brass (including French horns, trombone and *pistons*—instruments similar to a euphonium), and percussion. *Berthelier Meets the Mormons*, performed at the same theater as *Mormons in Paris*, was also accompanied by an orchestra, as evidenced by the fact that specific instruments (that have largely fallen out of use today, like the saxotromba) are explicitly mentioned in the dialogue. The complete score can also be found in the BNF at the Richelieu site. A partial piano score to *Japheth's Twelve Wives* is available in the BNF's online repository, Gallica, and the complete piano score with lyrics can be found in several libraries in the United States. The composer of the music for *Japheth's Twelve Wives*, Victor Roger, composed dozens of operettas and began his career "under the auspices of Camille Saint-Saëns, a friend of his family."[84] Beginning in 1894 he also edited the theater reviews for the Parisian newspaper *Le Petit journal.* Given Roger's career and the type of composing he did, the original Parisian staging of *Japheth's Twelve Wives* likely had orchestral accompaniment, but only the piano score remains. Finally, *Stephana's Jewel* has only one vocal number accompanied by an onstage piano (in act II, scene 13), and the script mentions "musicians" that we assume would have performed, at the very least, in the background or between acts. The voice of Marguerite Gallayx, the actress who first played the role of Stephana, is compared to the voice of the well-known singer and vaudeville actress Céline Chaumont, suggesting that she was selected for the role, at least in part, for her vocal talents.[85]

Following the Revolution, musical societies flourished in France as men and women sought new forms of sociability while the Catholic Church lost its influence to structure people's lives and relationships. Choral groups, bands, and orchestras sprang up in cities and villages all over France with backing from mayors and prefects who saw them as powerful unifying influences in their communities.[86] The mania for music, marching bands, and orchestras is on full display in these plays. In *Berthelier Meets the Mormons*, a women's battalion marches to the sound of drums and brass, alerting the Mormon prophet of their revolutionary intentions. And *Japheth's Twelve Wives* features show-stopping choruses like "We've Just Arrived from America" and "Since We've Been Invited to the Ball," sung by all the wives together.

We have tried to make the translations clear to contemporary readers and have at times avoided some technical references to nineteenth-century French institutions. However, in some cases we have left these references in the translations and explained them in the notes. French verse length is not based on meter or stress, rather it is based on syllable count. In our translation of song lyrics, we have attempted to maintain the same number of syllables as in the originals (largely octosyllabic). We have often kept the same rhyme schemes, though, given English's difficulties when it comes to rhyming, we have occasionally opted for AABB in lieu of some ABAB rhymes in the original.

MORMONS IN PARIS

LOUIS LEROY AND ALFRED DELACOUR

Vaudeville Comedy in Four Acts

Premiered at the Théâtre des Variétés, August 6, 1874

We learned of the existence of *Les Mormons à Paris* by reading an 1874 *New York Times* review of the play where it was described as a "broad, extravagant farce . . . calculated to excite roars of laughter."[1] In France, A. de Bragelonne, writing for *Le Voleur*, called it "a very pleasing, very engaging, very funny play."[2] *L'Univers illustré* described the reaction to the play in these terms: "The public could only ask one thing of the actors, that they make them laugh; and the public laughed, laughed a lot, especially in the first two acts where funny lines and comical situations abound."[3] Other reviewers were less kind. *Le Journal des débats politiques et littéraires* praised the performance of Aline Duval in the role of Madame Chamboran but concluded by noting that the play's authors had often been more inspired.[4] Robert Nuay, writing for *La Fantaisie parisienne*, was the harshest critic, lamenting that *Mormons in Paris* was primarily interesting because of "beautiful women and bawdiness." He attacked the playwrights for lacking wit and predicted that the musical would barely last until the end of the month.[5] We find this review a bit cynical, as the play, in addition to offering insights into gender roles and the family in 1870s France, provides plenty of humorous situations and laughs.

Co-authors Louis Leroy and Alfred Delacour were both experienced playwrights when they wrote *Mormons in Paris*. Leroy had just written two successful plays with Eugène Labiche, easily the most celebrated boulevard playwright: *Il est de la police* in 1872 and *Brûlons Voltaire* in March 1874. Leroy also wrote articles for satirical newspapers, including *Le Journal amusant* (a paper that regularly parodied Mormons) and *Le Charivari*. He may be best known for coining the term *Impressionisme* to describe the art of Sisley, Pissarro, Monet, Morisot, Renoir, and others.[6] Significantly, this humorous article on Impressionism, published several months before the premier of *Mormons in Paris*, is written in dialogue, like a scene from a play. For his part, the prolific Alfred Delacour authored twenty-five plays from 1852 to 1876 with Labiche (and was one of his most frequent collaborators) and wrote 127 plays in all.[7] Leroy's and Delacour's plays were performed in all the big theaters in Paris: Palais Royal, Gymnase, Opéra Comique, Odéon, Gaîté, and, of course, the Théâtre des Variétés.

Created before the legalization of divorce, this play centers on the legality and binding nature of the marriage contract. It begins and ends with people on the cusp of beginning and ending their respective marriages. The play's main character, a French lawyer named Albert Savarin, has been married six times as the play begins. His challenge, and the nexus of the plot, is to legally rid himself of the five wives he married during a visit to Utah in order to avoid prison and to win back the affections of his new French bride, Mathilde, and the respect of his mother-in-law, Madame Chamboran. Instead of the plot trajectory of a traditional romantic comedy—love, misunderstanding, explanation, and marriage—this play begins with a marriage and then follows the couple from understanding to misunderstanding as Albert lies about, hides from, and then parts ways with his former wives before ultimately reconciling with wife number six.

The play opens at a ball where Albert and Mathilde have just married. Couples dance and flirt all around them. The word "flirt" actually appears in the first scene of the play. As Adeline Daumard reminds us, flirting in the late nineteenth century was a practice only recently "imported from England."[8] Albert soon learns that two of his Mormon wives have followed him from America, and one of them, Eva, comes to the hotel where Albert is celebrating his wedding to Mathilde.

After another one of Albert's Mormon wives makes an appearance at the new couple's apartment in act II, the action moves to the Parisian suburb of Chatou for act III where legal proceedings begin and where characters celebrate the "Mormon Festival." In the lead-up to that festival (the play's most spectacular moment), there is a reference to the holiday known as mid-Lent, a celebration where women, notably laundrywomen, were elevated as royalty. In French, the celebration was called both *mi-carême* (mid-Lent) and *la fête des blachisseuses* (Festival of the Laundrywomen). Men and women celebrated in masks and disguises, and theater, music, and drinking featured prominently. An article in the French press from March 22, 1873, chronicles the festival the year before the premier of *Mormons in Paris*. It tells of women parading through Paris singing, "One doesn't die from love" at the top of their lungs, and it ends with this description of the festivities:

> A large crowd prowled the boulevards all day long. From time to time, a carriage passed filled with masked passengers or with merciless scallywags playing cornetts. Horn players in neighboring apartments responded by playing out their windows. It was painful for delicate ears. Beginning at 10 P.M. it became nearly impossible to travel on the boulevards: they were filled with masked revelers going to the Opéra, to Valentino [a popular nineteenth-century dance hall], to Tivoli-Vauxhall [a theater], etc. The owners of these establishments must have been happy with their box office earnings since every *chicard* [a dancing carnival character] and would-be-tramp came out for this carnival revival.[9]

The Mormon Festival in this play can be read as a reflection of Parisian mid-Lent celebrations and of the broader carnival theme in all these Mormon-centered plays. It reflects both a cultural praxis associated with Mormons of challenging the status quo and a latent willingness to upend traditional power structures.

After this moment of carnival upheaval, the action returns to Paris for the final act, set in a costume shop where a pseudo-trial helps sort out the messiness of Albert's family life (see the introduction for an analysis of act IV). In the end, everyone's inner French character bests their Mormon characteristics. Though many of the characters pine for and miss certain aspects of Mormonism, the denouement provides a legal restoration of a traditional French family structure while the surfeit of wives is equitably distributed among other characters.

CAST:[10]	ROLE CREATED BY:[11]
Albert Savarin	Pierre-Eugène Grenier[12]
Jonathan	Deltombe[13]
Dubouloy	Baron[14]
Raphael	Cooper
Varequet	Blondelet
Gontran	Lanjallay
Falandard	D. Bac
Trinqueballe	Bordier
Servers	
Eva	B. Legrand
Madame Chamboran	Aline Duval[15]
Nadeje	Priston
Mathilde	A. Gérard
Mouchette	Varez
Boulotte	Louisa
Reseda	Bouttiez

ACT I

A small salon in the Grand Hotel. Three large doors upstage open onto a second ballroom. There are other doors on both the left and the right.

SCENE I

PERSIAN, servers, guests, DUBOULOY, EVA, GONTRAN

(*As the curtain rises a ball is in full swing; servers come and go with refreshments.*)

CHORUS[16]

SERVER, *holding a tray of ice cream, to the Persian who has a fur coat over his arm and holds a fur hat.*

Monsieur, would you like to check your furs?

PERSIAN

In a cloakroom? That's a joke! At the Frascati Hotel, I turned in my sable fur coat and they returned an old tattered frock with the humiliating label, "Custom Made."[17]

SERVER

That may happen at the Frascati, but it wouldn't happen here in the Grand Hotel, at a ball organized by a group of Americans.

PERSIAN

I'm not convinced. I'll leave my furs with the servant in the reading room. (*He exits.*)

DUBOULOY, *entering, to the server as he takes some ice cream.*

Is he a foreigner?

SERVER

A Persian that the Shah abandoned in Paris. He lives here in the hotel.

DUBOULOY, *sees Eva enter with Gontran.*

Ah! What a lovely woman!

SERVER

She's American. She lives in the hotel, as well. You live here, too, I presume?

DUBOULOY

Me? No. I live on the rue Vendôme, number twenty-six.

SERVER, *with disdain.*

Very middle class . . . a two-bit room. (*He turns his back on Dubouloy and exits.*)

GONTRAN, *standing next to Eva.*

Waltzing is so much fun. I could do it my whole life!

EVA

That would be a long dance.

GONTRAN

With you, mademoiselle, time would fly.

EVA

I must insist, call me *madame.*

GONTRAN

I see. You're married?

EVA

Of course. I've come to France to find my husband.

GONTRAN

Is finding him really necessary?

EVA

Ah! Schoking![18] (*They continue their conversation in a whisper.*)

DUBOULOY, *aside, watching Eva and Gontran.*

In English they call that "flirting." They are flirting.

EVA, *to Gontran.*

Oh, so you're rich. How much are you worth?

GONTRAN, *surprised.*

How much am I worth? Do you want to sell me?

EVA, *to Gontran.*

No. I'm asking for your net worth.

GONTRAN

Enormous. In the west there's an entire department that has my name.

EVA, *standing.*

Really! What's your name?

GONTRAN

Calvados . . . Gontran de Calvados. (*The orchestra begins warming up; Gontran offers his hand to Eva.*) Ah madame.

EVA

What?

GONTRAN

Don't you hear the orchestra warming up?

EVA

But we just danced.

GONTRAN

A waltz, yes. But this is a polka. It's completely different.

EVA, *smiling.*

Let's go! You can talk me into anything.

GONTRAN, *gallantly.*

Don't say that! You'll make me even more demanding. (*They exit upstage left.*)

DUBOULOY

Indubitably, they're flirting!

SCENE 2

DUBOULOY, MADAME CHAMBORAN

DUBOULOY

Ah! My sister.

MADAME CHAMBORAN

Another ice cream? You'll make yourself sick!

DUBOULOY

I never get sick when it's free. Where's the wedding celebration?

MADAME CHAMBORAN

All around us.

DUBOULOY

And the newlyweds?

MADAME CHAMBORAN

I just left them. They're in the ballroom. My son-in-law is giving my daughter a tour of the venue.

DUBOULOY

It's superb. I think I'll come spend a night here for a vacation.

MADAME CHAMBORAN

It's still not as nice as the Veau qui Tette restaurant.[19] There were some lovely parties there in the day, not to mention their famous mutton shanks in hen sauce.

DUBOULOY, *wistfully.*

Mutton shanks! Another flame that's been extinguished.

MADAME CHAMBORAN

And they weren't expensive there. Whereas here . . .

DUBOULOY

It's reasonably priced.

MADAME CHAMBORAN

The meal perhaps, but what about the ball?

DUBOULOY

They added it free of charge!

MADAME CHAMBORAN

What?

DUBOULOY

Thanks to my clever negotiations. When I came to book the meal, I learned that an American group was organizing a ball the same evening. I had an idea. I stipulated that the best-dressed people of our wedding party would be able to dance with the Americans. So we didn't have to pay for musicians or refreshments.

MADAME CHAMBORAN

I should have invited more people!

DUBOULOY

Remember to tell everyone that the refreshments are free.

MADAME CHAMBORAN

Do that yourself. I'm preoccupied with my daughter. Alas!

DUBOULOY

Don't worry about her. Albert Savarin is a charming young man. He's a lawyer and nowadays people need lawyers all the time. On top of that he's wealthy, educated, and remarkably well traveled.

MADAME CHAMBORAN

Yes, he was in America for a long time. But he doesn't like to discuss it. What was he up to over there?

DUBOULOY

He told me he was studying the Code Noir.[20] Apparently, he knows it inside and out.

MADAME CHAMBORAN

Why would he need to know that?

DUBOULOY

I don't know. Maybe slavery will be re-established at some point. (*He sees Albert and Mathilde entering.*) Ah! Here's the new couple.

SCENE 3

The same, ALBERT, MATHILDE, the SERVER

MATHILDE

Oh, Mother, it's beautiful!

ALBERT

Magnificent! And now that we've seen everything, I think we can go back to our place.

MADAME CHAMBORAN

What? At ten-thirty on your wedding night?

ALBERT

All the more reason to leave. If it weren't our wedding night, we would stay . . . But we have so many sweet nothings to whisper to each other.

MATHILDE

No, we don't. We're at a ball, I want to dance.

ALBERT

We can dance at our place, too.

MADAME CHAMBORAN

You're so impatient!

ALBERT

Cripes! Listen my dear Mother—may I call you Mother?—It's difficult to walk around all day long with a lovely woman on your arm who is yours and who . . . and who . . .

MADAME CHAMBORAN

Albert!

ALBERT

And I don't like to leave things unfinished. (*Taking Mathilde's arm.*) Let's go!

MATHILDE, *pulling away.*

Not until we've danced!

DUBOULOY, *whispering, to Albert.*

Nephew, have some ice cream. It will give you patience. (*To a server.*) Give some to this gentleman. (*To Albert.*) Eat as much as you'd like. It's free!

(*Everyone takes ice cream.*)

ALBERT

So be it. I'll be patient and I'll overeat. But at eleven o'clock . . .

(*Cheering and applause offstage.*)

DUBOULOY, *to a server.*

What's that cheering?

SERVER

A conference is ending in the green ballroom.

DUBOULOY

A conference?

SERVER

Yes, a Mormon apostle was preaching.

ALBERT, *aside, agitated.*

A Mormon!

MATHILDE, *to Albert.*

What's a Mormon?

ALBERT

Savages, I think . . . redskins.

SERVER

He's right over there.

(*Jonathan crosses the salon upstage followed by a crowd; they seem to be praying. Albert recognizes him.*)

ALBERT, *aside.*

Jonathan, here?

MATHILDE

Oh, he's frightening.

ALBERT

He is. Let's go . . . let's go!

MATHILDE

Let's go dancing?

ALBERT

Yes, yes, let's dance.

MATHILDE

May we, Mother?

MADAME CHAMBORAN

Of course, my child. (*Albert exits brusquely, pulling Mathilde with him.*) Mormons! Aren't they the horrible men newspapers speak of so often?

DUBOULOY

I think they're members of a temperance society.

MADAME CHAMBORAN

Ah! But look at him. His nose is a bit too red for a teetotaler.

(*Jonathan enters right, followed by the crowd. He is wearing a long coat with tails and glasses and has long hair. His nose is bright red.*)

SCENE 4

DUBOULOY, MADAME CAMBORAN, JONATHAN, the crowd, AN OLD MAN, servers.

JONATHAN, *to the crowd.*

Yes, my sisters and brothers, I've just arrived from the shores of the Great Salt Lake. (*He takes a glass of rum punch from a tray.*)

And I've come to bring you the light. We will now address the question of marriage.

THE CROWD, *enthusiastically.*

Ooh! Ahh!

JONATHAN

In Salt Lake City . . . (*To the server, taking a second glass.*) Don't go far, brother sommelier. (*He drinks.*)

MADAME CHAMBORAN

Why is he drinking so much?

DUBOULOY

Well, it's awfully salty where he's from.

JONATHAN, *putting down his glass.*

Where was I? Oh, right. In France, marriage is a petty, narrow thing. People look for happiness in a union of two people . . . sometimes three . . . rarely four. It's unfortunate. Overseas, in the land of new horizons, the union of souls is more complex. There, my sweet gazelles, your sisters aren't afraid to join with ten, twenty, or even one hundred others to make one man happy.

THE CROWD

Oh!

MADAME CHAMBORAN

One hundred wives!

JONATHAN

And that's not too many. (*He drinks.*)

MADAME CHAMBORAN

It's monstrous!

DUBOULOY

Pipe down! (*Aside.*) This idea's appealing.

JONATHAN

In my modest dwelling, I have thirty-three legitimate wives.

THE CROWD, *surprised.*

Oh!

MADAME CHAMBORAN

It's deplorable.

DUBOULOY

But they're legitimate . . .

JONATHAN

And had I accepted all the offers women have made to me, I wouldn't have room for my staff. And yet . . .

DUBOULOY

He wishes he had more.

JONATHAN

I often suffer from this conjugal shortage.

THE CROWD, *laughing.*

Ha! Ha!

JONATHAN

But, nothing can be done. I'm learning to be happy with what little I have.

DUBOULOY

He's like a rabbit!

MADAME CHAMBORAN

It's horrible. Ernest, your arm.

DUBOULOY

Let's hear him out.

MADAME CHAMBORAN

I can't listen anymore. (*She drags Dubouloy out.*)

DUBOULOY, *aside, exiting.*

Thirty-three wives . . . I'll be back to learn more.

JONATHAN, *to the server.*

Leave the tray here. (*To the crowd.*) As for you, sisters . . .

THE CROWD

Stop! Enough!

JONATHAN

If I have deposited the seed of belief in your souls . . .

THE CROWD

No! No! Kick him out!

JONATHAN

If my healthy doctrines on spousal abundance . . . [21]

THE CROWD

That's enough! (*They knock him over as they exit, leaving Jonathan alone with one old man, his eyes fixed on Jonathan.*)

CHORUS

JONATHAN

As calm as a summer evening, I will only respond to this violence with the tranquility of a pure soul.[22] (*Looking around.*) Well, they're gone. (*Noticing the old man.*) You alone, brother, have remained faithful. I've had my eye on you for an hour.

THE OLD MAN, *cupping his hand to his ear.*

Speak up!

JONATHAN, *dejectedly.*

I only have one listener and he's deaf. (*Screaming in his ear.*) Good evening!

THE OLD MAN

Oh! We're done. Excellent. (*He exits.*)

SCENE 5

JONATHAN, then DUBOULOY

JONATHAN, *alone.*

Zip, nothing, zero! Fortunately, I have a few other candidates in reserve that will suit me.

DUBOULOY, *returning.*

What? It's over? Too bad.

JONATHAN

Is it possible, good brother, that I planted the seed in you?

DUBOULOY

I won't hide the fact that what you said piqued my curiosity. You say you have thirty-three wives?

JONATHAN

No more, no less.

DUBOULOY

Impressive.

JONATHAN, *aside.*

He's taking the bait. (*Aloud.*) Please sit down. (*They sit down on opposite sides of a table that has glasses of rum punch on it.*)

DUBOULOY

Cheers!

JONATHAN

Are you single?

DUBOULOY

It's impossible to be more single than I am.

JONATHAN

Excellent. Being single predisposes you to marriage.

DUBOULOY

It's strange . . . The thought of having a wife has always scared me, but the thought of having several appeals to me.

JONATHAN

The more there are, the more appealing it becomes. (*Aside.*) He's taking the bait.

DUBOULOY

But I don't understand how your institution works.

JONATHAN

It's really quite simple.

DUBOULOY

For starters, how many wives can you have?

JONATHAN

You can have as many wives as you can feed.

DUBOULOY

That must be nice for the wealthy.

JONATHAN

It's nice for everyone. Food costs next to nothing over there. We think of it as an act of charity to remove a bison's hump.

DUBOULOY

I've heard it tastes delicious.

JONATHAN

Exquisite. And now a supposition: You've had a good year and sold your crops for a good price. A batch of young women becomes available. You think, "I have enough to feed them." And you marry the whole lot.

DUBOULOY

What an advanced civilization!

JONATHAN

You start out modestly with a half dozen or so.

DUBOULOY

Right, a starter kit.

JONATHAN

You put this first batch to work behind a plow or growing potatoes. You earn money from that crop and the next year, thanks to the revenue brought in by the first batch, you marry a second batch.

DUBOULOY

And it snowballs from there.

JONATHAN

So much so that after thirty or forty years . . .

DUBOULOY

Your little family is well stocked.

JONATHAN

Precisely!

DUBOULOY

It's entirely patriarchal . . . But how do you avoid jealousy among the wives?

JONATHAN

Nothing could be easier. You arrange your wives by height and assign each one a number.

DUBOULOY

Like we used to do in the National Guard.[23] Number one has guard duty, then number two. But what if you want someone to report for duty out of order?

JONATHAN

Oh, it's forbidden! (*Changing tone.*) But you can make it work by mixing up the numbers. My number twenty-seven, for example, has a button nose and is very cute, and somehow her number comes up three times more than the others. On the other hand, numbers fourteen and twenty-three are a bit on the old side and have no chance.

DUBOULOY

You can't imagine how much you're making me dream! (*He sees servers enter.*) Someone's coming. Quiet!

JONATHAN

I'll bring you a little pamphlet.

DUBOULOY

Here's my card.

JONATHAN

Here's mine. (*They exchange cards.*) What time do you eat breakfast?

DUBOULOY

At eleven. And we dine at six.

JONATHAN

Noted.

DUBOULOY, *taking a glass and drinking.*

To your health! I'm looking forward to reading your pamphlet.

JONATHAN

Go, Brother, and water the seed!

DUBOULOY, *exiting.*

Thirty-three wives! He's like a rabbit!

SCENE 6

JONATHAN, then ALBERT

JONATHAN, *taking a drink.*

Watering the seed is the key. (*Taking out his notebook.*) He swallowed the bait. I'll take down this old simpleton's name. (*He writes.*)

ALBERT, *entering.*

While Mathilde is dancing the polka, I absolutely have to ward off this imbecile Jonathan.

JONATHAN

I hear my name.

ALBERT

It's him!

JONATHAN

What is this? Renegade! Impious deserter!

ALBERT

Quiet! People might overhear.

JONATHAN

So what if they hear me? Savarin, what did you do to your wives?

ALBERT

Will you shut up?

JONATHAN

What have you done to your five wives?

ALBERT

It's true! I abandoned them. So what? I've come back to France to collect an inheritance from my uncle.

JONATHAN

What about your responsibilities to your wives?

ALBERT

Do those marriages even count? I was traveling in Mormondom to study their culture. I was told that in order to stay I had to adopt the local customs. The next thing I know I'm stuck with three wives.

JONATHAN

A modest start.

ALBERT

Since I didn't want to offend my hosts, I accepted them. Later they offered me two more, contending that my wealth authorized this addition. They were nice, so, naturally, I accepted them. I made them happy for six months. What more could anyone want?

JONATHAN

If I may . . .

ALBERT

I adopted the customs of the land. I married conscientiously; I have nothing to be ashamed of. Did they think that when I came back to France I would bring all of my little households with me to Paris? Not a chance!

JONATHAN

You scoundrel! Without me what would your five widows have become?

ALBERT, *laughing.*

You married them?

JONATHAN

I took them in. To distract them I took them for walks with my wives. That made thirty-eight in all, nineteen for each arm.

ALBERT, *laughing.*

An entire boarding school!

JONATHAN

Yes, but we blocked the road while I tried to lecture them.

ALBERT

They've remarried?

JONATHAN

Not all of them. Only numbers two, three, and five.

ALBERT

Bravo! Five minus three leaves two. It's a good start. What about the other two?

JONATHAN

One and four are inconsolable. When they heard I was being sent to France as an apostle, they insisted on coming with me.

ALBERT

You brought them?

JONATHAN

Of course. They were burning with desire to see their other half. I thought it wise to yield to their pleas for the good of the cause.

ALBERT

And they're here?

JONATHAN

Your number one left us when we set foot in Paris, and I don't know what has become of her. But number four has remained faithful. Eva is here.

ALBERT

What do you mean, here? Where here?

JONATHAN

At this ball!

ALBERT

Oh no . . .

JONATHAN

Tomorrow we were planning to go to the lost-and-found office at police headquarters in order to claim you. But since you're here, I'll go get her and bring her to you.

ALBERT, *restraining him.*

Wait a minute.

JONATHAN

Her place is under your roof. I'll be back with the most beautiful flower in your garden.

ALBERT, *restraining him.*

Dang! It's that . . .

JONATHAN

You'll be happy just smelling her perfume.

ALBERT

On second thought, yes . . . go.

JONATHAN

My child.

ALBERT

It's true, I have missed her.

(*Jonathan exits.*)

SCENE 7

ALBERT, then DUBOULOY, MADAME CHAMBORAN, MATHILDE

ALBERT, *very agitated.*

If he thinks I'm actually going to wait for him, him and his flower . . . I'm off to the cloak room. In five minutes we'll be home and tomorrow we're off to Italy for a short trip of two or three years. I'm paying the price for my five lapses in judgment.

DUBOULOY, *entering upstage with Madame Chamboran and Mathilde.*

We've been looking for you!

ALBERT

And I've been looking for you. Let's go. It's eleven o'clock.

MADAME CHAMBORAN

Let's stay a little longer, my son-in-law.

ALBERT, *getting angry.*

It's eleven o'clock. Didn't we agree to leave at eleven? Yes, we did! So let's go! I'm going to get my coat. (*He exits.*)

SCENE 8

DUBOULOY, MADAME CHAMBORAN, MATHILDE, then EVA, then ALBERT

MATHILDE

It seems Albert's angry.

MADAME CHAMBORAN

Yes, what's gotten into him?

DUBOULOY, *maliciously.*

Well, obviously, what's gotten into him is that it's eleven o'clock.

MATHILDE

So?

DUBOULOY

The time has come.

MATHILDE

What time?

DUBOULOY

You ask too many questions.

EVA, *entering left.*

It's so hot! (*She fans herself.*)

DUBOULOY

Say, it's the American. (*To Eva.*) Would you like some ice cream or something to drink?

EVA

How do you say, thank you?[24]

DUBOULOY, *surprised.*

What?

MATHILDE

She's thanking you in English.

DUBOULOY, *to Eva.*

Oh! A thousand pardons. I'm still not familiar with your language.

EVA, *to Mathilde.*

Do you speak English?

MATHILDE

Oh, very little, Madame. Just a few words. (*They speak to each other but can't be heard by the audience.*)

ALBERT, *peeking in, his hat and coat in hand, aside.*

Here? Now? What am I seeing? Eva! Curses!

EVA, *to Mathilde.*

Really, just married today?

MADAME CHAMBORAN

This morning at eleven o'clock.

DUBOULOY

A neophyte.

MADAME CHAMBORAN, *to Eva.*

You're upset?

EVA, *to Mathilde.*

The wreath in your hair brings back so many memories for me.

DUBOULOY

If the memories are swelling in your breast, they must be pleasant.

MADAME CHAMBORAN

Shush, Brother! (*To Eva.*) Are you married?

EVA

I've been married for four years. But three and a half years don't count.

MADAME CHAMBORAN

Oh, did your husband pass away?

EVA

He abandoned all of us.

MADAME CHAMBORAN, *surprised.*

All of you?

EVA

His other wives and me.

MADAME CHAMBORAN

How many did he have?

EVA

Only five.

MADAME CHAMBORAN

A Turk!

EVA

No. A Frenchman who came to America and joined the Mormons.

MADAME CHAMBORAN

And you're a Mormon?

EVA

Yes.

DUBOULOY, *aside.*

Well, well . . .

MADAME CHAMBORAN

The horror! Come, my daughter. Come, Ernest. Let's get out of this den of iniquity.

DUBOULOY, *aside.*

Very nice, the young thing. If they're all like that . . .

(*They exit.*)

SCENE 9

EVA, then ALBERT

EVA

What's her problem?

ALBERT, *entering from the reading room, his hat and coat in hand, aside.*

I don't understand anything anymore . . . Eva!

EVA

Albert! (*Running to him.*) My Albert!

ALBERT, *stopping her with his hand.*

You're wrong, madame. I'm not Albert.

EVA

But I recognize you so well! I know your face, your lovely face.

ALBERT

That doesn't prove anything. Everyone in Paris has a lovely face. Let me pass.

EVA

Jonathan will recognize you too. (*Calling.*) Jonathan! Jon . . .

ALBERT

Will you be quiet? Fine, yes, I recognize you, my little goose. It's me. Ha! Ha! Are you happy?

EVA, *kissing him.*

Oh, it's so good, it's so good!

ALBERT

Eva, restrain yourself. The lights are on.

EVA, *tenderly.*

I can't wait to turn them out. We won't ever be apart again, my little goose, my dear darling.

ALBERT

Manners, Eva! We're in public.

EVA

We can leave if you want. Let's go right away.

ALBERT

Go where?

EVA

To your place.

ALBERT

Impossible! I'm having it painted. It smells of paint.

EVA

Then come to my place. I'm in this hotel on the sixth floor, room 798.

ALBERT

Two less than eight hundred. Very well. I'll remember. Go up right away. I'll join you soon.

EVA

Oh no! Let's go together.

ALBERT

I would, but . . . I've promised the first waltz to the ambassador's wife. People are counting on me.

EVA

Okay, go dance then. I'll take your hat and coat as a deposit to make sure I see you again. (*She takes them quickly.*)

ALBERT

What? Wait!

EVA

I don't want you to leave without me.

ALBERT

But . . .

EVA

There's only one exit. I'll wait for you there.

ALBERT, *trying to take back his hat and coat.*

C'mon, Eva, my little Eva.

EVA

No, I'm going to be watchful this time.

ALBERT, *cajoling her.*

Leave without you, my silly little one? I'm too happy to have found you again.

EVA

Really?

ALBERT, *glancing to the side.*

Oh!

EVA

What?

ALBERT, *aside.*

My mother-in-law! (*Aloud.*) People are coming.

EVA

Who? Your dance partner?

ALBERT

Yes. The ambassador's wife. Go wait in your room.

EVA

No, over there in the hall! (*She exits with Albert's hat and coat.*)

SCENE 10

ALBERT, then MADAME CHAMBORAN, MATHILDE, DUBOULOY with his hat and coat and a giant book under his arm

ALBERT

Here comes trouble!

MADAME CHAMBORAN

Albert, we've been looking for you for an hour! Come on, let's go!

ALBERT

Yes, let's go. (*Aside.*) And the other one who's keeping guard . . .

DUBOULOY

Where are your hat and coat?

ALBERT

They're . . . in the reading room. (*Aside.*) There must be another way out. (*Aloud.*) We'll get them on the way out. (*He takes Mathilde's arm.*)

MADAME CHAMBORAN

Let's go!

(*Eva enters upstage and sits down with Albert's hat and coat on her lap.*)

ALBERT, *aside.*

Oh, Eva! (*He runs into the reading room.*)

MATHILDE, *surprised.*

What?

MADAME CHAMBORAN

What has gotten into him today?

DUBOULOY

Getting married has affected his brain. He'll be much calmer tomorrow. (*Aside, pointing to the book.*) He gave me the pamphlet with an inscription. (*Smiling.*) A little light reading. (*They follow Albert out.*)

SCENE II

EVA seated upstage, GONTRAN

GONTRAN, *entering.*

Where is my American hiding? I've got to find her. It was starting too well for it not to end even better. (*Looking around.*) Hey, there she is! But why does she have a man's hat and coat in her lap? Does she work in the cloakroom? If that's the case, I'll check myself there!

(*He walks toward Eva. She stands, preoccupied, and crosses the room upstage, looking for someone, then exits momentarily. Gontran follows her, smiling.*)

SCENE 12

DUBOULOY, MATHILDE, MADAME CHAMBORAN, then ALBERT, then EVA, GONTRAN, then JONATHAN

DUBOULOY, *emerging from the reading room.*

I swear, he's crazy!

MADAME CHAMBORAN

I've never seen such strange behavior: trying to convince us we're on the ground floor so we'll climb out through the window.

MATHILDE

He's frightening me!

ALBERT, *entering wearing the Persian's fur coat and fur hat.*

Are we all here? I'm ready to go.

MADAME CHAMBORAN

Oh my! What is that?

ALBERT

I can't seem to find my coat, but I don't want to catch a cold, so I borrowed these furs from the clerk in the cloakroom. (*Aside.*) Who was asleep. (*Aloud.*) Your arm, my dear Mathilde.

MADAME CHAMBORAN, *spying Eva entering upstage.*

That woman again! Let's go!

(*Albert takes Mathilde by the arm and walks sternly in front of Eva and bows to her. She doesn't recognize him in the furs.*)

GONTRAN, *entering.*

Oh, Eva, do you see him?

EVA

I can't find him. Where did he go?

GONTRAN, *to Eva.*

Stop looking. A lost husband always reappears too soon. (*Eva mutters something in English.*)

(*As Albert, Mathilde, Madame Chamboran, and Dubouloy exit right, Jonathan enters upstage left. He has a woman on his arm who has another on her arm, who has linked arms with a third, and so on, forming a long line of women stretching offstage.*)

JONATHAN

To the future! Thirty-three plus twelve equals forty-five. (*He continues walking with his wives.*)

(*Curtain.*)

ACT II

The stage represents an elegantly furnished boudoir with two doors at left, two at right, a loveseat, chairs, and a fireplace upstage.

SCENE I

NADEJE, RAPHAEL

(*As the curtain opens, Nadeje is seated on the loveseat at left. There is a lamp next to her on a side table. She is sewing. There is a second lamp on the mantle. Raphael is placing curlers in a box on the table.*)

NADEJE, *as the clock sounds the half hour.*

Eleven thirty. Hurry Raphael!

RAPHAEL, *putting the curling cloths in the box.*

It's done.

NADEJE

The new couple will be here soon, and if we're alone, what's our story?

RAPHAEL

I have a pretext: I'm here to get my hair iron and the box of hair extensions that I left this morning when I did the bride's hair.

NADEJE

You've got it all worked out!

RAPHAEL

When a man gives his heart to a woman, he can work anything out!

NADEJE

But you haven't given me a thing!

RAPHAEL

Really? (*He walks behind her and takes her by the waist.*) Then I'll take it!

NADEJE

Don't touch me, I bite!

RAPHAEL

I'm attracted to danger. (*As he tries to kiss her she pricks him with a needle.*) Ouch!

NADEJE

You deserved it.

RAPHAEL

That's the thanks I get for finding you this good job?

NADEJE

A good job? We'll see. I've only been here a few hours. Come back in a year or two, and I'll tell you then.

RAPHAEL

I can feel these things. I've only known you for a week, but seeing you negotiate a good price for a false braid with my boss, I said to myself right away, "This woman suits me." I can feel these things. (*He rubs the spot Nadeje pricked.*)

NADEJE

You said that to yourself, did you?

RAPHAEL

The proof is that when you told me you were looking for a job as a maid, I beat the bushes through the entire neighborhood to find a position for you.

NADEJE

That's very kind of you. And I enjoy your company.

RAPHAEL

I'm fun to talk to, aren't I?

NADEJE

You're quite brilliant.

RAPHAEL

In the neighborhood people call me the fireman.

NADEJE

You were a firefighter?

RAPHAEL

No, it's because I light people's hearts on fire.

NADEJE

I see.

RAPHAEL

It's too bad you weren't born into a better situation.

NADEJE

That's life.

RAPHAEL

If only I had my own hairdressing salon on rue de la Paix . . . with six large windows on the façade, a desk made from exotic wood . . . You know what I'd do?

NADEJE

You'd go bankrupt.

RAPHAEL

But before that, I'd give you a job there!

NADEJE

Enough daydreaming. Tell me, fireman, what are the newlyweds like? I only know what Madame Chamboran told me yesterday.

RAPHAEL

The bride and groom?

NADEJE

Yes, what's the bride like?

RAPHAEL

A little birdlike, but she'll do.[25]

NADEJE

And the groom? I don't even know his name.

RAPHAEL

His name? Wait . . . I know it's a food . . . Ah!
Savarin.[26]

NADEJE, *shuddering.*

What? What did you say?

RAPHAEL

Navarin, Tabarin . . . umm . . . something like that.

NADEJE

Have you seen him?

RAPHAEL

Yes, I saw him for the first time this morning.

NADEJE

What's he like?

RAPHAEL

Let's see . . . he was with his four witnesses, all wearing black suits and white gloves, and I never did figure out which one was the groom. But I think he was the tall, handsome man with a thick mustache.

NADEJE

Oh, you gave me a fright.

RAPHAEL

A fright? I scared you?

NADEJE

No . . . a fright from far away. (*She begins working again while singing an African tune by Henri Potier.*[27])

Was born in Mozambique
With African mystique
And my old father dear,
He always kept me near.
A merchant once did come
From Europe to our dock
And started making some
Knives and jewels to hawk.
Oh, oh, oh, oh! Hee, hee, hee, hee!
Oh, how shiny, oh, so lovely!

RAPHAEL

What are you singing?

NADEJE

An African song that someone dear to me would often hum.

RAPHAEL

A woman?

NADEJE

Of course.

RAPHAEL and NADEJE, *together.*

Oh, oh, oh, oh! Hee, hee, hee, hee!

NADEJE, *stops singing as the clock chimes.*

I hear horses in the courtyard. Quick! Go down the servants' staircase.

RAPHAEL

As you wish. Goodbye, Miss Nadeje.

NADEJE

Goodbye.

RAPHAEL

True love conquers all. (*He exits.*)

SCENE 2

NADEJE, then MADAME CHAMBORAN

NADEJE

He's a bit crazy, the fireman . . . But he's not bad for a hairdresser.

MADAME CHAMBORAN, entering.

Oh good, you're here, mademoiselle. What time did you arrive?

NADEJE

At eight o'clock like you asked.

MADAME CHAMBORAN

Is everything ready in my daughter's room?

NADEJE

Yes, madame.

MADAME CHAMBORAN

Perfect. Take this lamp in there and trim the night light. Oh!

NADEJE

Madame?

MADAME CHAMBORAN

Don't forget to place a heating pan in the bed. Only on my daughter's side. Don't bother on the other side.

NADEJE

Yes, madame.

SCENE 3

MADAME CHAMBORAN, then MATHILDE, ALBERT, and DUBOULOY

MADAME CHAMBORAN, *watching Nadeje exit.*

Well mannered . . . She's no genius, but she has the necessary dignity of her profession.

ALBERT, *entering with Mathilde, followed by Dubouloy, the large book still under his arm.*

Ah, we're finally home.

MADAME CHAMBORAN

You took your time coming upstairs!

ALBERT

The coachman wanted to debate the amount of his tip.

DUBOULOY

Those people are never happy. One day I wanted to see what it would cost to get a thank you from one of them. I gave him some money, then more, and more, and more, without succeeding.

ALBERT

How much did you give him in all?

DUBOULOY

Oh! At least three cents, and he didn't even begin to say thank you.

ALBERT

Inexplicable!

MADAME CHAMBORAN

My dear son-in-law, how do you like the apartment I've prepared for you?

ALBERT

It's delightful, Madame Chamboran, absolutely delightful!

MADAME CHAMBORAN

There's the bedroom.

ALBERT, *passionately to Mathilde.*

Right! There's the bedroom . . .

MATHILDE, *scandalized, stepping toward her mother.*

Oh! Mother!

MADAME CHAMBORAN

Don't worry. (*To Albert.*) And this is the boudoir.

ALBERT

No need to continue. This apartment is identical to yours just below.

DUBOULOY, *switching the book to his other arm, aside.*

Damned pamphlet! It's heavy!

MADAME CHAMBORAN

And there's the bathroom, your slippers, and your robe . . .

ALBERT

Yes, my second mother, yes. Goodnight. Time to go. Goodnight.

MADAME CHAMBORAN, *aside.*

Such impatience! (*Aloud.*) Come here, Malthide.

MATHILDE

Yes, Mother.

ALBERT, *stopping Madame Chamboran.*

If you please, a simple observation: Now that we are married, be kind enough to call my wife Mathilde like everyone else does. I would appreciate it.

DUBOULOY

He's right. You know her name is spelled Malthide, but we pronounce it Mathilde.

MADAME CHAMBORAN

How dare you try to teach me my own daughter's name? Come Malthide.

ALBERT

That's enough. The door is right over here, Mother-in-law.

DUBOULOY, *to Mathilde.*

And don't I get a kiss goodnight?

MATHILDE

Of course, my uncle! (*She kisses him.*)

DUBOULOY

My child, the time has come when the timid dove . . .

MADAME CHAMBORAN

Enough!

DUBOULOY

You don't know what I was going to say to the dove.

MADAME CHAMBORAN

I can guess. But that's my role. Come, Malthide.

ALBERT

Go ahead, *Malthide*. (*Madame Chamboran and Mathilde exit.*)

SCENE 4
ALBERT, DUBOULOY

ALBERT

Since she insists . . . (*To Dubouloy, who shifts the book to his other arm.*) So, what have you been carrying under your arm for the last hour?

DUBOULOY

A work on Mormon marriages.

ALBERT, *aside.*

Mormon marriages!

DUBOULOY

I'm going to read a few pages before I fall asleep. I'll have sweet dreams.

ALBERT

Where the hell did you get it?

DUBOULOY

The apostle gave it to me . . . free of charge.

ALBERT

What apostle?

DUBOULOY

At the Grand Hotel.

ALBERT

You spoke with him?

DUBOULOY

He may even come to breakfast.

ALBERT

You invited him?

DUBOULOY

I gave him my card along with our mealtimes, and he gave me the tome. (*He opens the book and skims it.*)

ALBERT, *aside.*

Oh great! What luck! At eight o'clock Mathilde and I will be on the express leaving here as fast as possible.

DUBOULOY, *thumbing through the book.*

Say!

ALBERT

What is it?

DUBOULOY

Very interesting . . . A list of Mormons . . . with the number and names of their wives.

ALBERT, *agitated.*

What?

DUBOULOY, *laughing.*

Ah, wow! (*Reading.*) Romanoff, forty-one wives. Look at this! (*Reading.*) Heloise, Anna, Marie, etc., etc., etc. It fills the whole page.

ALBERT, *with a forced laugh.*

Ha! Ha! Very funny.

DUBOULOY

Romanoff . . . He must be from the north. (*Reading.*) Salomon, twenty-two wives . . . (*Speaking.*) Still not bad. (*Surprised.*) Oh!

ALBERT

What?

DUBOULOY

Your name. Look. (*Showing him the book.*) A. L. B. Savarin. Albert Savarin.

ALBERT, *coolly.*

No. A.L.B. It must be Alberic Savarin, one of my uncles.

DUBOULOY

Bah! You have a Mormon uncle?

ALBERT

I have . . . That is, I had . . . he was very old.

DUBOULOY, *reading the book with disgust.*

Oh! Only five wives.

ALBERT

Damn! That's a lot for a man over eighty.

DUBOULOY

That's his excuse? (*Reading.*) Hey, Jonathan didn't lie. Thirty-three wives!

MADAME CHAMBORAN, *offstage.*

Yes, my child, see you tomorrow.

ALBERT, *energetically.*

Madame Chamboran! Hide that! (*Dubouloy closes the book. Aside.*) Yes, we are definitely leaving tomorrow.

SCENE 5

The same, MADAME CHAMBORAN

MADAME CHAMBORAN

There, that's done.

DUBOULOY

Were your goodbyes emotional?

MADAME CHAMBORAN

They were what they should be: tender on Malthide's part, energetic on mine. As for you, my son-on-law, no need to remind you of your duties.

ALBERT

No need at all, mother-in-law, I'm up to speed on the subject.

DUBOULOY

Not too fast, I hope.

MADAME CHAMBORAN

Dubouloy, shut up! I'm consulting my heart.

DUBOULOY

What does it say, dear mother?

MADAME CHAMBORAN, *with emotion.*

Albert, my friend, be strong.

ALBERT

Rest assured, I'm overflowing with strength.

MADAME CHAMBORAN

Remember that I'm just below, nothing but a floorboard between us, and if you need anything . . .

ALBERT

No, no, we'll manage.

MADAME CHAMBORAN

My son! (*She embraces him.*)

ALBERT, *pulling himself away, aside.*

Ah! So clingy! (*Aloud.*) That's enough, goodnight, goodnight. I'm going to remove my boots. (*He exits to his study.*)

MADAME CHAMBORAN

It's strange. I left my daughter without the least bit of emotion, and I'm turned inside out saying goodbye to my son-in-law. Is that stupid?

DUBOULOY

Yes, it's rather stupid.

MADAME CHAMBORAN

I remember my poor Chamboran. On our wedding day he was more uncomfortable than I was.

SCENE 6

MADAME CHAMBORAN, DUBOULOY, NADEJE, ALBERT in his study.

NADEJE, *entering, carrying a candlestick.*

Madame, the nightlight is trimmed and everything is ready.

MADAME CHAMBORAN

Very good. You can go up to your room.[28]

NADEJE

Goodnight, madame. Goodnight, monsieur.

(*With the door to the study slightly ajar, Albert can be heard singing.*)

ALBERT, *singing.*

Oh, oh, oh, oh! Hee, hee, hee, hee!
Oh, how shiny, oh so lovely!

DUBOULOY, *laughing.*

He's singing to get his strength up!

NADEJE, *stopping, aside.*

Oh my! That's his voice!

ALBERT

Oh, oh, oh, oh! Hee, hee, hee, hee!
Oh, how shiny, oh so lovely!

NADEJE, *aside.*

Without a doubt, that's him!

MADAME CHAMBORAN, *to Nadeje.*

Why are you still here? Scurry off to bed!

NADEJE

Yes, madame, I'm going.

MADAME CHAMBORAN

Don't forget the key so that you can come in without waking them up in the morning.

NADEJE

Yes, madame, I have it. (*Aside.*) And I know how I'll use it . . . Ah! The traitor! (*She exits.*)

SCENE 7
MADAME CHAMBORAN, DUBOULOY, then ALBERT

DUBOULOY, *ogling Nadeje.*

Not bad. She'd make a nice addition to a batch.

MADAME CHAMBORAN

What's that?

DUBOULOY

Oh, nothing.

ALBERT, *enters wearing a robe.*

What, still here? Your pillow must be sick with worry.

MADAME CHAMBORAN

We were waiting for the maid to leave. Goodnight, my son-in-law.

ALBERT

Goodnight, Mother-in-law! (*To Dubouloy.*) I'll see you tomorrow, Uncle.

DUBOULOY, *picking up the book.*

They call this a "pamphlet" in America!

MADAME CHAMBORAN, *with emotion.*

Remember, a simple floorboard is all that stands between us.

ALBERT

And if I need you I'll stomp. It's agreed.

MADAME CHAMBORAN, *crying as she exits.*

My heavens, the most beautiful day of my life is certainly ugly! (*Dubouloy and Madame Chamboran exit.*)

SCENE 8

ALBERT, then MATHILDE, then NADEJE

ALBERT, *alone.*

Finally! Free and alone. Let me think. (*He paces for a moment, then stops.*) Even if you've been down this road before, the heart still beats with anticipation—thump, thump, thump, thump . . . I need to think . . . (*He continues pacing.*)

MATHILDE, *enters wearing a white robe.*

Mother! Mother!

ALBERT

Why do you want her? She's gone.

MATHILDE

I was scared all alone in the bedroom.

ALBERT

You should have called for me.

MATHILDE

I wouldn't dare.

ALBERT

You're so sweet. (*He tries to kiss her.*)

MATHILDE, *pushing him away.*

Oh!

ALBERT, *aside.*

Too soon. (*Aloud.*) Let's sit here for a moment and chat like two friends . . . that just happen to be of the opposite sex.

MATHILDE

I'd like that, monsieur.

ALBERT, *rebuking her.*

Monsieur? Today say, "my dear," tomorrow, "my love." And show more affection each day.

MATHILDE

Yes, my dear.

ALBERT, *passionately.*

Oh, Mathilde!

MATHILDE

What is it?

ALBERT, *passionately.*

Everything, Mathilde, everything!

NADEJE, *entering behind a tapestry; she sings but can't be seen.*

Oh, oh, oh, oh! Hee, hee, hee, hee!

ALBERT

What? What's that?

MATHILDE

Ignore it. That's just the maid going back to her quarters.

ALBERT, *aside.*

That melody! She must have heard me humming it. (*Calmly, aloud.*) Let's get back on topic. Where were we, Madame Savarin?

MATHILDE

It's funny to be called "Madame."

ALBERT

Tell me you love me.

NADEJE, *like before.*

Oh, oh, oh, oh! Hee, hee, hee, hee!

ALBERT

That song again?

MATHILDE

I forbid you from being so uninhibited with me, monsieur.

ALBERT

Yes, yes, we'll come back to that. (*He takes her hands.*) Now, did your mother give you any advice before she left?

MATHILDE

Yes, she told me to be careful not to hurt your feelings.

ALBERT

Then why would you resist holding my hand?

MATHILDE

You're really that sensitive?

ALBERT

Like a barometer. The slightest frustration sets my nerves on end.

MATHILDE

Really?

ALBERT

So you must be kind with me and always obey me. (*He kisses her hands.*)

MATHILDE, *aside.*

I mustn't frustrate him.

ALBERT

And if I want to kiss you . . .

MATHILDE, *pulling away abruptly.*

Oh, no, not that!

ALBERT

Oh! You're hurting my feelings!

MATHILDE

Too bad for your feelings!

ALBERT, *embracing her.*

Come now, Mathilde . . . my little Mathilde.

MATHILDE

No, monsieur!

ALBERT, *noticing Nadeje staring at him, he stands in shock and represses a scream.*

Ah!

MATHILDE, *without seeing Nadeje.*

What's wrong?

ALBERT, *moves away from Mathilde, complying with a hand signal from Nadeje.*

With me? Nothing.

MATHILDE

Are you frustrated?

ALBERT

Yes . . . Yes . . . excessively frustrated.

MATHILDE, *aside.*

It's my fault. I hurt his feelings. (*Aloud.*) Please forgive me. Come back and sit here beside me.

ALBERT, *aside.*

She's intoxicating. (*He forgets about Mathilde, steps toward Nadeje, then backs up quickly when she motions for him to stop.*)

MATHILDE

Please come back. (*Aside.*) He's trembling. It must be his nerves. (*Aloud.*) That kiss you asked for, you can have it now.

ALBERT, *trembling.*

Oh . . . I can . . . kiss . . . you?

MATHILDE, *after a pause.*

Well, aren't you coming to kiss me? (*She stands.*) Then I'll come and kiss you! (*Walking toward Albert, she sees Nadeje who steps between them.*) Ah! You scared me.

NADEJE

You rang, madame?

MATHILDE

Me? No.

NADEJE

I thought I heard . . .

ALBERT

Yes, one often thinks . . . (*A glance from Nadeje makes him stop.*)

MATHILDE

Return to your quarters, mademoiselle.

NADEJE

Yes, madame.

MATHILDE, *aside as she exits.*

This girl is so tactless. I was just starting to be less afraid. (*She exits to the bedroom.*)

SCENE 9

NADEJE, ALBERT

NADEJE

It's just the two of us now.[29] (*She closes the door to the bedroom behind Mathilde.*)

ALBERT

What are you doing?

NADEJE

I'm closing the door to the nuptial chamber. Do you really think I'll let you perform the final act of this little comedy?

ALBERT

You're crazy!

NADEJE

Oh! You left me behind in America to come and marry another wife in Paris. And now that I've found you, you assume it's all over between us? No! You're going to spend your wedding night with me, my little coconut!

ALBERT

What?

NADEJE, *imitating Albert's voice.*

"Tell me you love me," you monster. (*She stomps her feet violently.*)

ALBERT, *frightened.*

Be quiet! You'll wake up my mother-in-law.

NADEJE

Good! (*Someone knocks on the floorboards.*)

ALBERT, *aside.*

And there we go. This isn't going to end well! (*Aloud.*) Come now, my little Nadeje.

NADEJE

Don't use your calm voice with me! So! You're sensitive like a barometer . . . The slightest frustration sets your nerves on end . . . And what about me?

ALBERT

Calm down, calm down! Let's be reasonable. What's happened to us is unfortunate. Neither of us can do anything about it.

NADEJE

What do you mean, we can't do anything about it?

ALBERT

It's too late! If I had seen you this morning, I wouldn't have gotten married this evening.

NADEJE

What about tomorrow morning?

ALBERT

Leave me alone with my wife.

NADEJE

Never!

ALBERT

What do you want?

NADEJE

It's simple. You had five wives in America. You'll have two in Paris.

ALBERT

Under one roof? Perfect. But when the prosecutor finds out, he'll speak with his friends in the police, and one morning we'll find ourselves in jail. No thank you.

NADEJE

Listen, do you still love me?

ALBERT

Do I still love you? How could you ever doubt it?

NADEJE

Prove it. I still have some coal left over from warming your bed. Let's die together!

ALBERT

That's one idea. But I must warmly refuse.

NADEJE

Then let's run off together before dawn. We'll take the train to Le Havre and set sail.

ALBERT

For where?

NADEJE

For America! We'll go back to Salt Lake City!

ALBERT

Thanks, but I've had enough of that place.

NADEJE

You refuse?

ALBERT

Precisely.

NADEJE

And if I insist?

ALBERT

By what right? After all, we aren't married.

NADEJE

We aren't married?

ALBERT

Over there, perhaps. But not in France.

NADEJE

What difference does that make?

ALBERT

Do those bulk marriages even count?

NADEJE

Oh, they don't count?

ALBERT

Speak with my lawyer. He'll tell you that the courts will . . .

NADEJE

You want to drag me to court? (*Angrily.*) That's too much! (*She upends the side table.*)

ALBERT

You're crazy! You'll wake the entire building!

NADEJE

I truly hope so! Here! Take this! (*She runs through the apartment knocking over chairs and rings the bell used to call the maid. Someone knocks on the ceiling. Mathilde, knocking on the door from her room, shouts, "Mother! Mother!"*)

ALBERT, *dazed.*

Stop it! You're out of control! Fine, yes, we'll leave together.

NADEJE

When?

ALBERT

Tomorrow.

NADEJE

No, right now. Let's go.

ALBERT

We can't. Someone's coming up the stairs.

NADEJE, *pointing at the service stairway.*

Then let's go this way.

ALBERT, *listening.*

Someone's coming up those stairs, too. (*He pushes Nadeje toward the sofa.*) Quick! Hide under the couch.

NADEJE

There's not enough room!

ALBERT

Uh . . . Lie down on it! (*She hesitates.*) What do you want?

NADEJE

Run away with me.

ALBERT

Yes, I swear. (*Nadeje lies down on the sofa. Albert covers her with the fur coat. Madame Chamboran and Dubouloy enter at the same time from opposite sides.*) Just in time! (*He tries to block Nadeje from their view.*)

SCENE 10

The same, MADAME CHAMBORAN, DUBOULOY in pajamas, then MATHILDE

MADAME CHAMBORAN

What's all this noise? What's going on?

DUBOULOY

Why is all the furniture upended?

ALBERT

I can explain.

DUBOULOY

You were playing hide-and-seek?

ALBERT

Exactly . . . Before going to bed.

MADAME CHAMBORAN

But my daughter . . . Where is she?

MATHILDE, *offstage.*

Mother! Mother!

MADAME CHAMBORAN

She's locked in? (*She unlocks the door.*)

MATHILDE, *throwing herself in her mother's arms.*

Oh, Mother, if only you knew.

MADAME CHAMBORAN

I can guess. He beat you!

ALBERT

Listen, Mother-in-law! (*He tries to move toward her. Nadeje grabs him from under the coat.*)

MADAME CHAMBORAN, *sobbing.*

My dau . . . My daughter. Ah! Your mother is about to pass out.

DUBOULOY, *catching Madame Chamboran.*

There, there . . . Oof, she's heavy! (*He drags Madame Chamboran to the sofa and drops her on top of Nadeje.*)

NADEJE, *crying out.*

Ah!

ALBERT, *aside.*

The jig is up!

MADAME CHAMBORAN

What's that?

DUBOULOY, *aside.*

The chambermaid!

MADAME CHAMBORAN

This girl alone with my son-in-law? (*To Nadeje.*) Get out!

NADEJE

Get out? Excuse me? I'm staying here in my husband's house.

MADAME CHAMBORAN, MATHILDE, DUBOULOY

Her husband!

ALBERT, *aside.*

And that's that.

NADEJE, *pointing to Albert.*

He married me in America. We'll celebrate our fifth anniversary this summer.

MADAME CHAMBORAN

Bigamist!

NADEJE

Oh, if it were just me! But he married many others . . . in Mormondom!

MADAME CHAMBORAN and MATHILDE

A Mormon!

DUBOULOY, *opening his book.*

Wait! So it is him!

ALBERT

Mathilde! Mother! I promise . . . it's not what you think! I swear. I can explain.

MADAME CHAMBORAN, *holding Mathilde in her arms.*

Get away from us, polygamist!

SCENE II

The same, JONATHAN, EVA

JONATHAN, *opening the door.*

It's me!

ALBERT, *aside.*

Jonathan! The plot thickens.

DUBOULOY

The apostle!

JONATHAN, *to Albert.*

We found your card in your coat pocket. (*He points to Eva, who enters carrying Albert's hat and coat.*) I'm returning your wife.

ALBERT, *aside.*

The end of the line!

MADAME CHAMBORAN

Another one?

DUBOULOY, *looking in his book.*

He had five. (*Reading.*) Nadeje.

NADEJE

Here!

DUBOULOY, *reading.*

Eva.

EVA

Here!

MADAME CHAMBORAN

And he married my daughter!

JONATHAN

That makes six. That's reasonable. (*To Albert.*) Don't you agree?

ALBERT

Go to hell!

MADAME CHAMBORAN

Let's leave this den of iniquity, my daughter. (*To Albert.*) I'll see you in an hour with my lawyer and in a month in a courtroom . . . an eternal separation! (*She exits with a weeping Mathilde.*)

DUBOULOY

The sly dog. He knew how to pick wives.

ALBERT, *falling on the sofa.*

A separation! Ah! I'm paying a high price for those five lapses of judgment!

NADEJE and EVA, *sitting on each side of Albert.*

My darling!

JONATHAN, *standing behind the sofa with his arms outstretched around Eva and Nadeje.*

Be happy my children!

(*Curtain.*)

ACT III

The action takes place outside of Paris in Chatou. The stage represents a garden bordered by a hedge upstage. There is a small staircase that leads over the middle of the hedge to a towpath that runs along the Seine. Over the stairs a sign reads "Marine Restaurant." There is a rustic house to the right and downstage, against the house, a brick storeroom. There is a stable on the left. Near the house, on the right, is a chair with a towel over it.

SCENE I

RAPHAEL, then ALBERT, then DUBOULOY

RAPHAEL, *sharpening a razor and thinking aloud.*

As I shave Monsieur Savarin maybe I'll get some news about Nadeje. I don't know what's become of her. A week ago I went to her hotel to do her hair. I'd been going there since she left Madame Chamboran's employ. The concierge told me that Monsieur Savarin left with his two companions. Where to? Don't know. Even the police don't know. Then this morning I traveled here to deliver a blond hairpiece to the winner of last year's Miss Chatou contest and I came face to face with an unkempt beard belonging to Monsieur Savarin. I offered my services, he accepted, and . . . Oh! Here he is.

ALBERT, *coming out of the house.*

Are we ready, Figaro?[30]

RAPHAEL

Ready when you are.

ALBERT, *sitting.*

Go ahead. I put some water on the stove.

RAPHAEL, *placing the towel around Albert's neck.*

Ah! You take care of the house yourself? You don't have any help?

ALBERT

I'm completely alone.

RAPHAEL

What about Mademoiselle Nadeje?

ALBERT

Mademoiselle Nadeje hopes no one speaks with me about her while I'm shaving. It would double the pain of being shaved.

RAPHAEL, *aside.*

Oh! He's speaking evil against my angel! (*He tightens the towel around Albert's neck.*)

ALBERT, *loosening the towel.*

Careful! You're strangling me.

RAPHAEL

But I have a light touch.

ALBERT

I can tell.

DUBOULOY, *entering upstage via the garden.*

Monsieur Savarin, please.

ALBERT, *sitting up abruptly.*

Uncle! (*To Raphael.*) You'll shave me later.

RAPHAEL

It's not a problem. I can work while the two of you chat.

ALBERT

No. Take a walk and come back in an hour.

RAPHAEL, *aside as he exits.*

I will definitely be back. I never imagined becoming so attached to a woman's false braids! (*He exits upstage.*)

SCENE 2

ALBERT, DUBOULOY

ALBERT, *shaking Dubouloy's hand.*

It's nice of you to come.

DUBOULOY, *looking around to make sure they are alone.*

Be careful! And hide your wives!

ALBERT, *laughing.*

My wives?

DUBOULOY

Yes, your spouse overage. You don't have much time. You heard that at the request of your mother-in-law the court ordered an investigation? It's taking place today. I'm just a few minutes ahead of my sister. She'll be here soon with a first-rate prosecutor who is in charge of investigating your past.

ALBERT

Thank you, Uncle. Madame Chamboran will get very little for her troubles. And her prosecutor can search as much as he wants.

DUBOULOY

You've unloaded your wives?

ALBERT

Yes, but lovingly. What can you tell me about Mathilde?

DUBOULOY

She's still very upset.

ALBERT

I'll talk her down.

DUBOULOY

I hope so. Shh! Here's my sister with the long arm of the law.

ALBERT

Oh! Very solemn!

SCENE 3

The same, MADAME CHAMBORAN, FALANDARD, TRINQUEBALLE

(*Madame Chamboran enters escorted by Trinqueballe, a rural police officer wearing a cavalry sword, and by Falandard, a bald prosecutor wearing a black robe, a white collar, and gold-rimmed glasses.*)

MADAME CHAMBORAN, *to Dubouloy.*

You're already here?

DUBOULOY, *ill at ease.*

Yes . . . I wandered around a bit on the way, so I'm ahead of you.

ALBERT, *trying to embrace Madame Chamboran.*

Mother-in-law, may I?

MADAME CHAMBORAN, *pushing Albert away.*

Get away, monsieur! You may not do anything, and I forbid everything! Especially in this den of iniquity.

ALBERT

Oh, Madame Chamboran.

DUBOULOY

"Den of iniquity" is a bit strong, Emilie.

MADAME CHAMBORAN

If I knew a stronger expression, I would use it. But that's beside the point. (*With emotion.*) This is Master Leon Falandard, our supporter, our defender. (*Falandard bows.*) Announce the motive of our visit.

ALBERT, *aside, looking at Falandard.*

Have I seen this cue ball somewhere?

FALANDARD, *taking some snuff.*

We hereby declare, monsieur, that you have six wives.

ALBERT

No, monsieur, we do not declare it.

FALANDARD

They are all young and pretty, no doubt?

ALBERT

I refuse to answer.

FALANDARD

Let's just agree that they are varied. How many are you currently keeping in your harem?

ALBERT

My harem?

MADAME CHAMBORAN

My poor Malthide, an adolisque![31]

FALANDARD, *correcting her.*

"Oda," madame, "odalisque."

MADAME CHAMBORAN, *surprised.*

What?

DUBOULOY

The gentleman is correct. One writes adolisque, but it's pronounced odalisque.[32]

FALANDARD, *to Albert.*

Please call your wives to come out.

ALBERT, *laughing.*

For a square dance?

FALANDARD, *with severity.*

To appear before us. Let me advise you to be more restrained in your language and in your behavior.

ALBERT, *aside.*

Where in the hell have I seen his mug before?

FALANDARD

Exhibit, monsieur, the victims of your intemperance.

MADAME CHAMBORAN

Exhibit!

ALBERT

Dammit! I'm telling you I'm alone here! I don't even have a maid.

FALANDARD

Very well. Mathilde counts as one spouse. (*Gravely.*) I await the other five, monsieur.

DUBOULOY

Forgive me for intervening, but this interrogation is all wrong. Albert has answered all your questions, and you're responding as though he were speaking rot.

FALANDARD

The responses of the accused are only reliable when they confess.

MADAME CHAMBORAN

Obviously.

FALANDARD

Otherwise, what would be the point of an interrogation?

ALBERT

I deny everything. Next?

MADAME CHAMBORAN

The all-seeing eye of justice will uncover traces of your crimes.

FALANDARD

Even if they are invisible! (*He points to the brick storeroom.*) What's this mysterious hideout?

ALBERT

It's a storeroom for cheap wine, potatoes, and rats.

FALANDARD, *walking toward the storeroom, backs up quickly when Albert mentions rats.*

Rats, you say? Trinqueballe, go inspect.

TRINQUEBALLE

Yes, your lawyership. (*He enters the storeroom.*)

DUBOULOY

He clearly didn't put wives in bottles.

TRINQUEBALLE, *emerging.*

Spiderwebs. Nothing else.

FALANDARD, *pointing to the stable.*

And what about this other hideout, the one giving off . . . dubious emanations?

ALBERT

It's a stable.

FALANDARD, *walking toward the stable, stops.*

Are there rats?

ALBERT

Sorry, yes, but they are happy and friendly rats. They only want to play. You can check in on them.

FALANDARD, *walking back from the door.*

We are not here to frolic with rodents.

MADAME CHAMBORAN, *aside.*

"Rodents!" These lawyers have the best words.

DUBOULOY

And it's unlikely he put his wives in the straw.

MADAME CHAMBORAN

There's a first time for everything.

FALANDARD

Let's move on to the house.

ALBERT

Go ahead and search. I'm happy to accompany you. (*He offers his arm to Madame Chamboran.*) Mother-in-law, my arm?

MADAME CHAMBORAN

No thank you! My two arms suffice. What's more, your presence isn't necessary. We can open doors and drawers ourselves.

ALBERT

As you wish.

FALANDARD

Trinqueballe, you're part of our detachment. Follow us.

TRINQUEBALLE

Yes, your lawyership.

MADAME CHAMBORAN, *to Dubouloy, indicating Albert.*

Brother, keep an eye on him. (*To Falandard, who is on the porch of the house.*) Master Leon Falandard, after you.

FALANDARD

No, after you, madame.

MADAME CHAMBORAN, *entering.*

As you wish. (*Falandard follows her in. Trinqueballe wanders into the garden.*)

SCENE 4

ALBERT, DUBOULOY

DUBOULOY

So there's no danger? They won't find anything?

ALBERT

Absolutely nothing. By now my two hangers-on are in sight of New York.

DUBOULOY

How did you get rid of them?

ALBERT

It wasn't easy. I first tried to reason with them. That's always a bad idea with women.

DUBOULOY

An excessively bad idea.

ALBERT

Then I had a stroke of genius. I proposed returning immediately to Salt Lake City together. They accepted. And the next day we set off for America.

DUBOULOY

I see! And you've already made your way back from New York?

ALBERT

Let me explain. Once we boarded the ship, I helped my traveling companions to their cabin, where they soon began to suffer from seasickness. I went to the captain and told him that they were my sisters and that I didn't want to leave them until the last possible moment. I asked him to help them get to their destination, then I got into the tugboat and returned to Le Havre. From there, I came to Chatou, where I've been tranquil and free from hangers-on for five days.

DUBOULOY

Very cunning!

ALBERT

So when the trial comes, I can prove that three of my Mormons are remarried and that the other two acknowledged the invalidity of their claim when they left for America. The court will wipe my slate clean and nullify the separation from Mathilde. Mathilde will happily forgive me, and Madame Chamboran will get over her jaundice once and for all.[33]

DUBOULOY

Oh, she gets that every year.

ALBERT

Well, this year she'll have it twice. It has been a banner year for jaundice.

DUBOULOY

Shh! Here they come.

SCENE 5

The same, MADAME CHAMBORAN, FALANDARD, TRINQUEBALLE

FALANDARD

Nothing. Absolutely nothing.

MADAME CHAMBORAN

That's disappointing.

FALANDARD

Wait, madame. (*To Albert.*) Albert Savarin, two of your wives crossed the sea to throw themselves into your arms. Do you acknowledge that you had an interest in getting rid of them?

ALBERT

Of course.

FALANDARD

The court is within its rights to ask the whereabouts of these two innocent victims.

MADAME CHAMBORAN

They must be found!

TRINQUEBALLE

Nobody leaves!

DUBOULOY, *aside.*

The plot thickens.

ALBERT

Since you insist, I can tell you that the two people in question are on their way back to Salt Lake City.

FALANDARD

Alone and of their own free will? That sounds highly unlikely.

ALBERT

I took them to Le Havre, and we set out for America that evening.

FALANDARD

And you, you've finished setting out?

ALBERT

Obviously I stayed behind.

FALANDARD

He confesses! (*Writing in his notebook.*) I'm taking note. We are making great strides toward the light.

ALBERT

But wait! I haven't confessed anything at all.

FALANDARD

Too late. I never cross anything out once it's written it down. With this first admission by the accused, everything else can be deduced: probable poisoning of both victims.

ALBERT, *infuriated.*

Outrageous! You know I didn't poison anyone.

FALANDARD

Poisoned or stabbed, it's all the same.

MADAME CHAMBORAN

Do more digging. We'll find the victims.

DUBOULOY, *wiping his brow.*

It's all moving so quickly!

FALANDARD

To summarize: Albert Savarin, you stand accused of a capital offense. Produce your two wives or face the consequences!

ALBERT

You're really starting to annoy me. Now it's my turn. I hereby summon you to follow me to the mayor's residence. He will probably be less absurd than you.

FALANDARD

I was just going to say that. Let's go see the mayor. If you resist, we'll take you by force. (*To Trinqueballe.*) Guard! Seize this man!

TRINQUEBALLE, *grabbing Albert by the neck.*

En route, quickly!

ALBERT

Hands off or I'll make you swallow your sword!

FALANDARD, *to Madame Chamboran.*

We're on the brink of a cause célèbre!

DUBOULOY

It's all moving so quickly!

FALANDARD, MADAME CHAMBORAN, TRINQUEBALLE, *singing.*

Now let's all go to city hall!
The crime's more than subliminal.
The darkest case in all of Gaul
Requires stopping this criminal!

DUBOULOY, ALBERT, *singing.*

Now let's all go to city hall!
The crime's merely subliminal.
The fake-est case in all of Gaul,
We'll prove it's wholly fictional!

(*They all exit upstage.*)

SCENE 6

RAPHAEL, then JONATHAN, MOUCHETTE, POMPONNE, BOULOTTE, RESEDA, FRIQUETTE, eight young women, GONTRAN, NADEJE, EVA

RAPHAEL, *watching the others leave.*

Birds of a bourgeois feather stick together! It will be hard to shave his beard now. (*Laughter offstage.*) Look at this! Girls from a boarding school with a male teacher. (*Jonathan enters upstage with a young woman on his arm and eleven others lined up beside her.*) Hey, it's Jonathan!

CHORUS

Let's race to this flowery space
Of open-aired pleasure and grace.
With a guide we all could embrace,
Have fun like in Paris, let's race![34]

MOUCHETTE

It's lovely here.

BOULETTE

What a view.

RAPHAEL, *seeing Nadeje.*

Nadeje! I'm so happy to see you!

NADEJE, *striding across the stage and surveying the audience.*

Where is that scoundrel? Show yourself!

RAPHAEL, *following Nadeje.*

It's really you! I've found you!

NADEJE

Hello, hairdresser, hello. (*To Jonathan.*) Where's Albert?

JONATHAN

He stepped out. But he'll be back.

EVA, *storming back and forth.*

Oh! I'm so angry!

GONTRAN, *following her.*

My angel, I've become a Mormon apprentice for you!

EVA, *nonchalantly.*

Very well . . . Very well. What a bore.[35]

RAPHAEL, *following Nadeje.*

I thought I'd lost you forever.

NADEJE

You found me, nothing more. (*Walking to the front of the stage.*) I'm sharpening my claws!

EVA, *stopping.*

I want to claw his eyes out!

JONATHAN, *coming between them.*

Understood. You'll scratch him! But calm down first.

NADEJE

He lives here, right?

JONATHAN

Yes, this is his cottage.

EVA, *to Gontran.*

My good young man.

GONTRAN

Yes, mistress?

EVA

Run to the train station and fetch my luggage.

GONTRAN

I won't run, I'll fly! (*He runs out upstage.*)

NADEJE, *to Raphael.*

You, too, bring my bag. But be careful, it's heavy.

RAPHAEL, *exultantly.*

Not heavy enough. Love gives strength! (*He exits upstage.*)

NADEJE, *agitated.*

Ah! I want to break things, to pulverize something!

EVA, *in the same vein.*

He made us seasick for nothing!

MOUCHETTE

Ah! Men! All unreliable!

BOULOTTE

And then they complain when we hold them accountable.

POMPONNE

I ask you all, what are they good for?

JONATHAN, *to the young women.*

Don't answer. You're not supposed to know yet.

MOUCHETTE

Ah! It's hot.

RESEDA

I'm thirsty.

FRIQUETTE

I'm hungry.

NADEJE

Ladies, we invite you to dine with us.

ALL

Bravo!

NADEJE

Empty the pantry and the hen house.

EVA

And the wine cellar.

JONATHAN

What a great idea! Today is the anniversary of our founder's one-hundredth marriage. It's Mormon Day!

NADEJE

That's right!

EVA

It's a party over in Salt Lake City.

JONATHAN

Albert probably forgot about it. Let's remind him by celebrating it here.

FRIQUETTE

But what if he disapproves?

NADEJE

We don't care. This is our house!

EVA

It all belongs to us.

NADEJE

Cut the flowers, lay waste to the garden, pillage the house. I authorize it.

EVA

So do I!

JONATHAN

A great Mormon holiday in Chatou!

NADEJE

Help us trample the traitor!

ALL

Yes! Yes!

NADEJE

Chorus

Vengeance! Vengeance!
Let's dance in France,
Lay waste and devastate!
This is how we celebrate
Our annual Mormon festival.
A huge party's on the docket
For the all-powerful prophet.
Let's get revenge while having fun
And pillage till the day is done.
Make lovely garlands for our heads
By tearing up the flower beds.
So now let's cut, steal, crush, and break,
Trample anything you can't take!

ALL, *singing the chorus.*

Vengeance! Vengeance! etc.

EVA

The little rat in Mormon-land
Convinced us that he loved us well.
"I love you, dear, please take my hand.
Je vous aime, I love you, my belle!"
But like you say right here in France,
"*Au revoir mon amie, c'est la vie*!"
He left without a second glance.
We'll take revenge on him with glee!

ALL, *singing the chorus.*

Vengeance! Vengeance! etc.

JONATHAN

Celebrate the hundredth marriage
By destroying Albert's houses.
Let's party! Let none disparage
As we praise the king of spouses.
Were he here, he would exhort you
To drink, to dance, and not relent.
The more we brew and ballyhoo,
The more we make our boss content!

ALL, *singing the chorus.*

Vengeance! Vengeance! etc.

NADEJE

Let's go ladies. You take the garden. We'll attack the house!

ALL, *singing the chorus.*

Vengeance! Vengeance! etc.

SCENE 7

JONATHAN, then DUBOULOY

JONATHAN

Everything is going so well. My only worry is the meal.

DUBOULOY, *entering upstage.*

What's this? A henhouse on vacation? Ah, Brother Jonathan.

JONATHAN

Brother Dubouloy! What a happy coincidence!

DUBOULOY, *ogling the women as they exit.*

Are all these young hens yours?

JONATHAN

It's a batch of emigrants I'll be dispatching soon. Not many items, but all high quality and guaranteed.

DUBOULOY

That gives you time to trade them.

JONATHAN

Too many blonds, unfortunately.

DUBOULOY, *walking upstage, ogling.*

In Paris, blonds are in demand.

JONATHAN

Over there their stock is down according to the wives-market news I read yesterday. (*He takes a notebook out of his pocket and reads.*) Brunettes rally and remain a solid investment; blonds are plentiful, and the market is weak; red heads are flagging but may bounce back.

DUBOULOY

By the way, what brings you here?

JONATHAN

I'm planning a surprise for our dear Albert. But what has become of him?

DUBOULOY

He's at city hall squabbling with my sister's lawyer. I was bored to tears, so I left. What's your surprise?

JONATHAN

Have you had a chance to look at that little book I gave you?

DUBOULOY

I'm devouring it. But I'm only on page 773 of the introduction.

JONATHAN

If you want fruit, you have to climb the tree! Did you read the description of the Mormon Festival?

DUBOULOY

I know it by heart. Page 499.

JONATHAN

Well, we're planning to celebrate it here.

DUBOULOY

Great idea. I'm with you!

JONATHAN, *eyeing Dubouloy.*

Wait a second. Yes. You have his nose, his majestic silhouette, his eagle eye. It's surprising I haven't noticed the resemblance before.

DUBOULOY

Resemblance?

JONATHAN

Between you and our great leader!

DUBOULOY

I look like him?

JONATHAN

You're like two peas in a pod! Has the seed I planted in your soul taken root?

DUBOULOY

Do you need to ask? I dream about it every night. It has taken root and started to grow!

JONATHAN

I knew it! Bow down then.

DUBOULOY

I bow before you!

JONATHAN

I have something to bestow upon you.

DUBOULOY, *still bowing.*

Is this far enough?

JONATHAN

A little lower. There, that's far enough. (*He gives Dubouloy a light whack.*)

DUBOULOY, *surprised.*

Are we playing tag?

JONATHAN

No. Don't move. (*With solemnity.*) Brother Dubouloy, you will hereby represent our illustrious founder at the ceremony.

DUBOULOY

The man with one hundred wives! Oh yes!

JONATHAN

Such an honor! Don't you agree? Such an honor!

DUBOULOY

Is the ordination finished?

JONATHAN

Yes, you can stand at ease.

DUBOULOY

So now I'm the great leader?

JONATHAN

To you, the laurels! To you the hymns!

DUBOULOY

I'll have my sister return to Paris alone, and I'm all yours. I admit I'm excited to wear the regalia of my high position.

JONATHAN

One way to increase the pomp would be to order a heap of food from the local restaurant.

DUBOULOY, *proudly.*

I'm off. You'll see how well I can serve my people!

JONATHAN

Most importantly, remember we need to moisten the seed. That's key.

DUBOULOY

Argenteuil first growth, all-you-can-eat fried food, and veal.[36]

JONATHAN

That's good. And don't forget Madeira, Clicquot, coffee, liqueurs, cigars, and the rest!

SCENE 8

JONATHAN, RAPHAEL, GONTRAN

JONATHAN

Our culinary prospects are looking up. Concocting that resemblance story was a stroke of genius. He swallowed it hook, line, and sinker. (*Seeing Raphael.*) Ah! The minions of those two ladies are back. Put the bags over there, little Casanovas.

GONTRAN

Whew! It's hot!

RAPHAEL

This is really heavy!

JONATHAN

Come on. Let's go join our sisters and organize the parade.

GONTRAN

Will we eat after that?

JONATHAN

Yes, my young gelatinous friend. And the feast will be extensive.

RAPHAEL

Sounds good to me. I love extensive feasts.

(*They exit.*)

SCENE 9

ALBERT, NADEJE, EVA

ALBERT, *alone.*

I can finally catch my breath. I managed to get rid of that beastly attorney with his stupid accusations. He really wound me up. At first, the mayor didn't believe that my parasitic wives had left town. Fortunately, I still had the receipt for their transatlantic tickets. When I produced it, I was declared innocent on the spot. Madame Chamboran was still complaining, but I finally remembered where I had seen Master Falandard. He's a regular at Mabille and a defender of women who have problems with their landlords.[37] I quietly informed him that I knew of a certain young woman named Mouchette who borrowed his robes for a mid-Lent costume.[38] He promised me that his inquiry would completely clear me. (*Gleefully.*) What a wonderful day! (*He hums a tune, then stops short.*) What's this? Those bags look vaguely familiar. (*Reading the tags.*) Nadeje! Eva! Oh no! The savages have returned to Robinson Crusoe's island! (*He backs away from the bags, and, at the same time, Nadeje and Eva surround him from behind.*)

NADEJE

Indeed, they have returned!

EVA

Oh yes!

ALBERT, *aside.*

Oh no! Someone opened their cage.

NADEJE

Your little wife is still alive, you monster!

EVA

You didn't plan on our ship docking in England, did you?

NADEJE

That little stunt you pulled with the captain made it difficult.

EVA

He refused to let us off.

NADEJE

But we sweet-talked him.

EVA

We had no choice.

ALBERT, *ironically.*

Well, how nice of you to come back. Congratulations.

NADEJE

Thank you. And this time we've got you.

EVA

And we won't let you go again.

ALBERT

My little lambs, you have stupidly returned only to fall into the jowls of the wolf. Here's a subpoena for you and one for you. You're looking at six months in prison.

EVA

Us?

NADEJE

Why?

ALBERT

Because you entered the conjugal domicile. You're wanted by the law. The police were here less than an hour ago.

NADEJE and EVA

The police?

ALBERT

In full dress uniform. I have one piece of advice for you: leave immediately.

NADEJE

Come on . . . This is just a ruse to get us away from you again.

EVA

We're innocent.

ALBERT

So was Joan of Arc, but we all know how that ended.

EVA

You're like the English.

NADEJE

More like an English jester.[39]

ALBERT

Ladies, you forget your place.

NADEJE

Isn't our place in your home?

EVA

We're here to celebrate Mormon Day.

ALBERT

On the day of the investigation? (*Ironically.*) I'd like to see that.

NADEJE, *pointing to the garden.*

It's the parade!

SCENE 10

All the characters, then MADAME CHAMBORAN, FALANDARD, TRINQUEBALLE

(*A crowd gathers upstage; they raise banners made of garlands and brightly colored fabrics. The orchestra plays a triumphant march. Dubouloy makes a majestic entrance. He has a bouquet in each hand and wears a large crown of white roses and orange blossoms. Six long white ribbons extend from his crown and are carried by six young women. Raphael is holding a large parasol over Dubouloy's head. Gontran is fanning him with peacock feathers. Jonathan precedes him, dancing and playing cymbals. Two young women throw flowers in front of the great leader.*)

WOMEN'S CHORUS

Glory, praise, and honor
To our benefactor!
He walks with such daring
And a noble bearing.[40]

ALBERT

The scoundrels have stolen my landlord's knickknacks!

DUBOULOY, *to the young women holding ribbons.*

Hey, don't pull so hard to the left.

ALBERT, *recognizing Dubouloy.*

Uncle Dubouloy?

DUBOULOY

In the flesh, my friend. Bow before his majesty!

ALBERT

It's the feast of fools.

(*Madame Chamboran, Falandard, and Trinqueballe enter upstage.*)

MADAME CHAMBORAN, *to Falandard.*

What is this? Clowns performing at my son-in-law's house?

DUBOULOY, *to the young women holding ribbons.*

My dear sisters, do I look all right? Am I majestic enough?

MADAME CHAMBORAN

Is that my brother? Am I seeing things?

DUBOULOY, *aside.*

Emilie . . . Drat! This wasn't in the script.

MADAME CHAMBORAN

I'm losing my mind. I think I'm going to pass out.

ALBERT

This spectacle is killing you. Let me help you.

MADAME CHAMBORAN

Don't touch me! I forbid it! (*Recognizing Nadeje and Eva.*) Those two! The monster's accomplices! Master Falandard, arrest them!

MOUCHETTE, *to Falandard.*

Leon, I forbid it!

(*The Mormons surround Falandard.*)

MADAME CHAMBORAN

My attorney, arm in arm with prostitutes?

FALANDARD

Clients, madame. They're just clients. If you knew me better, you'd be arm in arm with me too.

MADAME CHAMBORAN

It's the end of the world! Where can I run? Where can I hide?

ALBERT

Come here with me, Madame Chamboran. It's the safest place for a mother.

MADAME CHAMBORAN

Behind me, criminal! It's no longer a misdemeanor trial that awaits you, it's a felony trial!

ALBERT, *outraged.*

That's how it's gonna be? I'll take you to court too. I'll argue the case myself and unfortunately for you, I'll be in fine voice.

(*Madame Chamboran tries to escape upstage. Gunshots scare her back downstage. Frenzied, she falls into Jonathan's arms.*)

(*Curtain.*)

ACT IV

The stage represents a costume shop near the Palais de Justice.[41] *There is a counter upstage with doors on each side leading to a covered passageway. There are smaller counters on the left and on the right with chairs and boxes in between. Legal robes hang on hooks around the stage.*

SCENE I

THE COSTUMIER, then DUBOULOY

THE COSTUMIER, *arranging robes.*

The Palais is crowded today. The correctional court is packed and I've rented almost all my robes. (*To Dubouloy, entering.*) How may I help you, monsieur?

DUBOULOY

I'd like a judicial cap, a robe, and a collar.

THE COSTUMIER

I haven't seen you at the Palais before. Are you from a provincial circuit?

DUBOULOY

Not exactly. I could have been a lawyer, I suppose. It doesn't require a lot of money up front. But to tell you the truth, I'm not.

THE COSTUMIER

But you want a robe?

DUBOULOY

I can explain. There's a trial right now that involves my family. My nephew is a lawyer, and he's representing himself. At first it was amusing. He was tormenting his mother-in-law every way possible. But it got tiring, and I left to protest how he was airing his dirty laundry in public.

THE COSTUMIER

I see.

DUBOULOY

Then I remembered there was a spicy trial in the courtroom next door.

THE COSTUMIER

I've heard.

DUBOULOY

I love spice. Unfortunately, the room is completely packed. They're only letting in attorneys wearing their robes.

THE COSTUMIER

And you want to pass yourself off as an attorney?

DUBOULOY

Precisely.

THE COSTUMIER

People do that all the time. (*Giving him a robe.*) This one's your size. Would you like to try it on?

DUBOULOY

Yes, give me a hand. (*He puts it on.*) It fits like a glove. Ha! Ha! It makes me want to run off at the mouth!

THE COSTUMIER

Yes, it's contagious.

DUBOULOY

Now the cap.

THE COSTUMIER, *pointing at the boxes.*

Choose whatever you'd like.

DUBOULOY

I'm not picky. (*He pulls a jester's hat out of a box.*) What's this?

THE COSTUMIER

Oh! My apologies. I've been diversifying by renting out costumes for Carnival. Take this instead. (*He gives him a legal cap.*) Look at yourself in the mirror.

DUBOULOY, *admiring himself.*

Perfect. Do you want a deposit?

THE COSTUMIER

Oh no, monsieur. You look trustworthy.

DUBOULOY

It's true, I look trustworthy. I'll be back soon, monsieur. (*He exits upstage.*)

SCENE 2

THE COSTUMIER, then MATHILDE, MADAME CHAMBORAN, and others

THE COSTUMIER, *throwing the jester's hat into an open box on the left counter.*

Mixing jesters and lawyers . . . Typical for my assistant. The other day, he put a fake nose in the pocket of a robe. During his closing argument, Master Falandard reached for a handkerchief to wipe his tears and ended up flinging the fake nose at the judge. The judge threatened him with contempt of court and gave his client the maximum sentence. (*A loud noise is heard offstage.*) What's that? Something's happening in the passageway. (*He looks out the doors upstage.*) A woman has passed out!

MATHILDE, *entering urgently.*

Monsieur, can my mother rest in here for a moment?

THE COSTUMIER

Of course, mademoiselle. (*Madame Chamboran is carried in by several people. They help her to a chair that has a legal robe draped over it.*) A few drops of water on her face and she'll be fine.

MATHILDE

Thank you so much, monsieur.

THE COSTUMIER, *with a glass of water he just filled.*

But I don't want to ruin her dress. Wait. (*He puts the lawyer's robe on Madame Chamboran.*) There. Now we can spritz her. (*He throws water on her face.*)

MADAME CHAMBORAN, *sneezing.*

Achoo!

THE COSTUMIER

It's working! (*He continues splashing her face with water.*) It never fails.

MADAME CHAMBORAN

Achoo!

MATHILDE, *stopping him.*

I think that's enough.

MADAME CHAMBORAN

Where am I? Achoo! Ah! Oh, I see where I am. Has the criminal finished vilifying me?

MATHILDE

Calm down, Mother.

MADAME CHAMBORAN

Not until I've ripped him to shreds. Give me something to drink.

THE COSTUMIER, *to Dubouloy entering upstage.*

Already back?

SCENE 3

The same, DUBOULOY

DUBOULOY, *wiping his brow.*

How embarrassing!

MATHILDE, *seeing Dubouloy.*

Uncle!

DUBOULOY

What are you doing here?

MADAME CHAMBORAN

What's with the costume?

DUBOULOY, *vexed.*

I'll explain. I wanted to study a case being tried in courtroom number six.

MADAME CHAMBORAN

What case?

DUBOULOY

The case . . . of a . . . philanthropic association. I rented this robe to blend in with the attorneys. But I had barely entered when the presiding judge rose and declared in a menacing voice: "I've just learned that people who do not belong to the bar have slipped into my courtroom. I warn them that they will be subjected to several days in prison if they don't leave immediately."

MATHILDE

That sounds serious.

DUBOULOY

On top of that, I was right next to a huge bailiff, who was glaring at me. I got up and left while people in the audience laughed and jeered.

MATHILDE

By yourself?

DUBOULOY

No, with one other fake lawyer, whom I recognized as a grocer from my street.[42]

MATHILDE

Poor uncle!

DUBOULOY, *whispering to the costumier.*

It's too bad. Things were getting interesting. They were about to question the Baroness of Château-Margaux, an extremely deceptive creature.

SCENE 4

The same, ALBERT

ALBERT, *entering upstage.*

This cap is too small. I need to exchange it.

MADAME CHAMBORAN, *leaping up.*

Him again!

ALBERT

Say, it's the entire family!

MADAME CHAMBORAN

Yes, you monster. The family you'll never, ever be part of. Never!

ALBERT

We'll see about that.

MADAME CHAMBORAN

Over my dead body!

ALBERT

That would certainly make things easier.

MADAME CHAMBORAN

Felon!

MATHILDE

Oh, Mother . . .

DUBOULOY, *calming her.*

Come now . . .

MADAME CHAMBORAN

He dares threaten my life!

DUBOULOY

Of course not. He's merely expressing a desire, a simple wish.

MADAME CHAMBORAN, *to Albert.*

I can't believe your lack of respect for mothers-in-law and how you spoke about them in the courtroom.

ALBERT, *very animated.*

You'll hear even more when the trial resumes. The court will tremble.

MADAME CHAMBORAN, *furious.*

What more could you possibly add?

ALBERT

What would I add? (*Leaping behind the counter at right and beginning his oral argument.*) I would say that of all the plagues Providence has sent to afflict humanity, not one is more pernicious, more monstrous than the frightening institution of mothers-in-law!

MADAME CHAMBORAN, *furious.*

Really. Well, I would respond . . . (*She leaps behind the counter at left and begins her oral argument.*) I would tell the court that I won't allow my daughter, my child, the fruit of my collaboration with Chamboran, to be kidnapped. And by whom, I ask? (*Without paying attention she reaches into the open box on the counter, takes the jester's hat, and puts it on her head.*) By whom? By a depraved Sardanapalus![43]

MATHILDE

Oh, mother!

MADAME CHAMBORAN, *with authority.*

Silence, Malthide! Silence!

ALBERT, *pounding his fist on the counter.*

You hear it, incorruptible magistrates, this so-called mother doesn't even know the name of her own child!

THE COSTUMIER, *laughing.*

Ha, ha, ha! (*Abruptly changing tone.*) Silence, gentlemen!

MADAME CHAMBORAN

What? I don't know Malthide's name?

ALBERT

Malthide! Always Malthide! Does this not suffice, gentlemen, to establish our intellectual and moral superiority over this childish dowager who became a mother through an incomprehensible stroke of luck and who, in her guilty ignorance, misunderstands both the laws of grammar and maternity!

MADAME CHAMBORAN

Such insolence!

DUBOULOY, *now standing behind the counter upstage as if he were the presiding judge.*

Do not interrupt!

MADAME CHAMBORAN

But I'm being insulted!

DUBOULOY

It's the defense's right. You'll insult . . . (*Correcting himself.*) You'll respond in turn. (*To Albert.*) Please continue.

ALBERT

Let us get to the facts of the case. What is our crime? Of what do we stand accused?

MADAME CHAMBORAN

Your five marriages!

ALBERT

I deny them. Introduce the subpoenaed witnesses. (*To the costumier.*) Bring in the coachman.

DUBOULOY

The coachman?

ALBERT

He is undoubtedly with the local wine merchant. Go fetch him. (*The costumier exits.*) Allow me to take advantage of this short break granted by opposing counsel to say to the sweet young woman listening with fear and trembling: Oh Mathilde! (*He blows kisses to her.*) Here! Here!

MADAME CHAMBORAN

I forbid you to blow kisses to my daughter!

MATHILDE

But Mother, I didn't accept them.

MADAME CHAMBORAN

That's the only thing still missing from this circus!

ALBERT

Naive child! Then I'll do it again. (*He blows more kisses.*) Here, here, here!

MADAME CHAMBORAN

Your honor, I object!

THE COSTUMIER, returning.

Silence! (*Announcing.*) Number 14312!

SCENE 5

The same, JONATHAN dressed as a coachman.

JONATHAN, *entering.*

Oh . . . huh? The trial's here? Hey, Albert, how are you?

ALBERT

Address the court!

JONATHAN

Ah! Old man Dubouloy . . . (*He goes to shake Dubouloy's hand.*) Nice to see you.

DUBOULOY

Witness, keep your distance.

ALBERT, *to Jonathan.*

Please state your name.

JONATHAN

You know me.

ALBERT, *emphatically.*

State your name for the court.

JONATHAN

You know perfectly well . . . Isidore Plâtreaux. I went by the name Jonathan in the days of my prosperity and eloquence.

ALBERT

Your profession?

JONATHAN

Well, when I ran out of money, I sent a telegram to Salt Lake City requesting more funds. They cabled back that I was an ass.

ALBERT and DUBOULOY

An ass?

JONATHAN

That I was impure! And they politely added that there was a price on my head.

ALBERT

These details aren't important. What is your profession?

JONATHAN

A fallen apostle whom misfortune has forced into the horse and buggy business.

ALBERT

Communist, please tell the court what you think of Mormons.[44]

JONATHAN

They kicked me out. They're a farce.

ALBERT

And their institutions?

JONATHAN

A joke.

MADAME CHAMBORAN

And your opinion of their marriages?

JONATHAN, *looking around nervously.*

Oh, please! There are some scary-looking men here.

MADAME CHAMBORAN

I order you to explain yourself.

JONATHAN

Fine! Getting married there is about as serious as drinking a pint of ale here.

(*Laughter.*)

THE COSTUMIER, *laughing.*

Ha, ha, ha! (*Abruptly changing tone.*) Silence, gentlemen!

DUBOULOY, *to Jonathan.*

Continue.

JONATHAN

A spouse over there is like an acquaintance here. You have one, you have two, you have three, you have . . .

DUBOULOY

Enough! Enough!

JONATHAN

Personally, I had . . .

ALBERT

Take your seat!

JONATHAN

Yes, bourgeois. (*He gives a bill to Albert.*) Number 14312, two francs an hour, the tip isn't included. (*He looks at his watch.*) It's five after noon now.

ALBERT

As you see, gentlemen of the jury, the accusations of bigamy, of trigamy . . . of quadrigamy are fabrications made up by the opposing counsel!

MADAME CHAMBORAN

Fabrications? What about the two wives who followed you to Paris? What about Eva?

ALBERT

She has been subpoenaed. Have her called.

DUBOULOY

Have the witness shown in. (*The costumier exits.*)

JONATHAN

She's waiting outside. I drove her here.

THE COSTUMIER, *returning.*

Silence! (*Announcing.*) Monsieur and Madame Calvados!

SCENE 6

The same, GONTRAN, EVA in a wedding dress, followed by grooms and bridesmaids

MADAME CHAMBORAN

A wedding dress! Is that all she does?

ALBERT

Isn't this wardrobe the most eloquent defense? The veil, the orange blossoms, nothing is missing.

EVA, *looking down.*

Monsieur!

GONTRAN

Dear Eva! As for Monsieur Savarin who summoned us, the proof that he never had a legitimate claim to madame is that I just married her. And I forbid this gentleman from besmirching my chaste companion any longer by referring to her as his wife!

ALBERT

He renounces any claim on her.

GONTRAN

It's about time!

ALBERT

The incident is hereby vacated. Monsieur Savarin yields before the overwhelming evidence. (*He bows to Eva and Gontran.*)

GONTRAN

That is wise. (*He leads Eva to a chair.*) Dear Eva, you have only ever been mine; the judgment is clear.

EVA, *looking down, whispering.*

Oh yes. The evil villain!

MADAME CHAMBORAN

What about that Nadeje you introduced into the conjugal domicile?

EVA

Nadeje? She's here.

ALBERT

Show in the witness.

SCENE 7

The same, NADEJE in a wedding dress, RAPHAEL, grooms, and bridesmaids

MADAME CHAMBORAN

What? Another wedding?

NADEJE

It's already done. We just left the Batignolles city hall.[45]

RAPHAEL

Raphael Trumeau, hairstylist and barber, first-class laureate. Here are the addresses of my salons, "Venus's Braid." (*He presents his card.*) I've also included pricing: men's beards, twenty-five cents; women's beards, one franc fifty cents.

ALBERT

The presence of these two young maidens, arm in arm with their tender husbands, in their wedding gowns, with an abundance of orange blossoms in their hair, should suffice, I hope, to enlighten the court.

DUBOULOY

Say no more, your case has been made. I order the prosecution to submit a retraction to the court.

MATHILDE

Oh yes, mother. Can't you see he's innocent?

MADAME CHAMBORAN

Innocent? Innocent? A . . . Ach . . . Achoo!

ALBERT, *aside.*

This head cold is calming her down.

MADAME CHAMBORAN

Well, since I must . . . My son-in-law, come to my arms.

ALBERT

Just a minute. First give me the keys to our apartment. These pretty little keys that . . . that . . . well, I think I make myself clear.

MADAME CHAMBORAN, *pulling an enormous set of keys from her pocket.*

Here they are. Now embrace me!

ALBERT

With pleasure!

(*Madame Chamboran opens her arms, Albert moves toward her then changes course and embraces Mathilde passionately. Laughter.*)

MADAME CHAMBORAN

Still mischievous!

THE COSTUMIER, *laughing.*

Ha, ha, ha! (*Abruptly changing tone.*) Silence, gentlemen!

DUBOULOY

Court is adjourned . . . until the next separation.

ALL, *protesting.*

Never! Never!

ALBERT, *holding his wife tightly.*

Oh, my one and only love.

MATHILDE

You'll never love anyone else?

ALBERT

I swear! Mormonism is an awful, horrible institution! (*Aside.*) But it had some good things here and there.

JONATHAN

And now, let's go water the seed![46]

(*Curtain.*)

BERTHELIER MEETS THE MORMONS

UNKNOWN

Sketch in One Act

Performed at the Théâtre des Variétés, June 1875

Less than a year after the premiere of *Mormons in Paris*, the Théâtre des Variétés staged the one-act play *Berthelier chez les Mormonnes*. It appears to have been improvised quickly in June 1875 for a one-night performance to showcase Jean-François Berthelier (1830–1888; figure 7), a well-known comic actor who performed in theaters all over Paris and created a number of roles for Jacques Offenbach's comic operas. According to the *Annales du Théâtre*, upon learning of devastating floods in southern France Berthelier decided to donate proceeds from the evening's performance to the victims.[1] The handwritten manuscript does not list an author nor do any of the reviews, though, given the theme, it is likely that the same team who wrote *Mormons in Paris*, Louis Leroy and Alfred Delacour, also wrote *Berthelier*. A review of the play in *La Comédie* reports that Berthelier, "surrounded by the most beautiful women of the troupe, was applauded with delirium when he made his entrance. The unanimous and repeated applause seemed to take Berthelier aback. The good man had never seen such a raucous party. The actors had to let the audience cheer on . . . and their heartfelt appreciation threatened to bring the house down."[2] The evening's entertainment also featured a number of musical numbers, a one-act comedy titled *Les Giboulées* by Charles Nuitter and Jules Prével, and one satirically performed act of Joseph Bouchardy's 1840 drama *Lazare le pâtre*.[3]

FIGURE 7 Photo of Berthelier. (BnF Gallica)

CAST:[4]

Berthelier
Prophet Oscar, head of the Mormons[5]
Bibifrong, Oscar's confidant

Ridonbeth, Oscar's confidant
Pichenette, Parisian
Myrrha, Italian
Lodoïska, Polish
Dolores, Spanish
Ellen, English
Lisbeth, Swiss
Other Mormon men and women

The stage represents an elegant pavilion open on all sides and surrounded by lush vegetation. Upstage a sign reads: "Utah; Mormon capital; 35,000 kilometers to Nanterre."

SCENE I

PICHENETTE, MYRRHA, LODOÏSKA, DOLORES, LISBETH, and ELLEN

CHORUS

It's deplorable! It's out of hand!
The fate of women in this land . . .
It's revolting and indecent
That we suffer such poor treatment!

MYRRHA

It's an indignity!

LODOÏSKA

A monstrosity!

DOLORES

A horror!

PICHENETTE

Enough platitudes! Let's cut to the chase. The prophet is depraved!

MYRRHA

Twenty-seven wives for his personal use!

DOLORES

It's revolting!

PICHENETTE

Oh, why did I leave Paris? There, at least, I had Oscar's affections all to myself. Oscar was a talented artist's apprentice! He left for California and I followed. When he arrived in this city overrun with Mormonism, Oscar learned he could have several wives. He decided to go no further, and he became a Mormon. Last year he was named prophet. Oh! How I miss the Luxembourg Theater and the crêpe stand at the Gymnasium Theater.

LODOÏSKA

It's true that women lead a very unhappy existence here.

MYRRHA

Sharing one man with twenty-seven women, is that a social position to be proud of?

ALL THE WOMEN

No! No! No!

PICHENETTE, *striking her chest.*

My degraded sisters, do you have heart?[6]

ALL, *repeating the gesture.*

Yes! Yes! Yes!

PICHENETTE

See, all so courageous! In the name of Pichenette, I don't understand why you still put up with this.

LODOÏSKA

What else can we do?

DOLORES

These vicious men have strength on their side.

LISBETH

And they take advantage of it.

PICHENETTE, *forcefully.*

I swear that if you all felt the same righteous indignation in your bones that I feel in mine, we would soon change the order of things.

LISBETH, upstage.

Silence! The prophet and his confidants are on their way.

PICHENETTE

Let's keep our rebellion secret!

SCENE 2

The same, PROPHET OSCAR, BIBIFRONG, and RIDONBETH

(*Prophet Oscar, followed by his confidants, enters majestically; he slowly climbs onto a thronelike armchair.*)

CHORUS[7]

PROPHET OSCAR, *on his armchair.*

Spiritual wives, gather 'round.

PICHENETTE, *aside.*

So pretentious! So pretentious!

BIBIFRONG, *in a falsetto voice.*

Silence!

OSCAR

Spiritual wives, I am here to confess, without artifice, that my affection for you has dropped to many degrees below zero, and I feel the need to choose a twenty-eighth companion to brighten my existence. (*Bibifrong pulls him by the sleeve.*)

PICHENETTE, *aside.*

Let's keep our rebellion secret! (*Aloud.*) O beloved master, ray of sunshine! (*Aside.*) Savoyard![8] (*Aloud.*) Your words are sweet as honey and we could not be happier.

OSCAR

Naturally. Now serve me by sewing the buttons on my flannel vests and spare me your delicious but unbearable presence. Go!

PICHENETTE, *aside.*

So pretentious! So pretentious!

CHORUS

(*As the chorus sings, the wives prostrate themselves one by one before the prophet and then exit upstage.*)

SCENE 3

OSCAR, BIBIFRONG, and RIDONBETH

OSCAR, *descending from his armchair.*

To be the prophet is grand, beautiful, and vast! My friends, if I were offered the direction of the Théâtre de l'Odéon,[9] I would turn it down!

BIBIFRONG

And you might be right.

OSCAR

And when I think that just two years ago I was leading a dismal existence on the cobblestones of Paris . . . what a transformation.

BIBIFRONG

Master, you are a superior man!

OSCAR, *modestly.*

I'm chic, nothing more.

RIDONBETH, *entering upstage.*

My lord, a stranger I have never met is quickly approaching.

OSCAR

A stranger, you say? What is he doing here?

BIBIFRONG

Could he be coming to uncover our mysterious customs?

OSCAR

We shall find out soon enough. Let's step away and return to interrogate him later!

SCENE 4

BERTHELIER

(*He enters upstage in a travel suit; his clothes are untidy, his hair is messed up, and he is dragging a trunk.*)

BERTHELIER

Where am I? What is this strange place? (*Greeting the audience.*) Pardon me . . . I'm Isidore Berthelier, born in 1835 in Saint-Denis, comic at the Théâtre des Variétés.[10] I left Paris two months ago with Léonce and Aline Duval[11] to perform in America. Everything was going well, but when traveling nearby, we were attacked by Indians. Léonce is being held by Black Cat and Aline has fallen into the hands of Brave Rabbit. I managed to escape. For two days I've wandered over hill and dale with my trunk (*Showing his trunk.*) that has all my costumes. (*Opening his trunk.*) Here they are. Oh, Paris! Will I ever see you again? Will I ever see the Obelisk again or Hyacinthe's nose, Paris's two greatest monuments![12] In the meantime, which way should I go? Ah! Here is a sign. (*Reading.*) "Utah; Mormon capital; 35,000 kilometers to Nanterre." I'm in Mormon territory! (*Looking to the left.*) Oh, my goodness! What is that?

CHORUS

Men with beards,
Beards are coming,
Beards are coming.[13]

SCENE 5

BERTHELIER, OSCAR, BIBIFRONG, and RIDONBETH

OSCAR, *to Berthelier.*

Who are you? What do you want? Where are you from? Where are you going?

BERTHELIER

Rub-a-dub-dub, three men in a tub!

OSCAR

Three men in a tub? He needs to be taught some respect! Throw him in the Great Salt Lake!

BERTHELIER

Wait! My name is Berthelier. I'm from France and would like to return home. What's the quickest way back to the Théâtre des Variétés?

OSCAR

That's impossible. You've entered our inner sanctum. You can't leave now. Would you like to become Mormon?

BERTHELIER

That's a kind offer, but I'd rather not.

OSCAR

Very well. Throw him in the Great Salt Lake!

BERTHELIER

Wait! (*Aside.*) Can he say anything but "Great Salt Lake"? (*Aloud.*) Since I have no choice, make me a Mormon, and let's be done with it.

OSCAR

Pay attention! This is your initiation. Turn around.[14]

BERTHELIER, *worried.*

What's he doing?

OSCAR, *kicking him in the pants.*

Pow! You're a Mormon.

BERTHELIER, *rubbing his backside.*

I'm touched . . .

OSCAR

You're a Mormon, I say! From this moment on you enjoy the innumerable rights associated with your new status. They can all be summed up in one: the right to obey me! The first time you oppose my will, I will have you thrown . . .

BERTHELIER

In the Great Salt Lake . . . I get it. (*Aside.*) He's going too far!

OSCAR

Now, we'll need to furnish you with wives. How many would you like?

BERTHELIER

Well, I don't know.

OSCAR

If I give you six, will that do?

BERTHELIER

Six? That should be more than enough for me.

OSCAR

Very well. (*Aside.*) Here's where I unload some of my stock . . . (*Aloud.*) Have my spiritual wives shown in!

SCENE 6

The same, PICHENETTE, LODOÏSKA, MYRRHA, DOLORES, LISBETH, and ELLEN

OSCAR

My young Mormon friend, consider your prize:
A flock of women with brown and blue eyes.
What do you think?

BERTHELIER

Charming! Had I more talents,
Each one would receive a hefty allowance!

OSCAR

Very well. Now my sweet Mormon beauties,
Watch this man fulfill his Mormon duties.
Admire with me his curly brown hair,
His plump body, and his clueless, blank stare.
Answer me, truly, are you not awed?
Does he not look the part of a fallen Greek god?
Don't answer. I have a new plan for your lives:
I hereby declare you . . . husband and wives!
I'll leave you newlyweds to your romance
As I depart with pomp and circumstance.
Now, let's go. Hey! That's too much bass drum!

(*Oscar departs upstage with his confidants; Berthelier walks them out.*)

SCENE 7

BERTHELIER upstage; PICHENETTE, MYRRHA, LODOÏSKA, DOLORES, ELLEN, and LISBETH downstage

PICHENETTE

Ladies, all six of us have just been pawned off on one man. It's intolerable!

ALL

Yes, yes, it's intolerable!

PICHENETTE

I propose taking revenge on this man for all the wrongs we've suffered. Are you with me?

ALL

We're with you!

BERTHELIER, *returning.*

Here I am with six wives! I'm feeling such incredible emotion. They are lovely. The blonde is well rounded, and the brunette . . . a beautiful woman. Good heavens! Good heavens! I don't know if it's the climate, but I'm tingling all over. Good heavens!

MYRRHA, *stepping toward Berthelier.*

Our dear husband, before getting closer, we need to be sure you know your duties.

BERTHELIER

Oh! I know my duties.

LODOÏSKA

Silence! You don't know anything at all.

PICHENETTE

We have changed the order of things and have written this new code.[15]

ARTICLE I:

Given that women
Are delicate creatures
And love is the liniment
That enhances their features,
This judgment we render:
Husbands must be knightly
And constantly tender,
Treating us politely.

ALL

It's so perfect! It's so perfect!
This new code
Is solid gold.
It's so perfect! It's so perfect!

The code's correct:
We demand respect.

PICHENETTE

ARTICLE 2:
Women are a bit coquettish,
And no one will deny
That to bejewel and embellish
Must be done both far and nigh.
To have a calm domestic life,
We require you to know
That men get all the toil and strife
And women all the dough.

ALL

It's so perfect! It's so perfect!
This new code
Is solid gold.
It's so perfect! It's so perfect!
The code's correct:
We demand respect.

PICHENETTE

ARTICLE 3:
Women are all very wise.
They're never known to fail.
And since some men we must advise,
Here's how we will prevail:
Should we disagree or fight,
We'll sing this little song,
"The wife is always right
And the husband always wrong!"

ALL

It's so perfect! It's so perfect!
This new code
Is solid gold.
It's so perfect! It's so perfect!

The code's correct:
We demand respect.

PICHENETTE

Do you accept our demands?[16]

BERTHELIER

I do.

PICHENETTE

Very good. My little husband.

BERTHELIER

My little wife.

PICHENETTE

I give you permission to take me by the waist.

BERTHELIER

I couldn't ask for more.

LODOÏSKA

Me too! My turn!

BERTHELIER

I'll be right with you.

ELLEN, LISBETH, MYRRHA, and DOLORES

My turn, my turn.

BERTHELIER

Here you are, there you go, let's go.

PICHENETTE, *turning her cheek.*

I give you permission to kiss me.

BERTHELIER

Delighted. (*He kisses her and tries to kiss each wife as they request his affections.*)

MYRRHA

My husband.

BERTHELIER

My wife.

MYRRHA, *turning her cheek.*

My turn.

BERTHELIER

Here I am.

DOLORES, *turning her cheek.*

My husband.

LODOÏSKA, *turning her cheek.*

My husband.

BERTHELIER

I'm on my way, I'm on my way. Be patient.

ELLEN

My turn.

LISBETH

My turn.

BERTHELIER

Hold on! (*Aside.*) Good heavens, this is exhausting!

PICHENETTE, *turning her cheek.*

Our cheeks are getting cold.

ALL, *turning their cheeks.*

Get to work!

(*Berthelier, followed by his wives, doesn't know which way to turn and finally escapes upstage and exits; the women follow and exit, chasing him.*)

SCENE 8

OSCAR, then BERTHELIER

(*As the women exit, Oscar enters stage right, holding a photograph of Berthelier dressed as a woman. He advances slowly, gazing at the portrait.*)

OSCAR

A woman! I was deceived! It was a woman! This photograph that he . . . I mean . . . that she dropped proves that he's here . . . I mean . . . that she's here. It proves that she's an Italian named Barbarinia Barbarini.[17] She's gorgeous in this dress! Ah! I'm crazy about her. (*Kissing the photograph.*) What a revelation!

BERTHELIER, *enters stage left.*

I made a sharp turn and gave them the slip. Phew.

OSCAR

It's her!

BERTHELIER

Oh no! This old fogey again.

OSCAR

Oh! Stay there. Don't move. Let me look at you.

BERTHELIER

What's gotten into him? He's fluttering his eyelashes.

OSCAR

No, my first twenty-seven don't add up to half the woman you are. You are a shining star. But I don't need to tell you that.

BERTHELIER

You're too kind, Father What's-your-name.

OSCAR

Please, call me Oscar. It's my pet name. (*He pinches Berthelier's waist.*) Barbarini.

BERTHELIER

Barbarini!

OSCAR

Yes, I have had a revelation. You are a woman, an Italian, the woman of my dreams. (*Pinching Berthelier's waist.*) You are an angel. (*He embraces Berthelier.*)

BERTHELIER

Stop! You're tickling me. My dear man, I'm sorry to dash your hopes.

OSCAR

Enough. We have embraced. This means you will be my twenty-eighth and have the place of honor and authority. I will do everything you desire, everything you want. Command, order, your slave will obey. You are so beautiful, a revelation! Stay here. I'll come back to get you soon. (*He exits left.*)

SCENE 9

BERTHELIER, then PICHENETTE, LODOÏSKA, MYRRHA, DOLORES, ELLEN, and LISBETH

BERTHELIER, *alone.*

What an idiot. Me, a woman? That's a good one. But I'm still worried. You may not believe me, but I would rather be memorizing difficult lines right now.[18] My six wives are exhausting.

LODOÏSKA

There he is!

BERTHELIER

It's them! I'm caught! (*He tries to flee.*)

PICHENETTE, *a riding crop in hand.*

Running away? You coward! Stop him, ladies!

ALL

On guard!

BERTHELIER

Stop it! I've had enough! I'd appreciate it if you all got lost.

PICHENETTE

He's insulting us! Take revenge! Raise our whips, ladies, we must make an example of him! (*They all raise riding crops.*)

BERTHELIER

My wives are going to beat me!

PICHENETTE, *singing as the women whip Berthelier.*

We must avenge our sex;
We must do so right away!
For too long we've been vexed,
Forced to constantly obey.
So arm ourselves with riding crops!
We'll strike at the same time.
And if our cowardly husband drops,
We'll repeat this little rhyme:
"Whip, whip, whip, whip!
This is how we right the ship!
Whip, whip, whip, whip!
This is how we right the ship!"
We'll use our whipping talent
To make our husband gallant
So he will caress us,
Gently seduce us,
And most of all obey us.
With our whips

At our hips
In our house,
Our spouse
Won't grouse!

BERTHELIER
Have mercy!

PICHENETTE
This is only the prologue of what we have in store for you.

BERTHELIER
The prologue? I'll never survive to the final act. (*Aside.*) How can I get out of this? Ah! I have an idea. The prophet's so-called revelation. Yes. (*Aloud.*) Ladies, I have to tell you a secret.

ALL
A secret? What secret?

BERTHELIER
Shh!!!

ALL
Shh!!!

BERTHELIER, *whispering.*
You all think that I'm a man, right?

PICHENETTE
What? You aren't?

BERTHELIER
Shh!!!

ALL
Shh!!!

BERTHELIER
I look like a man, it's true.[19] But I am a woman!

ALL
A woman!

BERTHELIER
Completely.

PICHENETTE
Then why this outfit?

BERTHELIER
Why? It's . . . It's because of an unfortunate event. I was traveling through a virgin forest when I was abducted by a

warrior from the tribe of the Staring Dogs. He took me to his wigwam, in other words, to his bedroom.

PICHENETTE

Poor little thing. I'm beginning to understand.

BERTHELIER

Rest assured that I still merit the adjective of the virgin forest I was in.

PICHENETTE

What a relief. Continue your story.

BERTHELIER

My abductor left to attend the bonfire council. I rifled through his dresser, found these clothes, and put them on.

PICHENETTE

I see. Well, since you are one of us, it's your turn to hear a secret.

LODOÏSKA

You'll be discreet?

BERTHELIER

Quiet as a mouse.

PICHENETTE

We have organized a petticoat uprising.

BERTHELIER

I'm ready to break all the streetlamps for your cause![20]

PICHENETTE

Bravo! What enthusiasm! Ladies, I propose granting her command of our new campaign.

ALL

Yes! Yes!

PICHENETTE

Unanimously, we declare our loyalty. Long live our commander!

ALL

Long live our commander!

BERTHELIER

Dear colleagues, I am touched. Believe me. (*Forcefully.*) This is the most beautiful day of my life!

ALL

Bravo! Bravo!

PICHENETTE

Commander, you must wear the insignia of your sex.

BERTHELIER

That's simple. My clothes are in my trunk.

PICHENETTE

Let's march! I'll attach your pins.

BERTHELIER

I won't say no . . . as long as you let me return the favor.

ALL

Forward, march!

CHORUS

Let's prepare for a war that's just.
Soon our Iroquois will eat our dust!
Every brave will answer to a squaw.
At the point of a sword, we'll dictate our law.

(*They exit with Berthelier in the lead.*)

SCENE 10

PROPHET OSCAR, BIBIFRONG, RIDONBETH, several Mormons

OSCAR, *entering.*

Here we are. Come, let me introduce you. (*Looking around the vacant stage.*) Wait. She's gone. Could she have tried to deprive me of her love by fleeing?

BIBIFRONG

It is certainly possible.

OSCAR, *emphatically.*

Don't tell me that. I could be happy with nothing but her and a handful of coal.

RIDONBETH

You love her that much?

OSCAR

I'm crazy about her. Ah, my children, this Italian is so attractive, I would give my treasures and my existence for her. (*A loud fanfare sounds offstage.*) What's that?

RIDONBETH

What's that strange tune?

OSCAR

Is that a tuba I hear?[21] Where is it coming from? (*He looks upstage.*) What is that?

RIDONBETH

What do you see?

OSCAR

I don't know. That's why I asked.

BIBIFRONG

Clearly.

OSCAR

No, it's not clear.

RIDONBETH

It's getting closer.

BIBIFRONG

I see flags and colorful costumes.

OSCAR

What color?

BIBIFRONG

All colors!

OSCAR

Could they be Apache warriors?

PICHENETTE

Intrepid Mormons, onward!

CHORUS

Rat-a-tat-tat, rat-a-tat-tat

PICHENETTE

For too long we've been conquered.

CHORUS

Rat-a-tat-tat, rat-a-tat-tat

PICHENETTE

To restore our authority and influence

CHORUS

Boom ba-da-boom, ba-da-boom boom boom

PICHENETTE

We'll make our masters watch us dance

CHORUS

Boom ba-da-boom, ba-da-boom boom boom

PICHENETTE

We will vanquish, I'm not lying.
We will vanquish or die trying.

CHORUS

Ba-da-boom, ba-da-boom boom boom
Zing-zang boom boom.

SCENE 11

OSCAR, BIBIFRONG, RIDONBETHER, PICHENETTE, MYRRHA, LODOÏSKA, DOLORES, ELLEN, LISBETH, a dozen Mormon women

(*All the Mormon women are armed; there is a drummer in front.*[22])

PICHENETTE

Halt! Left face! Present arms!

OSCAR

What does this mean? Who will explain this riddle to me?

SCENE 12

The same, BERTHELIER

BERTHELIER, *making a dramatic entrance in his Italian dress with a rifle and a Turkish sabre.*

I will!

OSCAR

Her! It's her. Here she is . . . in her Italian dress. How pretty you are.

BERTHELIER

Hands off! And listen to our ultimatum.

CHORUS MEMBER[23]

We maintain,
Yes, we claim
The total end of your reign.
La-oo-la-la!

That here and now
Old man, and how!
Our reign you must avow.
La-oo-la-la!
In Paris,
That lovely terrace—
A beautiful slice
Of paradise—
With flair
Women wear
Seditious crinoline.[24]
And we maintain
That its glorious reign
Shall never end.
Yes, everything drops
And all sound stops
In sight of the queen
With the golden sheen.
La-oo-la-la!
Her suitors slink,
Admirers wink,
As they gather 'round her;
And with a coy
Coquettish ploy
She drops white gloves behind her.

FULL CHORUS

Her suitors slink,
Admirers wink,
And promise to always be true.

BERTHELIER

La-oo-la-la!
La-oo-la-la!
She can choose on a hunch
Whom she wants from the bunch.

CHORUS

Get out the broom.
Let's sweep the room.

And change this state of affairs!
La-oo-la-la!
Get out the broom.
Let's sweep the room.
And change this state of affairs!
La-oo-la-la!
Get out the broom.
Let's sweep the room.
And change this state of affairs!
La-oo-la-la!
It's our turn to gather rose buds.
La-oo-la-la!
Husbands wear the toiler's duds,
Here we've come to settle scores,
And now the worries are yours.

BERTHELIER

That is our ultimatum!

OSCAR, *mechanically.*

I accept. I will only ever love you. Here is my hand.

BERTHELIER

I will only offer you my hand in front of the flag in the city hall of Paris's fourth arrondissement.

OSCAR

I consent. Let's leave for Paris.

BERTHELIER

And I'm bringing Pichenette as my companion.

OSCAR

So be it. I'll put on my scarf, and we're off! (*He puts on his scarf and picks up his umbrella.*)

BERTHELIER, *to Pichenette.*

Here's my plan: once in Paris, I'll lose him in the construction.[25] As for you, Pichenette, stay calm. I'll protect you.

PICHENETTE

You! A woman!

BERTHELIER

A woman! (*He takes her hand and runs it under his chin.*)

PICHENETTE

Ouch! It's prickly.

BERTHELIER

Shh! I'll look out for you. I'll help you land a role at the Bouffes-Parisiens.[26]

OSCAR

Let's go!

BERTHELIER

One minute. Let me say a few words to these ladies and gentlemen, and then I'll join you.

BERTHELIER and CHORUS

Away with me,
Leave shall we
My friends, and sing this ditty:
Afar we'll be
And soon shall see
Dear Paris, our fair city!
Away with me,
Leave shall we
etc., etc.

(*Curtain.*)

JAPHETH'S TWELVE WIVES

ANTONY MARS AND MAURICE DESVALLIÈRES
MUSIC BY VICTOR ROGER

Vaudeville Operetta in Three Acts
Premiered at the Théâtre de la Renaissance, December 16, 1890

Les Douze femmes de Japhet opened in 1890 at the Théâtre de la Renaissance to rave reviews. *Le Ménestrel* called it "extraordinary," stating that Parisian audiences "have not laughed so hard in a long time." The same review called the music "charming" and predicted that it would "soon be in everyone's head" and that the play would enjoy "a long theatrical run."[1] The play was reprised in 1897 at the Eldorado in Paris, and, in the same year, a censored version was performed at the Josefstadt Theater in Vienna.[2] Writing about the 1897 reprise, Paul-Emile Chevalier notes that the play was staged in both Pisa and Milan with three fewer wives as the *Nove Moglie di Japhet* before returning to Paris.[3] It was also performed outside of Paris in Lille, a staging mentioned in 1908.[4]

Even the costumes received positive reviews and were featured on the richly colored posters promoting the operetta (figure 8). Writing in December 1890, Richard O'Monroy (pseudonym of Richard de L'Isle de Falcon de Saint-Geniès) provided detailed descriptions of the three different costumes worn by the wives in the three acts: "First costume: Short skirt with pleated yellow tulle revealing high brown spats, bodice of red velour with gold embroidery and wide sleeves. . . . Second costume of Japheth's twelve wives: Gray tight-waist smock with Havana satin lapels and large buttons; small red leather handbag; and a stylish fedora with peacock feathers. . . . Third costume of the twelve wives:

FIGURE 8 Poster for *Japheth's Twelve Wives.* (BnF Gallica)

Pink tulle skirt with an embroidered yoke, belt and bow in pink satin, pink feather fan, and on their heads a small pink plumed pouf."[5]

Written by Antony Mars and Maurice Desvallières with a score by Victor Roger, this vaudeville operetta is perhaps the best of the French Mormon musical comedies. Desvallières collaborated extensively with Georges Feydeau who, after Labiche, remains the most enduring of the

Boulevard playwrights. But Desvallières also collaborated frequently with Mars. A quick search of the Bibliothèque Nationale de France (BNF)'s database reveals that the two worked together on at least six plays.[6] Around the time he coauthored *Japheth's Twelve Wives*, Mars seems to have been inspired by marriage and divorce, writing plays with titles like *Les Maris sans femmes* (Husbands without Wives, 1889), *Les Surprises du divorce* (Surprises of Divorce, 1889), and *Les Vieux maris* (Old Husbands, 1890).

The first act of *Japheth's Twelve Wives* is set in Salt Lake City, Utah, at the home of Japheth Paterson, a canned-goods tycoon who has immigrated from France and married twelve wives. The representation of America as an exotic locale and the hypocrisy of French marriage stand as key themes in the opening scenes as Japheth is described as a sort of colonial master.

The play's second act is set in Paris at a police headquarters. Japheth's uncle, Baliveau, has been appointed police commissioner and prides himself on the luxurious nature of his cells and office space. Beginning in 1790, Paris had forty-eight commissioners with a responsibility of overseeing police activity and investigations in a district of the capital.[7] Historians Dominique Kalifa and Pierre Karila-Cohen identify two different types of commissioners in the French imaginary of the nineteenth century: those who are "benevolent and legitimate, a person of note in a community" and those who are "incompetent . . . arrogant and corrupt."[8] Baliveau borrows from both of these types. He is petulant and petty but prides himself on taking good care of his inmates. He knows the goings-on of his district and writes an anonymous column describing the many scandals he encounters. The only crimes he seems to investigate though are crimes relating to prostitution or adultery. He is wealthy and only accepts the position of commissioner so that he can better take revenge on the institution of marriage since his wife cuckolded him and left him for another man, Cassoulet.

The final act, set in a marriage agency, reflects the very real world of a widely used but often crooked profession in late nineteenth-century France. As mentioned in the introduction, over 25 percent of marriages in Paris went through agencies.[9] Kalifa points out that the police opened an investigation into these agencies in 1893 and "in 1911, a lawyer estimated that there were 150 agencies in the capital and at least ten in each large city outside Paris."[10] The most reputable agencies did not require any payment up front but only collected once a marriage was completed. Less reputable agencies specialized in "delicate" situations like the one in this play involving married women. These agencies often charged "exorbitant sums proportional to 'the gravity of the wrongdoing.'"[11] Women were classified by their appearance, dowry amount, age, and potential inheritance, while men were grouped according to their social position: "identity, place of residence, health, wealth, and family alliances."[12] These agencies often featured rather unscrupulous proprietors who frequently provided more than one service to maximize their revenue. Kalifa notes that these shops began as generic "business agencies" whose employees helped in real-estate deals, moneylending, travel arrangements, etc.[13] If the agent in this play, Cassoulet, opens another branch in his agency, it is completely in line with the reality of the industry in 1890 Paris.

Unlike the first two plays in this collection, *Japheth's Twelve Wives* was printed and published for distribution to other troupes that staged the play. A copy of the play is housed in the BNF, and images of the poster advertising the original staging of the play along with photos of the cast can be found in the BNF's online database, Gallica. Gallica also holds a piano score and detailed directions for the staging of the play, including sketches of the stage layout.

CAST:	ROLE CREATED BY:
Japheth Paterson	Victor Regnard
Briquet, his servant	Edouard Georges
Cassoulet, marriage agent	Victorin
Baliveau, Japheth's uncle, police commissioner	Bellot
Des Toupettes, Japheth's friend	Anthony Gildès[14]
John Smith, Mormon pastor	Corbières[15]
Ernest, police officer	Colleuille
Godet, a suitor	Gorby
Deborah, Paterson's wife	Irma Aubry
Arabella, Paterson's wife	Alice Berthier
Clary, Paterson's wife	E. George

Beatrice, Paterson's wife	Tylda Raphael
Rebecca, Paterson's wife	De Baeker
Zinna, Paterson's wife	F. Mayer
Mary, Paterson's wife	Lucy Albert
Elisa #1, Paterson's wife	Dubois
Elisa #2, Paterson's wife	Beckaert
Belly, Paterson's wife	Berthe Garry
Dorothy, Paterson's wife	Rosine
Adelina, Paterson's wife	Georgina

ACT I

A large room with a wide bay window upstage that opens onto an exotic countryside. Downstage left is a door to Deborah's room; just behind it another door leads to the rooms of the eleven other wives. Downstage right is a double door leading to the dining room. Between the two doors on the left sits a large cabinet divided into twelve compartments. Furniture is made of bamboo. Exotic plants can be seen. A bamboo table, front left, sits with chairs on each side. Front right are two large rocking chairs. Upstage, on the porch is a wide table with handicrafts: embroideries, tapestries, etc. The scenery is very sunlit.

SCENE I
BRIQUET

(*As the curtain opens, Briquet enters from the dining room at right. He is carrying a large basket filled with women's ankle boots. He takes them out of the basket and organizes them on the table on the left. Then he places the shoes in several bedrooms through the side doors.*)

BRIQUET, *alone.*

Number three. Number four. Number five. (*He crosses the stage.*) Number six. (*At number seven, he throws the ankle boots down the hall.*) Number seven. BAM! (*Returning.*) No! This isn't a life! It's three in the afternoon, and I'm just finishing the boots. I've been shining them all morning! Twelve pairs of boots. The boots of my twelve bosses. The twelve wives of Mr. Japheth Paterson, my master. No! He must be seriously hot blooded. Twelve wives! It might be fun for the masters, but it's exhausting for servants. (*He puts down the basket.*) Whew! (*He sits down at right.*) Mr. Japheth Paterson has gone out with his whole caravan. I can finally catch my breath for a moment. (*Standing.*) Oh, right, and I've forgotten the mail. (*He pulls a large stack of letters from the basket.*) Let's stuff them in here. (*He points to the cabinet at left.*) Each Mrs. Paterson has her own slot. (*He files the letters.*) Mrs. Paterson number one, Mrs. Paterson number two, Mrs. Paterson number three.

(*Des Toupettes enters upstage; he looks left and right, then decides to enter.*)

SCENE 2

DES TOUPETTES, BRIQUET

DES TOUPETTES, *entering.*

Excuse me, Mr. Paterson?

BRIQUET

Buzz off! He isn't here!

DES TOUPETTES, *aside.*

Buzz off? This servant is polite! (*To Briquet.*) But, my friend . . .

BRIQUET

If I tell you he isn't here, he isn't here! (*He turns around and recognizes Des Toupettes.*) Oh! I can't believe it! Monsieur Des Toupettes, my former master!

DES TOUPETTES, *surprised.*

Briquet!

BRIQUET

Briquet . . . Yes monsieur, your devoted Briquet.

DES TOUPETTES

Fancy meeting you here!

BRIQUET

Shocking . . . Just yesterday I was talking about you.

DES TOUPETTES

With whom?

BRIQUET

With myself!

DES TOUPETTES

My good Briquet! How do you like it here?

BRIQUET

I don't like it much, monsieur . . . I'm in Mr. Paterson's employ.

DES TOUPETTES

Life is funny! We said goodbye on the boulevard des Italiens in Paris and meet again on the shores of the Salt Lake.

BRIQUET

Yes, it's a bit farther away than Bougival.[16] Did you come here to sow your wild oats?

DES TOUPETTES

No! I've come seeking my fortune. I'm broke, my poor Briquet . . . not a penny to my name.

BRIQUET

Oh no! How did you lose it all?

DES TOUPETTES

Women, of course! Always women . . . I can't live without them. I gobbled through the fortunes of two uncles and five aunts for them.

BRIQUET

An entire family!

DES TOUPETTES

And now I'm eating crow.

BRIQUET

That's tough.

DES TOUPETTES

So, finding myself poor at winter's first roar, I left.[17] Six months ago I came to America. They say it's a land of promise for those of us who've gone bust! I started a business in San Francisco exporting canned goods.

BRIQUET

And how's business?

DES TOUPETTES

Not great, mostly because of this Paterson. In fact, that's why I'm here! I ordered three thousand cans of hare meat from his agent in San Francisco. And do you know what was in the cans of hare I received?

BRIQUET

No.

DES TOUPETTES

Plain old rabbit!

BRIQUET

It sounds like karma, monsieur . . . the revenge of the rabbits.

DES TOUPETTES

Laugh all you want, but your master is a crook!

BRIQUET

Monsieur, you can insult him all you want, but you won't come close to expressing what I think of him.

DES TOUPETTES

Things are that bad here?

BRIQUET

Oh monsieur, so much work! So many responsibilities! When I think back on our good life in Paris at your residence . . . That's where I was happy. You had your friends, I had mine. Never more than one woman to serve at a time, even though they changed often.

DES TOUPETTES

It's true, those were good times! Do you remember Ernestine, the star of the Folies-Parisiennes?[18]

BRIQUET

No monsieur . . . she must have been after my time.

DES TOUPETTES

Oh, what a great girl . . . pretty! And lively! And happy! And married!

BRIQUET

She was married?

DES TOUPETTES

She left him for me!

BRIQUET

And then you left her, monsieur?

DES TOUPETTES

No! She left me! She found work overseas . . . and the star left without even saying goodbye.

BRIQUET

A shooting star.

DES TOUPETTES

Believe what you will, she is the only woman I've ever missed.

BRIQUET

Well monsieur, men always regret the one that got away.

SCENE 3

The same, SMITH

(*Smith enters upstage wearing the formal garb of a Quaker: long tails, stiff collar, and glasses, with an umbrella under his arm. He has long hair and speaks with a slight American accent.*)

SMITH

Mr. Japheth Paterson, please.

BRIQUET

Well, Father Smith! (*To Des Toupettes.*) He's the local priest! (*To Smith.*) Hello, your eminence!

SMITH

Pastor, my friend, I'm just a pastor.

BRIQUET

Wait, what? Pastor or priest, it's the same!

DES TOUPETTES, *aside.*

This pastor has a good head on his shoulders. (*To Briquet.*) Introduce me!

BRIQUET

With pleasure! Mr. John Smith . . . Monsieur Des Toupettes, my former master: a Frenchman and a Parisian.

SMITH, *bowing.*

It's a pleasure to meet you, sir.

DES TOUPETTES

The pleasure is all mine.

SMITH

I won't even ask if you're married. But I will ask how many wives you have?

DES TOUPETTES, *laughing.*

What? How many wives I have? What a question. For now, none; I'm a bachelor!

SMITH, *extends his arm to shake Des Toupettes hand but pulls it back with disdain and speaks stiffly without looking at Des Toupettes.*

Ah! Good day, sir!

DES TOUPETTES, *surprised, aside to Briquet.*

Umm . . . What's gotten into him?

BRIQUET, *aside to Des Toupettes.*

Dang! You told him you're a bachelor. Bachelors are looked down on here in a land where everyone is married!

DES TOUPETTES

Everyone is married?

BRIQUET

This is Mormon territory!

DES TOUPETTES

That's right! I'm in Mormon territory! (*Enthusiastically.*) So, are there a lot of women here?

BRIQUET

Ah! I'd rather not talk about it. They multiply . . . like rabbits. Since we're on the topic, I'm going to ask our priest for news of his wives.

DES TOUPETTES

His wives? Priests are married too?

BRIQUET

They have the most wives! (*To Smith.*) How are your wives doing, Mr. Smith?

SMITH

Thank you. (*He pauses.*) I have . . . ten that are doing well . . . seven suffering from a mild cold . . . and four in a situation . . . How do you say? In short, they will soon make me a father!

DES TOUPETTES

Four at the same time?

SMITH

Indeed!

DES TOUPETTES, *laughing, aside.*

Dirty old dog!

SMITH, *to Briquet.*

But tell me, is Mr. Paterson in? He invited me to dinner.

BRIQUET

No, he went out with his ladies. He'll be home soon.

SMITH, *sitting, to Des Toupettes.*

You don't mind if I sit, do you, sir? I'm a bit tired. I performed seven marriages today. I've just left the last one, a marriage of the proprietor of the Salt Lake Hotel.

DES TOUPETTES

That's my hotel!

BRIQUET

What? He just got married last week and he's already taking a new wife?

SMITH

It's the law of the land . . . Multiply and replenish the earth, my good man. We mustn't let the glass go empty, as it were!

DES TOUPETTES, *laughing.*

Like at the café-concert![19] What a crazy place!

SMITH

You mean the ideal place. Man is born to be polygamous . . . And the proof is that in your old Europe, you marry only one woman, but since she's not enough for you, you take your friend's wife too.

BRIQUET

That's true.

DES TOUPETTES

Excuse me, we may have mistresses, but . . .

SMITH

And polygamy does away with mistresses . . . hence our morality . . . We are faithful to our wives.

DES TOUPETTES

You never cheat on them?

SMITH

Never! Our system can be summed up in these two principles: a lot of wives and no mistresses . . . At your service!

DES TOUPETTES

Thank you! But I prefer my own system . . . No wives and a lot of mistresses . . . At your service!

SMITH

Shocking!

DES TOUPETTES

And with that I'm off.

BRIQUET

Monsieur, aren't you waiting for Mr. Paterson?

DES TOUPETTES

No. I'm going back to my hotel. I'll return after dinner. (*To Smith.*) Good day, Mr. Smith. Delighted to have met you. (*Bowing.*) Best wishes to your wives! (*He exits upstage right.*)

SCENE 4

BRIQUET, SMITH

BRIQUET

Monsieur Des Toupettes is a fine young man. I spent two years working for him.

SMITH

I can't say I'm impressed . . . A man without even one legitimate wife!

BRIQUET

He gets by just fine without one.

SMITH

Man was created to multiply and replenish the earth.[20]

BRIQUET

Well, then, you should find me a wife. I want to multiply and replenish.

SMITH

You? Impossible! Servants don't replenish.

BRIQUET, *vexed.*

Fine. I'll just visit the local working girls.

SMITH

What do you mean by "working girls"?

BRIQUET

They are the wives of bachelors! (*Sounds of voices and laughter in the garden.*) Ah! Here come Mr. Japheth and all his wives.

SCENE 5

BRIQUET, SMITH, JAPHETH, all his wives except ARABELLA

(*The eleven wives enter upstage by twos, marching in military style. Deborah is at the head of the formation. They are all wearing the same outfit with straw hats. Japheth follows behind and a black boy carries the parasols. Japheth is dressed entirely in white in a fanciful costume and carries a large umbrella.*)

WIVES' CHORUS

We have just returned from a stroll.
Walking is so good for the soul.
We've spent a few hours out of doors,
Marching along the Salt Lake's shores.
Two by two we march in a row.
Our husband leads us where'er we go.

JAPHETH

Halt! Left face! (*The wives follow the order and face the audience.*) Dismissed! (*The wives break ranks and disperse.*)

DEBORAH

Whew! I can't take anymore. I'm hot!

JAPHETH

Deborah, stay calm! You're always moving.

DEBORAH

I'm hot!

JAPHETH

Wipe your brow in silence! (*Noticing Smith.*) Hello Reverend Smith. How are you? I've just finished walking my wives.

SMITH

You had a good walk?

JAPHETH

Excellent! We went to the Salt Lake and took a little walk around it!

BRIQUET

Yes, and paraded these women in front of the public.

JAPHETH

What's he singing about?

BRIQUET

I'm not singing, I'm just saying . . .

JAPHETH

Okay, that's enough, shut up!

BRIQUET

Yes sir.

JAPHETH, *taking the parasols from the boy and giving them to Briquet.*

And put these away. Now, I'll call roll to make sure no one is missing. One can easily misplace a wife.

BRIQUET

Dang! When you have twelve it's eleven too many.

JAPHETH

You're starting to annoy me. Get lost.

BRIQUET

Yes sir. (*Aside.*) But you have eleven too many. (*He exits with the parasols, followed by the boy.*)

JAPHETH

Attention for roll call! (*He takes a notebook from his pocket. To Smith.*) You're welcome to stay. (*He calls the first name.*) Clary!

CLARY

Here!

JAPHETH

Belly!

BELLY

Here!

JAPHETH

Elisa number one!

ELISA #1

Here!

JAPHETH

Elisa number two!

ELISA #2

Here!

JAPHETH, *to Smith.*

I have two Elisa's, so I've numbered them.

SMITH

Ingenious.

JAPHETH

It helps avoid confusion. Zinna!

ZINNA

Here!

JAPHETH

Dorothy!

DOROTHY

Here!

JAPHETH

Arabella! (*Silence.*) Arabella! (*More silence.*) What? She's not here? I've lost Arabella! (*To Deborah.*) Mistress Deborah, where is Arabella?

DEBORAH

How would I know?

JAPHETH

You should know. It's your duty to look after your colleagues. You're my oldest wife.

DEBORAH

As you remind me often.

JAPHETH

Because you seem to forget it.

DEBORAH

You remember well enough for both of us.

JAPHETH

All right, that's enough. (*Aside.*) She can be so annoying! (*Aloud.*) Let's see, ladies, who knows what has happened to Arabella?

CLARY

I know!

JAPHETH

You, Clary? Fine timing! You are a model spouse!

CLARY

Oh, I love you so!

JAPHETH

I know how you feel about me. Since we married I've had no reason to complain about you. If only all your colleagues were like you! Now, where is Arabella?

CLARY

She's at the theater café.

ALL

At the café?

CLARY

Yes. On our way home she saw some artists and cried out: "I'm going to have a beer with them!"

JAPHETH

She's having a beer? Ah! That woman! Always with artists!

SMITH

It's not surprising for a former operetta singer.

JAPHETH

That's no excuse!

(*Arabella enters carrying a copy of* La Vie parisienne.)

ARABELLA

Here I am!

ALL

There she is!

SCENE 6

SMITH, JAPHETH, all his wives
including ARABELLA

JAPHETH

There you are! Shame on you! You leave your companions for artists at the café.

ARABELLA

And? I can't say "hello" to friends? Why don't you put me on a leash? Oh, hello Father Smith.

SMITH
Ma'am.

ARABELLA
Your wives are well?

SMITH
Thanks for asking. Ten of them are healthy . . .

ARABELLA, *enthusiastically.*
Wonderful news!

JAPHETH
What's that newspaper you have?

ARABELLA
A Parisian paper, *La Vie parisienne.* Ladies, listen to this. (*All the wives gather around.*)

Rondeau

Look at this newspaper I bought.
It features the scandalous tale
Of an actress whose life was fraught
With details that made me go pale.
One night in her spacious bedroom,
She welcomed a handsome young beau.
He made way for a duke with whom
She stayed for an hour or so.
When this old nobleman took flight,
A young investor took his place
And spent a good part of the night
Till a senator upped the pace.
And an entire dozen came
Of every age, every estate.
On such a good roll, the fair dame
Never tired though it was late.
These customs are all our own!
She welcomed each, one by one,
With neither murmur nor moan—
Oh my!—till the work was done.
At Dawn, all the lovers in shame
Were hiding in the dame's armoire.
And then the debt collector came,

And locked them all in the boudoir.
Damn! To escape both lock and key
They paid her debts to the council.
Thus, they all got away scot-free,
Proving that the night brings counsel!

JAPHETH, *furious.*

I can't believe anyone would write such trash! (*Taking the paper.*) Confiscated.

ALL

Ah!

JAPHETH, *aside.*

I'll read it tonight in bed.

ARABELLA

Excuse me. My paper please.

JAPHETH

That's enough. Arabella, I'm very unhappy with you.

ARABELLA

What did I do?

JAPHETH

You sow discord in our household.

ARABELLA

If we can't even laugh anymore, what's the point?

JAPHETH

Laughter isn't forbidden, but there is a right time for everything. I'm going to finish the roll call. (*Looking at his notebook.*) Arabella!

ARABELLA

Here!

JAPHETH

Rebecca!

REBECCA

Here!

JAPHETH

Mary!

MARY

Here!

JAPHETH

Adelina!

ADELINA

Here!

JAPHETH

Deborah! (*Silence.*) Ahem. Deborah . . . answer!

DEBORAH, *bursting into tears.*

I . . . just . . . can't!

JAPHETH

What's wrong? Did you hurt yourself?

DEBORAH

No! I'm heartbroken . . . You don't love me anymore!

JAPHETH, *aside.*

Ah, she can be so annoying!

ARABELLA

Ha ha! That's funny coming from the old lady!

DEBORAH

"The old lady?" Did you say "old lady"?

JAPHETH, *separating them.*

Oh no! They're going to fight! Will you stop it!

DEBORAH

Strumpet!

ARABELLA

Strumpet? Damaged goods!

JAPHETH

Stop it! My God, what a household! What a household! (*To Smith.*) I'm sorry you have to witness these squabbles.

SMITH, *very calm.*

Oh, I'm used to it. My wives fight too.

JAPHETH

Listen up . . . Your commander speaks. Attention! (*The wives line up.*) Count off!

ALL, *counting off.*

One, two, three, four, five, six, seven eight, nine, ten, eleven, twelve.

JAPHETH, *positioning himself at the end of the row.*

Number four, suck it in!

DEBORAH

I can't.

JAPHETH

True . . . it's nature. Number seven, chest out!

BEATRICE

I can't.

JAPHETH, *to Smith.*

It's true, she's doing her best. Don't move! C'mon now, I ordered you to be still. Who's scratching her nose down there?

ADELINA

It itches!

JAPHETH

No comments, and don't move!

ARABELLA

Well . . . drat!

JAPHETH

Who said "drat"?

ARABELLA

I did!

JAPHETH, *aside to Smith.*

Not surprising! She's incorrigible! (*Aloud.*) And now, give me your undivided attention! Your husband, your dear little husband, will say a few words.

DEBORAH, *aside.*

Like every day!

ARABELLA, *aside.*

We know this speech by heart!

JAPHETH

Soldiers! (*Correcting himself.*) I mean . . . my dear wives . . . I am pleased with you. Fulfilling your conjugal duties is your principal obligation in the home.

ARABELLA, *quietly.*

"And I'm not afraid to say it . . ."

JAPHETH

And I'm not afraid to say it! If I fulfill my duties with justice and satisfaction, you fulfill yours with . . .

DEBORAH, *whispering.*

"Conscientiousness and celerity . . ."

JAPHETH

. . . conscientiousness and celerity . . . Always treat each other with harmony and goodwill . . . (*Interrupting his speech.*) Rebecca, stop kicking your neighbor.

REBECCA

She started it.

CLARY, *threateningly.*

Me? Say that again . . . say it to my face.

JAPHETH

Silence! (*Returning to his speech.*) And this goodwill, I say, makes the Paterson household the most tender and united . . .

ALL

In Salt Lake City!

JAPHETH

That's it! And now go remove your twelve hats in your twelve respective bedrooms.

WIVES' CHORUS, *reprise.*

We have just returned from a stroll.
Walking is so good for the soul.
We've spent a few hours out of doors,
Wandering along the Salt Lake shores!
Two by two we march in a row.
Our husband leads us where'er we go.

(*The wives exit upstage left.*)

SCENE 7

JAPHETH, SMITH

JAPHETH

Ah, my dear Smith . . . I am the happiest Mormon.

SMITH

You don't miss your old Europe?

JAPHETH

Let's not talk about it. It's heaven on earth here. A land where you can have an unlimited number of wives and where the penal code can't do anything to stop it! It's a dream come true! My wives are pretty and affectionate, and I owe it all to you, my good Smith. You picked them for me!

SMITH

Well, not all of them . . . your last, Arabella . . .

JAPHETH

That's true. Arabella was my choice. She is a bit lively, a bit whimsical . . . But what a woman! A compatriot from France. She has a certain presence, chic, an allure . . .

SMITH

And Deborah was your choice, too.

JAPHETH

That was different. I was forced to marry her.

SMITH

She tarnishes your collection.

JAPHETH

True. But you understand that when I arrived five years ago, I didn't take a forty-seven-year-old Mormon to wife for pleasure. It's because this old Mormon was the widow of the canned goods magnate Japheth Paterson . . .

SMITH

And in order to have his estate you needed to take the widow with it?

JAPHETH

His widow and his name! It was a clause in my predecessor's will. I took the whole lot.

SMITH

It was a bargain!

JAPHETH

It was . . . shh! It's her.

SCENE 8

JAPHETH, SMITH, and DEBORAH

DEBORAH

Oh, excuse me. Am I interrupting?

JAPHETH

You again?

DEBORAH

It's time for dinner.

JAPHETH

You're right . . . Go make sure everything's going well in the kitchen.

DEBORAH

No. I won't go. I'm always doing chores.

JAPHETH

Come on, Deborah. Be nice.

DEBORAH

Why would I be nice to you when you're not nice to me?

JAPHETH

Are you going to make a scene now? At least wait until we're alone.

DEBORAH

We never are.

JAPHETH

Ah!

DEBORAH

And Mr. Smith can listen in. He's a pastor.

SMITH

Don't mind me.

DEBORAH

It's obvious. You haven't loved me for a long time.

JAPHETH

But of course I love you. I love you, and I respect you.

DEBORAH

That's what I hold against you . . . my first husband, poor old Paterson, he respected me less. But he loved me more.

JAPHETH

Goodness! You were fifteen years younger then!

DEBORAH

The heart never grows old.

JAPHETH

That's a biological oversight.

DEBORAH

You weren't like that when you married me.

(*The orchestra begins to play.*)

JAPHETH, aside.

Oh no! She's going to start singing!

DEBORAH

I

In the past you were more tender,
You held me in such high esteem.
Your kindness filled me with splendor.
Your eyes made my life like a dream.
Now at the end of my lifespan,
Memories are all I have left.
I feel quite a bit like Saint Anne,
Seeing nothing, of love I'm bereft.[21]

II

In the past you spoke to please me.
Your love made you truly loquacious.
I asked you to be less steamy
Since your words were so audacious.
Now at the end of my lifespan,
Memories are all I have left.
I feel quite a bit like Saint Anne,
Seeing nothing, of love I'm bereft.

DEBORAH

I needed to open my heart to you.

JAPHETH

Well . . . close it back up now . . .

SCENE 9

JAPHETH, SMITH, DEBORAH, ARABELLA,
then the rest of the wives, then BRIQUET

ARABELLA

Aren't we going to eat soon? I could eat a horse.

JAPHETH

Arabella! Language!

ARABELLA

Did I say something wrong?

JAPHETH

Eat a horse?

ARABELLA

People say that.

(*The dinner bell chimes and the other wives enter.*)

CHORUS

We are called to dine by a bell,
And we certainly won't rebel.
We're famished and pray that somehow
You'll please bring our chow out right now!

BRIQUET, *entering from right.*

Dinner is served!

ALL

Ah! (*The wives move upstage.*)

SMITH

One moment! Before taking our seats, ladies, let us, as is our custom, sing the *Benedicite*.[22]

ALL, *annoyed.*

Ah!

CHORUS

To all Mormon children, God grants sacred pasture,
He gives us daily bread, saves us from disaster.
Let this well-earned meal
Give us health and zeal,
Sustenance,
Abundance.
And in our great felicity
We sing the *Benedicite.*
To all Mormon children, God grants sacred pasture,
He gives us daily bread, saves us from disaster.

JAPHETH

Very good! Now, let's eat! Let's eat!

ALL, *reprise of the chorus.*

To all Mormon children, God grants sacred pasture,
He gives us daily bread, saves us from disaster.

Let this well-earned meal
Give us health and zeal,
Sustenance,
Abundance.
And in our great felicity
We sing the *Benedicite.*
To all Mormon children, God grants sacred pasture,
He gives us daily bread, saves us from disaster.

(*All the wives exit to the dining room. Briquet and Smith follow them out. Japheth is about to exit with them when Des Toupettes enters upstage.*)

SCENE 10
DES TOUPETTES, JAPHETH

DES TOUPETTES

Excuse me, Mr. Paterson?

JAPHETH, *without turning around.*

He's going to eat!

DES TOUPETTES

I really need to speak with him.

JAPHETH

But sir . . . (*He turns around and recognizes Des Toupettes.*) What? Des Toupettes?

DES TOUPETTES

Beaujolais?

JAPHETH

You, here? Wow! What a surprise!

DES TOUPETTES

A complete surprise!

JAPHETH

I can't believe that you, a hardened Parisian, my old partner in crime when we sowed our wild oats, would be here on the shores of Salt Lake!

DES TOUPETTES

No kidding. You'd think all of Paris were here!

JAPHETH

The fact is that America is becoming a vacation destination.

DES TOUPETTES

A very long vacation!

JAPHETH

You haven't changed a bit!

DES TOUPETTES

Neither have you. My good Beaujolais, we haven't seen each other in five years.

JAPHETH

Not since I left. It's good to see you.

DES TOUPETTES

You too. But what are you doing here? Do you know this scoundrel, Paterson?

JAPHETH

Hey! Take it easy.

DES TOUPETTES

He's a friend of yours?

JAPHETH

My closest possible friend. I'm Paterson!

DES TOUPETTES

You, Beaujolais? You changed your name?

JAPHETH

Yes, when I assumed the business assets that came with the widow I married.

DES TOUPETTES

You're married?

JAPHETH

As married as can be.

DES TOUPETTES

I see. Your uncle must be happy. He was always upset at your carousing.

JAPHETH

What uncle?

DES TOUPETTES

The one in Paris. Didn't you tell me you had an uncle?

JAPHETH

Oh, I told you? Well, in that case I won't hide it. Yes, I have an uncle, but he doesn't know I'm married. He'd be furious if he ever found out.

DES TOUPETTES

How come?

JAPHETH

When I was forced to marry Mrs. Paterson I wrote my uncle to inform him of the upcoming nuptials . . . and when I returned from the ceremony I found an angry letter from him. He was completely against my marriage. Too late! It was done!

DES TOUPETTES

Why so much hostility for this particular sacrament?

JAPHETH

Because of his own marriage. After I left for America he married a beautiful young woman . . .

DES TOUPETTES, *laughing.*

Who then got to know him and left him!

JAPHETH, *laughing.*

After six months of marriage. It was his own fault. Marrying a young woman at his age was a fatal mistake.

DES TOUPETTES

Well, it's fatal at any age.

JAPHETH

He wrote that if I were to marry, my wife would certainly cheat on me, and he had already experienced that for the entire family. In short, if I had the misfortune of disobeying him, he would cut me out of his will.

DES TOUPETTES

What the devil? And is it a nice inheritance?

JAPHETH

Would you believe? It's . . . three million!

DES TOUPETTES

Gosh! So what did you do?

JAPHETH

I didn't tell him a thing, damn it! He thinks I'm still single, and I can continue living comfortably here.

DES TOUPETTES

With your little wife?

JAPHETH

With my little wives . . . I have twelve.

DES TOUPETTES

Twelve? For you alone?

JAPHETH

For me alone.

DES TOUPETTES

What? You married twelve wives in five years?

JAPHETH

Little by little, without realizing it. For starters, Deborah wasn't young anymore.

DES TOUPETTES

Who's Deborah?

JAPHETH

The widow!

DES TOUPETTES

Oh, right. The business.

JAPHETH

I wanted a second wife who was young and attractive.

DES TOUPETTES

For your personal pleasure.

JAPHETH

Exactly! So that made two. But here, if you don't have at least three, you're looked down on. So I took a third, then a fourth . . .

DES TOUPETTES

Then a fifth, then a sixth . . .

JAPHETH, *laughing.*

And that's how, going from wife to wife, I now have a dozen!

DES TOUPETTES

Having that many legal wives must be strange.

JAPHETH

Yes, it took some getting used to. For example, when I married Clary, my second, I felt awkward with Deborah. On our wedding night I hesitated to go into my new wife's room. It seemed like I was cheating on my first.

DES TOUPETTES

I can understand that!

JAPHETH

But I got used to it, and now it's natural.

DES TOUPETTES

Sounds like a lot of hard work.

JAPHETH

Oh, you know . . . Everyone buckles down and chips in. And I give myself two months off every year.

DES TOUPETTES

Two months off?

JAPHETH

Yes, my vacation!

DES TOUPETTES

And your wives let you leave?

JAPHETH

You're thick . . . I have a trick. But don't go telling anyone.

DES TOUPETTES

Of course not. What's your trick?

JAPHETH

Easy as pie. I write myself a letter through a correspondent. I ask myself to come to Paris. I find a pretext, whatever comes to mind. Last year it was the World's Fair, this year it's a canned goods conference.[23]

DES TOUPETTES

So your trip is coming up?

JAPHETH

I wrote the letter two weeks ago, and I'm waiting for the response. Then, with the excuse of a business trip . . .

DES TOUPETTES

You go on a vacation . . . a real bender, I bet! You sly dog!

JAPHETH

Oh, not at all. I relax. I stay in. I shock my uncle with my moral purity.

DES TOUPETTES

But that wouldn't necessarily prevent you from reliving the good old days, should the opportunity arise?

JAPHETH

That's true!

DES TOUPETTES

And you weren't always polite. You stole my mistresses away from me . . . Nini Plumeau, among others.

JAPHETH

Nini Plumeau! You're still bitter about that? That was ten years ago!

DES TOUPETTES

It's forgotten.

JAPHETH

By the way, how is Nini Plumeau?

DES TOUPETTES

She's still going! She's getting younger!

JAPHETH

And what about you? Still single?

DES TOUPETTES

Yes. And the better I know women, the less likely I am to marry one.

JAPHETH

I see. You got dumped, huh?

DES TOUPETTES

Ah, my friend, if you had known her . . . Her name was Ernestine. She sang operetta. I've been weeping for a year.

JAPHETH

That long?

DES TOUPETTES

She has gone to other pastures.

JAPHETH

You'll find her again.

DES TOUPETTES

I've lost hope.

JAPHETH

Then you'll replace her.

ARABELLA, *in the dining room.*

No, I won't dine. I've had enough!

JAPHETH

Here's one of my wives!

(*Arabella enters right, furious.*)

SCENE II

The same, ARABELLA

ARABELLA, *entering without initially seeing Des Toupettes.*

I can't believe this! They serve chicken and stick me with the bones.

DES TOUPETTES, *aside.*

Ernestine!

ARABELLA, *aside.*

Des Toupettes!

JAPHETH, *to Des Toupettes.*

What's wrong?

DES TOUPETTES

Nothing . . . nothing . . . just my cigarette . . . I'm okay.

JAPHETH, *introducing.*

My dear, Monsieur Des Toupettes, my best friend! Madame Arabella Paterson, one of my wives.

DES TOUPETTES

Madame . . .

ARABELLA

Monsieur . . . (*Aside.*) What's he doing here?

JAPHETH, *whispering to Des Toupettes.*

Well, what do you think?

DES TOUPETTES

She's charming!

JAPHETH

Let me introduce you to the others. (*To Arabella.*) My dear, would you please entertain our guest for a moment. I'll be right back.

DES TOUPETTES, *walking with him.*

Take your time, I'm in no hurry.

(*Japheth exits to the dining room.*)

SCENE 12
ARABELLA, DES TOUPETTES

ARABELLA, *running to him.*

Des Toupettes!

DES TOUPETTES

Ernestine, is it really you?

ARABELLA, *coldly.*

Excuse me, monsieur, but I'll ask you to be a little less familiar.

DES TOUPETTES

You're joking?

ARABELLA

I never joke about serious things.

DES TOUPETTES

Formalities with me, your little Des Toupettes, your little bow-wow as you used to call me?

ARABELLA, *severely.*

There's no more bow-wow, monsieur. I'm married.

DES TOUPETTES

And married to my friend, Japheth! But how the devil did you become his wife?

ARABELLA

It's simple, really. We came here to perform. I met Japheth at the theater. We saw each other, we liked each other.

DES TOUPETTES

And you married each other!

ARABELLA

Right!

DES TOUPETTES

So you're collecting husbands? If I'm counting right, Japheth is number three? You'd already had two, right?

ARABELLA

Yes. What do you expect? I've always had a thing for marriage.

DES TOUPETTES

But never for fidelity.

ARABELLA

You're not in a position to criticize! It's true. It's my fate. I cheated on my first husband with my second, and on my second with . . .

DES TOUPETTES

With yours truly! He even caught us, the scoundrel.

ARABELLA

In Robinson's tree![24]

DES TOUPETTES

On a Friday. It was bad luck. He divorced you, the coward.

ARABELLA

It doesn't matter. I found a third.

DES TOUPETTES

He married you even though he's number three?

ARABELLA

He doesn't know. Here, people get married without much pomp and circumstance: two witnesses, a blessing from the pastor, end of story.

DES TOUPETTES

And the name Arabella?

ARABELLA

My stage name. I took it to avoid compromising Ernestine.

DES TOUPETTES

I see. But for me you are—and always will be—Ernestine.

ARABELLA

Oh, you're not thinking clearly. You're my husband's best friend.

DES TOUPETTES

Of course. You're very reasonable.

(*Des Toupettes kisses Arabella's hands as Japheth enters right.*)

SCENE 13

The same, JAPHETH, then THE OTHER WIVES

ARABELLA, *aside, pulling away.*

My husband!

JAPHETH

Well?

DES TOUPETTES

Well! (*Nervously.*) You see, my friend, we are getting to know each another.

JAPHETH

And you're fast friends now?

DES TOUPETTES

Oh, completely.

(*Voices coming from the dining room.*)

DEBORAH, *entering with the other wives.*

A young foreigner!

JAPHETH

Ladies, allow me to introduce you to one of my good friends, Monsieur Des Toupettes. (*Introducing his wives to Des Toupettes.*) My wives!

DES TOUPETTES, *greeting them.*

Ladies!

(*The wives greet and surround Des Toupettes.*)

ALL

Monsieur!

WIVES' CHORUS

We are Paterson's wives,
How do you do? Welcome to our hive.
Please receive our bienvenue,
It's so nice to meet you!

DES TOUPETTES, *a bit dazed.*

Ladies, it's a pleasure!

CLARY

Our husband's friend is our friend.

DES TOUPETTES

Thank you, madame.

BEATRICE

Welcome.

DES TOUPETTES

Madame.

REBECCA

With our best wishes.

DES TOUPETTES

Madame.

DEBORAH

Please allow me to welcome you, too.

DES TOUPETTES, *backing up, whispering to Japheth.*

Ah! What's that?

JAPHETH, *whispering back to Des Toupettes.*

That's my first, the widow!

DES TOUPETTES, *whispering to Japheth.*

Oh, my poor friend. Your first wife is, umm . . . mature. (*To Deborah.*) Madame, it's a pleasure.

JAPHETH, *with satisfaction.*

Well, what do you think of my wives?

DES TOUPETTES

They're smashing. It almost makes me want to become a Mormon.

JAPHETH

If you feel inspired, you know . . .

DES TOUPETTES, *looking at Arabella.*

Thank you. Not now. I'll come back tomorrow. It's late. I'm off.

JAPHETH

Where to?

DES TOUPETTES

Back to my hotel.

JAPHETH

A hotel? Never. You're staying here.

DES TOUPETTES

Here?

ARABELLA

What? You . . . ?

JAPHETH

For heaven's sake! A dear old friend whom I haven't seen in five years . . . (*To Des Toupettes.*) There's a guesthouse in the park you can use. Don't you agree, Arabella?

ARABELLA

As you wish.

DES TOUPETTES, *aside.*

Bravo! I'll be closer to her.

JAPHETH

What did you say?

DES TOUPETTES

I'll go get my suitcase. (*Aside, while exiting.*) He's as dumb as the first two.

JAPHETH

I'll see you out. (*He accompanies Des Toupettes upstage.*)

SCENE 14

JAPHETH, THE WIVES

ARABELLA, *aside.*

Lodge Des Toupettes here? Wow. Husbands are all the same.

JAPHETH, *returning to his wives.*

My dear wives, now that we are alone, the time for effusion has come. Answer me: Are you still happy with your husband?

ALL

Oh yes.

JAPHETH

Very good. Does he fulfill his duties with justice and impartiality?

ALL, *except Deborah.*

Oh yes.

DEBORAH

Oh no.

JAPHETH

Be quiet! What unanimity! And just think that in France people can't get along in a simple ménage à trois. I authorize you to kiss me.

ALL, *running to him.*

Oh, my little husband!

JAPHETH, *stopping them.*

Oh, not like that. In order. Two by two. Even numbered wives on my right cheek, odd numbered wives on my left cheek! (*The wives line up upstage.*) And now, let the parade begin!

(*The wives proceed successively, marching military style to Japheth, who is at the front of the stage. Each one kisses him on the cheek and then returns to the back of the line upstage while singing.*)

WIVES' CHORUS

All in a row,
Here we go.
Hup, two, three,
Filled with esprit.
All in a row,
Here we go!

NUMBER 1

My little love!

NUMBER 2

My turtle dove!

NUMBER 3

My kind beauty!

NUMBER 4 (DEBORAH)

You're so snooty!

(*Japheth frowns and pushes her away.*)

NUMBER 5

My sweet treasure!

NUMBER 6

My dear pleasure!

JAPHETH

You're so charming,
It's disarming!
Thank you, misses,
For your kisses!
You're so charming,
It's disarming!
I'm the commander of your love!

Round two!

(*The parade begins again with the same song.*)

SCENE 15

The same, BRIQUET

BRIQUET, *enters upstage, a letter in hand.*

Monsieur.

JAPHETH

Animal! Can't you knock before entering?

BRIQUET

Am I disturbing you? Excuse me. I'll come back. (*He heads back upstage.*)

JAPHETH, *stopping him.*

What do you want?

BRIQUET

It's a letter.

JAPHETH

And you interrupt family time for a letter?

BRIQUET

Oh. I thought you said if a letter arrived from Paris . . .

JAPHETH

From Paris? (*Aside.*) My letter has returned! Show some emotion. Ahem. (*Opening the letter.*) Let's see. Just my luck.

ALL THE WIVES

What is it?

JAPHETH

Oh, my poor wives, I am so sorry. I have to leave you.

ALL THE WIVES

Leave us?

JAPHETH

Yes. The Canned Goods Association is meeting in Paris. (*He gives them the letter.*) See for yourselves. I've been invited, and I'll need to leave on the first ocean liner.

ALL THE WIVES

For Paris?

JAPHETH

Alas.

DEBORAH

Again?

CLARY

So you go every year?

JAPHETH, *sadly.*

Two months without seeing you.

ALL, *weeping.*

Two months! Boohoohoo!

DEBORAH

Take us!

JAPHETH

What?

ALL

Oh yes, take us.

DEBORAH

I've never traveled. It must be charming.

JAPHETH

Impossible! You would get in the way. Be brave.

CLARY, *weeping.*

It's easy for you to say! We'll be all alone.

JAPHETH

Oh, you won't be alone. You'll have Briquet.

BRIQUET

Impossible, sir. I'm leaving for Paris.

JAPHETH

You're leaving?

BRIQUET

I, too, just received a letter. The city councilor in my old neighborhood found a good position for me, and I regret to inform you that I'll be turning in my apron. The service has been too difficult with all these Mormon women. (*He exits, shooed out by the wives.*)

JAPHETH

Well, bon voyage! Now, be women, dammit! Dry your tears. I'm going to dine. I haven't had time yet. One other thing, who's on duty tonight? Where's my notebook? (*He takes it out and consults it.*) Let's see. Clary, check. Rebecca, check. Beatrice, Elisa, check, check. Ah! Arabella! (*To Arabella.*) My dear, you're on duty.

ARABELLA

Me? (*Aside.*) So close to Des Toupettes!

JAPHETH, *exiting, aside.*

Good. My plan is working. (*He exits right.*)

SCENE 16

The same, minus JAPHETH

ARABELLA

Ladies, would one of you take my place tonight? Rebecca?

REBECCA, *exiting.*

Oh, not me.

ARABELLA

What about you, Beatrice?

BEATRICE, *exiting.*

No thanks.

ARABELLA

Clary, my dear?

CLARY

I'm always filling in.

ARABELLA, *to the remaining wives.*

Any of you?

THE OTHER WIVES, *exiting.*

No! No!

CLARY, *following the others out.*

Everyone has to take their turn.

ARABELLA

Anyone?

DEBORAH

Oh, yes, I'll do it!

ARABELLA

You? He won't like it!

DEBORAH

Why not? I've been skipped three times under the pretext that months are twenty-eight days long.

ARABELLA

Very well, I'll try to get him to accept you.

DEBORAH

Oh, thank you! (*She steps forward enthusiastically.*) I'll make myself attractive.

SCENE 17
ARABELLA, then DES TOUPETTES

ARABELLA, *watching her leave.*

That won't be easy! (*Des Toupettes enters upstage, a suitcase in hand.*) It's him!

DES TOUPETTES

I'm here to get settled in. You're alone?

ARABELLA

Yes, Japheth is packing. He's off to Paris tomorrow.

DES TOUPETTES, *aside.*

Right, his yearly trip. Excellent. He'll be out of my way.

ARABELLA

What's up?

DES TOUPETTES

What's up, Ernestine, is that with your husband gone, nothing can keep us apart. You'll be my Ernestine again.

ARABELLA

And what about what I want?

DES TOUPETTES

What would hold you back?

ARABELLA

Well . . . my husband!

DES TOUPETTES

But he's leaving!

ARABELLA

And I should take advantage of his absence? That would be beneath me. This poor man is calmly, confidently leaving on business.

DES TOUPETTES, *laughing.*

You believe that?

ARABELLA

Of course! He's going to a conference for canned goods manufacturers.

DES TOUPETTES

He made this conference up. He's going to fool around.

ARABELLA

To fool around?

DES TOUPETTES

Like he does every year. He told me. He runs back to Nini Plumeau.

ARABELLA

Nini Plumeau?

DES TOUPETTES

An old lover that he stole from me.

ARABELLA

Oh, the traitor! The scoundrel! And he thinks he can get away with it? Des Toupettes, he's taking the first boat tomorrow. We'll take the second.

DES TOUPETTES, *aside, triumphantly.*

That's it. Game on!

ARABELLA, *calling out upstage.*

Ladies, come one and all!

SCENE 18

The same, THE WIVES, coming out of their rooms.

THE WIVES, *responding to Arabella.*

What is it?

ARABELLA

It is . . . that Japheth, our husband, is cheating on us.

THE WIVES

He wouldn't!

ARABELLA

He goes to Paris to carouse . . . to party!

THE WIVES, *furious.*

To party?

ARABELLA

But he won't do it this time. I'm going to follow him to Paris.

THE WIVES

Us too!

DES TOUPETTES, *surprised.*

You?

CLARY

Of course!

DEBORAH

We all stick together.

DES TOUPETTES, *dazed, aside.*

What? I'm going to have to take all this with me? I've made a terrible mistake!

ARABELLA, *to the other wives.*

And now, let's promise that if he cheats on us, we'll cheat on him.

THE WIVES, *raising their hands.*

We swear it! We swear it!

Such insolence
Requires vengeance.
We all swear,
Yes, we declare
That we will cheat on him!

(*The voice of Japheth can be heard offstage.*)

ARABELLA

We'll talk later. Here comes the traitor!

THE WIVES

Silence! Silence!

(*The women smile and line up at the back.*)

SCENE 19

The same, JAPHETH, SMITH, BRIQUET

JAPHETH, *entering arm in arm with Smith.*

Well, my good Smith, did you enjoy dinner?

SMITH, *a bit tipsy.*

Very much!

JAPHETH, *to Des Toupettes.*

Oh, you're back. I'm leaving.

DES TOUPETTES

I just heard.

ARABELLA

So it's certain? You're leaving?

JAPHETH

Yes, definitely. Tomorrow morning.

ARABELLA

But you haven't given us your address in Paris. How will we write you?

JAPHETH

Write to me at the Four Nations Hotel, rue de Moscou.

ARABELLA, *writing.*

Four Nations Hotel . . .

DEBORAH, *also writing.*

Rue de Moscou.

JAPHETH

That's where I stay when I visit Paris.

ARABELLA, *to Japheth.*

On another topic . . . I found someone else to take my place tonight.

JAPHETH

Who?

DEBORAH, *stepping forward.*

Me!

JAPHETH

You? Not on your life.

ARABELLA, *aside.*

Poor Des Toupettes!

DEBORAH, *aside.*

I'll win you back.

DES TOUPETTES, *aside.*

What? He's stealing his wife from me.

JAPHETH, *aside.*

And now, the Fontainebleau Adieux![25]

JAPHETH

I feel such sadness when I say goodbye.
As I leave you all, I sense my heartbreak.
To Paris I fly. I'll try to scrape by,
Grieving alone with a painful heartache.

WIVES

We feel such sadness when he says goodbye.
As he leaves us all we sense our heartbreak.
To Paris he flies. He'll try to scrape by,
Grieving alone with a painful heartache.

JAPHETH

When a husband leaves he doesn't
Want to say goodbye to his wife.
When I leave there's even more strife,
Saying "adieu" to a dozen.

WIVES

When a husband leaves he doesn't
Want to say goodbye to his wife.
When ours leaves there's even more strife,
He says "adieu" to a dozen.

JAPHETH

Oh, don't cry my dozen beauties.
Don't be sad my little cuties.
Two months will go by very fast.
You'll see me again at long last.
Wipe away your tears and sleep well.
Come and bid me a fond farewell.

(*To the audience.*)

I'm off to Paris!
So happy to go!
To Paris, to Paris I fly!

WIVES, *sadly.*

It's so hard to say goodbye!

JAPHETH

To Paris, to Paris I fly!

WIVES

Be happy and go

To Paris, to Paris you fly!

(*Curtain.*)

ACT II

The stage represents a very elegant police headquarters. The wall upstage is mostly windows. Midstage is a large double door covered in antique tapestries. The open door reveals an active courtyard. On the left are three doors numbered 1, 2, and 3. On the right, three more doors are numbered 4, 5, and 6. These doors are draped with rich curtains. Further back on the right at an angle is another doorway to the jail. At left, also at an angle, is a door leading to Baliveau's apartments. Here and there on the walls hang police decrees in felted frames. Far left, front, on a draped easel is the decree of the "Law against Public Intoxication" in a gold frame in the Louis XV style. Beside it is a sofa and a chair. At right is a small table and two chairs. Around the stage are elegant and expensive knickknacks, artwork, and furniture.

SCENE I

BALIVEAU, JAPHETH, ERNEST

(*As the curtain opens, Baliveau and Japheth are seated at the table at right. Ernest, a constable, with a tablecloth under his arm, is serving them lunch.*)

BALIVEAU, *wearing a vest.*

I recommend this Château d'Yquem, my dear Beaujolais. Thirty years in the bottle!

JAPHETH, *lifting his glass.*

I have great respect for the past, Uncle. (*He drinks.*) The past is tasty!

BALIVEAU

Do you smoke?

JAPHETH

But of course. A lunch without cigars is like a garden without roses.

BALIVEAU

You're waxing poetic!

JAPHETH

A good lunch inspires me, and yours was exquisite.

BALIVEAU

Ernest?

ERNEST

Commissioner!

BALIVEAU

Please fetch the cigars. You'll find them in my desk.

ERNEST, *aside.*

Top left drawer, I know. (*Aloud.*) I'll get them, commissioner.

JAPHETH

He's a good man, Ernest, and so deferential.

BALIVEAU

Ernest? He's my jack-of-all-trades. I couldn't find a competent servant, so now I have my housework done by the agent on duty.

JAPHETH, *laughing.*

Ha, ha! Very clever! And what nice digs! You know very few police commissioners are housed as well as you.

BALIVEAU

Yes, it's not bad, huh?

JAPHETH

Very nice! A flair, a chic, an elegance—it's a thoroughly modern police station!

BALIVEAU

You know, it wouldn't do to have a run-of-the-mill police station like the ones in poor neighborhoods. I only receive the crème de la crème here.

JAPHETH, *laughing.*

Right. Mostly beautiful women?

BALIVEAU

A lot of beautiful women. Part-timers, like they say.

JAPHETH

Part-timers?

BALIVEAU

Yes. But I still haven't shown you the whole place. (*Starting at left.*) First, here are the cells. (*He opens a door revealing a padded *cell.*) They're padded! (*Opening the angled door on the right.*) Here's the jail. (*The jail's interior is elegantly furnished with a sofa, a pouf, and a piano.*)

JAPHETH

Lovely! Wait, you have a piano in the jail?

BALIVEAU

It's an Érard.[26]

JAPHETH

I could live my whole life in that jail!

BALIVEAU

It's at your disposal. (*Pointing to the other doors at right.*) Here's my office. And there are three more cells each with different games: English billiards, Dutch Tops, etc.[27]

JAPHETH

My compliments, Uncle. It's charming! (*Admiring the whole place.*) And these curios, these paintings . . . (*Noticing the decree on the easel.*) What's this? (*He walks to it and reads.*) "Law against Public Intoxication." A police decree?

BALIVEAU, *pointing to the others.*

Yes. I frame all my decrees.

JAPHETH

As good as Meissonier.[28]

BALIVEAU

And much less expensive!

ERNEST *returns with the cigar box, which he places on the small table at left, then walks to the table at right.*

The cigars, commissioner.

BALIVEAU

Thank you, Ernest. (*To Japheth.*) You're going to love these cigars. They're from the black market.

JAPHETH

You smoke contraband cigars? But you're a commissioner.

BALIVEAU

Always! (*Opening the box.*) It's surprising how quickly they're disappearing. (*To Japheth.*) Say! Try one of these. (*He gives the box to Japheth.*) They're excellent! (*He gives the box to Ernest as he lights his cigar.*) Ernest, leave us.

(*As Ernest exits upstage, a courtyard can be seen through the open door.*)

BALIVEAU

Well, tell me. What do you think of the cigar?

JAPHETH, *sitting down.*

Exquisite, Uncle, exquisite! This place is paradise, you know?

BALIVEAU

And when you arrived two weeks ago you wanted to stay in a hotel?

JAPHETH

I didn't think you'd have room for me. I thought you were still in your little villa in Saint-James.[29]

BALIVEAU

You didn't expect to see me as a police commissioner, huh?

JAPHETH

No, I didn't.

BALIVEAU

It's only been six months. Were you surprised?

JAPHETH

A bit. And why wouldn't I be? What possessed you, in your situation and with your millions, to accept this position?

BALIVEAU

It's always been my dream! I must have Lecoq's blood in my veins![30]

JAPHETH

But it must be an exhausting job!

BALIVEAU

On the contrary, it's charming, entertaining, delightful. I'm up on all the local gossip, the little mysteries . . . I get to see drama. (*He goes to the library and returns with a newspaper.*) Look, I wrote about something in the morning paper.

JAPHETH

You write for a newspaper?

BALIVEAU

Every day! I sign my articles "A little, old policeman."

JAPHETH

Really? You're the little old policeman?

BALIVEAU

Yes!

JAPHETH

Uncle, you tell some doozies.

BALIVEAU

I write what I see. But even then I sanitize it. And that's not the only perk. There are the cases in flagrante delicto. I love seeing a husband cheated on by his wife.

JAPHETH

You enjoy that?

BALIVEAU

I was frequently cheated on myself!

JAPHETH

By that amiable person you married while I was away?

BALIVEAU

Yes . . . Ernestine. That rascal Ernestine. And that scoundrel Cassoulet!

JAPHETH

Cassoulet was her lover?

BALIVEAU

An actor, I'm told. Some hack singer . . . that I've never even met. If only she had stepped out with a man from our world, someone respectable.

JAPHETH

Yes, that would have been some consolation.

BALIVEAU

I say this without boasting: No one has ever been duped as badly as I've been duped. So you can imagine the exquisite pleasure I feel when I discover a brother in each newly cuckolded husband.

JAPHETH

It seems you're feeling a bit less happy about it now.

BALIVEAU

It's true.

JAPHETH

Well, take heart, you aren't the first.

BALIVEAU

Nor the last. Every husband is a cuckold.

JAPHETH

All? You go too far!

BALIVEAU

Yes, all of them, my dear Beaujolais. There are two kinds of husbands: those who are cuckolded and those who will be.

JAPHETH

Surely there are exceptions!

BALIVEAU

None.

JAPHETH

Hold on! I can tell you that if I were married . . .

BALIVEAU

You'd be duped too. I was.

JAPHETH

It isn't hereditary, Uncle.

BALIVEAU

Yes it is!

JAPHETH

No . . .

BALIVEAU

Of course it is! It's fate! There's only one way to avoid disaster: stay single! And when I think . . . when I think that if it weren't for me you would have wed.

JAPHETH

Me?

BALIVEAU

Well, yes. Five years ago with that American you were planning to marry.

JAPHETH

Oh, right . . . (*Aside.*) Shoot!

BALIVEAU

Fortunately, I was able to stop you in time.

JAPHETH

It's true. You stopped me. But what if, through circumstances out of my control, I had gone through with it.

BALIVEAU

I would have cut you out of my will!

JAPHETH

Really?

BALIVEAU

Of course! My word is my bond. If you marry, I'll never leave you my fortune.

JAPHETH, *aside.*

Goodness gracious!

BALIVEAU

But let's not get upset. Believe me, the secret to happiness is no wife.

JAPHETH

No wife . . . no wife . . . But that doesn't stop you. What about that little blond that came to see you yesterday?

BALIVEAU

Anais?

JAPHETH

Her name is Anais? It seems to me that Miss Anais is a bit like your wife.

BALIVEAU

Not in a legal sense! I allow that kind, no problem.

JAPHETH

If I understand correctly, you don't love one woman, you love women?

BALIVEAU

Exactly. (*Settling into the couch.*) Why get married? Look, aren't we happy like this? A good lunch, good drinks, a good cigar! This is the life, Beaujolais, this is the life!

JAPHETH

You might be right.

BALIVEAU

Of course I am!

ERNEST, *entering upstage.*

Excuse me, commissioner.

BALIVEAU, *standing.*

What is it?

ERNEST

Monsieur, it's the agent who is on duty today.

BALIVEAU

Oh good, the one who's replacing you. He was recently promoted and I hear he's quite good. (*A phone rings offstage left.*) There's the phone! (*To Ernest.*) Have the new officer come in. I'll be right back. (*Ernest exits.*) The telephone is such a nuisance. And my secretary is out.

JAPHETH

He's on vacation?

BALIVEAU

He's on his honeymoon! Another victim who has fallen into the marriage trap. Unbelievable! (*He exits via the angled door on the left.*)

SCENE 2

JAPHETH, then BRIQUET

JAPHETH

If he knew I've fallen into that trap twelve times! But no need to think about that now. (*He lies down on the couch.*) Just think this one thought: I'm a widower, a widower for two months! That's a nice thought, it's very good. No doubt about it. It's such a delicious feeling to know my wives are far away . . . very far away . . . extremely far away. My dear little wives are over there, at peace, thinking of me right now. (*Someone knocks at the door upstage.*) Come in! (*Briquet enters as a police officer.*) I can see them all . . . (*He closes his eyes. Briquet searches for the commissioner.*) Arabella, still just as lovely. Deborah, still just as ill-tempered and disagreeable! And Clary, and Rebecca, Beatrice, Zinna, and the others, the entire collection. But if my uncle ever found out . . .

(*Briquet sees him and approaches.*)

BRIQUET

Excuse me, commissioner?

JAPHETH, *without turning around.*

Have a seat! (*Briquet sits on the chair near the couch. Japheth continues daydreaming.*) But how would my uncle find out? Who would tell him? Salt Lake is far away. And thank God, nobody here . . . (*While speaking he sits up, turns around, and comes face to face with Briquet, shocked.*) What?! Briquet?!

BRIQUET, *surprised and overjoyed.*

Monsieur Japheth!

JAPHETH

Oh my, this is a problem! (*To Briquet.*) You . . . you! A police officer?

BRIQUET

Thanks to my city councilor, I was just appointed.

JAPHETH

And you're on duty in my uncle's precinct?

BRIQUET

What uncle?

JAPHETH

My uncle Baliveau!

BRIQUET

Your uncle! I should have known that the police commissioner was Mr. Japheth's uncle.

JAPHETH

Quiet! There's no Japheth here!

BRIQUET

Oh, right . . . Mr. Paterson!

JAPHETH

There's no Paterson!

BRIQUET

Oh. And how are your ladies?

JAPHETH

There are no ladies!

BRIQUET

Sorry . . . your wives!

JAPHETH

I don't have any wives. I'm a bachelor! I'm not Paterson. I'm Beaujolais!

BRIQUET

Beaujolais Paterson?

JAPHETH

And you don't know me, get it? You've never seen me.

BRIQUET

I haven't? I don't understand a word . . .

JAPHETH

You don't need to understand.

BRIQUET

Well, that's different.

JAPHETH

Quiet! Here comes my uncle.

BRIQUET

The commissioner! (*He salutes.*)

SCENE 3

The same, BALIVEAU

BALIVEAU, *returning.*

It's too much! These telephone operators are shameless. I ask what they want and they answer, "Nothing . . . We just want to make sure the line is working."

BRIQUET, *moving forward.*

Commissioner!

BALIVEAU

Ah! You're the new officer?

BRIQUET

Yes monsieur!

BALIVEAU

What's your name?

BRIQUET

Briquet!

BALIVEAU

That's a stupid name! What's your first name?

BRIQUET

Enguerrand Opportun Romuald!

BALIVEAU

I see . . . I'll call you Baptiste!

BRIQUET

Yes monsieur!

BALIVEAU

Your colleague brought you up to speed on the job?

BRIQUET

Yes, he explained everything.

BALIVEAU

I have to tell you that I don't have a housekeeper. You'll have to take care of the place. Do you know how to do housework?

BRIQUET

Oh, yes monsieur. I used to serve in the household of a man who has twelve wives!

JAPHETH, *whispering.*

Shut up, will you?

BALIVEAU

Twelve wives?! Was he a Turk?

BRIQUET

No, a Mormon!

JAPHETH, *whispering.*

Will you shut up?

BALIVEAU

Oh yes, I've heard of that! In America, right?

BRIQUET

Yes!

BALIVEAU, *to Japheth.*

Wait, you probably know some Mormons, don't you?

JAPHETH, *distressed.*

Me? No . . . Yes . . . I know one or two.

BRIQUET

Strange people! As soon as a woman catches their eye, bam! They marry her!

JAPHETH, *aside.*

Oh!

BALIVEAU

For me it's the opposite. When a woman catches my eye, bam! But I don't marry her!

BRIQUET, *delighted.*

The commissioner isn't married?

BALIVEAU

I'm a widower! And my nephew's a bachelor!

BRIQUET, *aside, stifling a laugh.*

A bachelor!

BALIVEAU

He despises marriage like me!

JAPHETH

It's true!

BRIQUET, *to Japheth, whispering.*

You hid your dozen from him? I see . . . (*He stifles a laugh. Ernest enters upstage.*)

BALIVEAU

What is it?

ERNEST

Commissioner, there is a man here requesting to speak to you.

BALIVEAU

Another complaint! And my secretary is still out. (*To Ernest.*) Show him in. (*Ernest exits. To Briquet.*) Tell him to wait. I'm going to put on my jacket. (*He exits left.*)

JAPHETH

Me too. I'll accompany you. (*To Briquet.*) Not a word! I'm counting on you.

BRIQUET

Put your mind at ease, monsieur.

JAPHETH

Thank you. (*He exits left.*)

BRIQUET, *alone.*

I'll keep quiet. But it's fun just the same.

SCENE 4

BRIQUET, CASSOULET

(*Cassoulet enters upstage led by Ernest who immediately exits. Cassoulet is well but gaudily dressed. He wears a large foreign decoration on his lapel. He is balding with his hair dyed black.*)

BRIQUET

Come in, monsieur. The commissioner will be here shortly.

CASSOULET

I'll wait. Actually, though, I'm not here to see him, but his secretary. I'm here for a small financial issue. I helped the secretary get married a few days ago.

BRIQUET

You're a mayor?[31]

CASSOULET

No, I'm a marriage agent. Cassoulet de Casabianca, marriage agent for men and women![32]

BRIQUET

Wow! What a name!

CASSOULET

It's really rather banal. I'm only named Cassoulet, but I added Casabianca to appear more exotic!

BRIQUET

That's the only way to succeed!

CASSOULET

I arranged some marriages that people thought were impossible. I'm proud to have brought people together that were not at all made for each other.

BRIQUET

And were they happy?

CASSOULET

Absolutely not! The Family Union does not get involved in those considerations.

BRIQUET

The Family Union! Is that the name of your joint?

CASSOULET

Of my agency. Alacrity! Discretion! Specializing in young women with a history! (*He takes out some flyers.*) Here's my brochure. In your role as a police officer perhaps you could distribute some for me in the street.

BRIQUET

I'll try. It must not be easy to marry people.

CASSOULET

So true! You have to show restraint and understand the ways of the world. But when you've lived in the upper crust like I have, when you've kept company with princes and dukes . . .

BRIQUET

Oh! You've kept company?

CASSOULET

With dukes? I *was* one! You are speaking with the former Duke of Nevers.

BRIQUET

Duke of Nevers?

CASSOULET

In the opera *The Huguenots*.[33] It was my best role when I sang at the Lyric Theater.[34] (*He sings.*)

I saved my sword from shame,
Here it is! Here it is!

(*He breaks his cane.*)

Oh no! I've broken my cane!

BRIQUET

You can glue it back together.

CASSOULET, *sitting on the couch.*

Ah, those were good times. They called me Cassoulet, the handsome Cassoulet!

BRIQUET

You've changed!

CASSOULET

My good man, I've seen a lot. Women threw themselves at me, they fought over the locks of my blond hair![35]

BRIQUET

Is that why you don't have any left?

CASSOULET

No, my last conquest made me lose my hair. Ernestine! A dramatic soprano that was too dramatic! (*He stands.*) She cheated on me. I had made the mistake of marrying her.

BRIQUET

And now you get revenge by arranging other people's marriages?

CASSOULET

You said it. (*He sings.*)

Yes, you said it!
Yes, you said it![36]

BRIQUET, *aside.*

He's being open with me! (*Aloud.*) Say, could you possibly get revenge on me? I'd like to try marriage out!

CASSOULET

Impossible! I only set up wealthy marriages!

BRIQUET

But that's precisely what I want!

CASSOULET

Well, I'll try. I'll advertise you in my paper, the *Family Union.* (*He takes out a notebook and writes.*) "Young man, well established in city police, seeking, etc., etc."

BRIQUET

Oh, thank you! (*Cassoulet puts out his hand. Briquet tries to shake it.*)

CASSOULET

That will be twenty francs.

BRIQUET

Oh, umm . . . (*Taking a coin from his pocket.*) Here!

CASSOULET

This is only twenty cents!

BRIQUET

Consider it a down payment! (*He walks upstage. Baliveau enters.*) Here is the commissioner.

CASSOULET, *greeting Baliveau.*

Monsieur . . .

BALIVEAU

Monsieur . . . (*To Briquet.*) Leave us Baptiste!

BRIQUET, *exiting.*

Yes commissioner!

SCENE 5
BALIVEAU, CASSOULET

BALIVEAU
How may I be of service?

CASSOULET
I'm a marriage agent. I arranged your secretary's marriage, and I came to collect my 5 percent.[37]

BALIVEAU
My secretary isn't here! He's on his honeymoon, but he's coming home today.

CASSOULET
Very well, I'll come back. A marriage agent must always be available to his clients.

BALIVEAU
Marriage agent! So you're a marriage agent?

CASSOULET
And proud to be one!

BALIVEAU
Good for you! It's a great profession! So do you enjoy making others suffer?

CASSOULET
You said it! Yes, I enjoy it! It's because I was once married, monsieur . . . Married and cuckolded!

BALIVEAU
Say! Like me!

CASSOULET, *extending his hand.*
Ah monsieur, nice to meet you!

BALIVEAU, *shaking his hand.*
My pleasure!

CASSOULET
From that day on, I swore to marry off as many imbeciles as I could. I get my revenge, and it pays the bills!

BALIVEAU
Well, it's strange, but I'm a police commissioner for the same reason!

CASSOULET

What a coincidence! My dear colleague!

BALIVEAU

My dear colleague! (*Pointing to the couch.*) Please, have a seat.

CASSOULET, *sitting next to Baliveau.*

How kind!

BALIVEAU, *sitting against the arm of the couch and laughing at Cassoulet.*

Ha! Ha!

CASSOULET, *doing the same.*

Ha! Ha!

BALIVEAU

Wow, you don't say . . . you were cheated on?

CASSOULET

Yes monsieur . . . like no one else!

BALIVEAU

Not as bad as me!

CASSOULET

Impossible!

BALIVEAU

I assure you, it is.

CASSOULET

No monsieur!

BALIVEAU

Well, let's just say we were each duped as badly as the other.

CASSOULET

If that makes you happy.

BALIVEAU

Who was the author of your misfortune?

CASSOULET

Oh! It's a long story . . . A garden-variety dandy named Des Toupettes!

BALIVEAU

In my case it was someone even worse! A minstrel, a performer who strutted around like a rooster!

CASSOULET

I know the type, a melodramatic hack!

BALIVEAU

Exactly!

CASSOULET

Ah . . . actors! I've never liked them. (*Naively.*) I was one!

BALIVEAU, *pulls a photograph from his pocket.*

If you had known her . . . My wife was so beautiful.

CASSOULET, *also takes out a photograph.*

So was mine.

BALIVEAU, *looking at his own photo.*

Her eyes!

CASSOULET, *looking at his own photo.*

Her mouth!

BALIVEAU

Her silhouette!

CASSOULET

Her legs! (*Showing his photo to Baliveau.*) Look!

BALIVEAU, *showing his photo to Cassoulet.*

Look!

BOTH, *jumping with surprise.*

My wife!

BALIVEAU, *furious.*

Your wife! So you're Cassoulet?

CASSOULET

But . . . you're Baliveau. (*Aside.*) I'm outta here!

BALIVEAU, *restraining him.*

It's you! I've got you now, you scoundrel! (*He goes to strike Cassoulet then suddenly stops, laughing.*) But wait . . . you married her. You married her, right?

CASSOULET, *sheepishly.*

Yes.

BALIVEAU, *laughing.*

And she cheated on you, like me?

CASSOULET

Yes!

BALIVEAU

Oh, my dear friend. Come here, dear Cassoulet.

CASSOULET, *embracing Baliveau.*

My dear Baliveau!

SCENE 6

The same, JAPHETH

JAPHETH, *entering left, formally dressed, hat in hand.*

What? My uncle is embracing a stranger?

BALIVEAU

Ah, here's Beaujolais! Let me introduce you to . . . to the man who stole my wife.

JAPHETH

And you embrace him for that?

BALIVEAU

Because he married her after me.

CASSOULET

And she cheated on both of us!

JAPHETH, *laughing.*

Ha, ha, that's funny!

BALIVEAU

Oh, she was a swindler!

CASSOULET

For sure!

JAPHETH, *laughing.*

Ha, ha!

CASSOULET

You'd understand if you saw her face. (*He holds out his photo of her.*)

JAPHETH

That's her picture?

CASSOULET and BALIVEAU, *showing him the two photos side by side.*

Yes, look!

JAPHETH, *aside, shocked.*

Arabella, my wife!

CASSOULET

What do you think?

BALIVEAU

Not bad, huh?

JAPHETH, *dazed.*

And you're both sure . . . you're sure . . . that's really your wife?

CASSOULET

Without a doubt!

BALIVEAU

As if I didn't know Ernestine!

JAPHETH, *aside.*

What? I married my uncle's wife!

BALIVEAU, *to Cassoulet.*

Since we're on the topic, do you know what's become of her?

CASSOULET

Not really. Someone told me she had married a third husband.

BALIVEAU

I'm not surprised. (*To Japheth.*) Some imbecile!

CASSOULET

A sucker like us.

BALIVEAU

Men can be so stupid! (*To Japheth.*) You're not laughing. Don't you think it's funny?

JAPHETH, *more and more dazed.*

Yes, yes! Very funny . . .

BALIVEAU

Well, that's marriage. Let it be a lesson to you.

CASSOULET

You might meet an Ernestine one day! (*To Baliveau.*) I'm off to run an errand. I'll come back later to see your secretary. (*He walks upstage.*)

BALIVEAU, *joining him upstage.*

Come by later and you are welcome to visit every day. We'll see each other often, my dear Cassoulet.

CASSOULET

My dear Baliveau! (*Baliveau walks Cassoulet to the door, shakes his hand and exits with him.*)

JAPHETH, *alone.*

How is this possible? Arabella had two husbands before me? Two husbands that she . . . Damn! And I left her back there! Not that! I'll have her watched. I need to go to the hotel and see if there are any letters from my wives. And I'll get the next boat out this evening!

BALIVEAU, *returning to Japheth who puts on his hat.*

You're leaving?

JAPHETH

Yes, I'm going to pick up my mail at the Four Nations Hotel.

BALIVEAU

At the Four Nations Hotel!

JAPHETH

Well, yes. I go to that hotel when I visit, and I gave that address to my, um, correspondents.

BALIVEAU

Well, you'll have to give another address to your, um, correspondents.

JAPHETH

Why? It's a tranquil and practical hotel.

BALIVEAU

It was, but ownership has changed. It's become a meeting place for call girls, an awful den run by an old escort named Nini Plumeau.

JAPHETH

You're sure?

BALIVEAU

So sure that we're conducting a raid there any minute now.

JAPHETH

Damn! And my letters?

BALIVEAU

You want me to send someone?

JAPHETH

No, I'd prefer to go myself. (*He exits upstage.*)

SCENE 7

BALIVEAU, BRIQUET

BALIVEAU

He'd prefer to go himself! And if he gets caught up in the bust? I gave the order to bring everyone from the hotel here, Nini Plumeau first and foremost, a real hustler, apparently.

BRIQUET, *entering left.*

Commissioner, your secretary has just arrived. He's waiting in the salon.

BALIVEAU

Oh good, he's back. This is great news. (*He exits left.*)

BRIQUET, *following him.*

He married a splendid woman . . . five feet tall with large red hands. (*He follows Baliveau out.*)

(*Just as Baliveau and Briquet exit, we hear the rumble of a coach. Ernest appears upstage.*)

ERNEST

Here's the police wagon. (*He opens the double door. We see the back door of the wagon. A municipal police officer opens it, and Ernest helps Japheth's wives get out.*)

SCENE 8

ERNEST, a PATROL OFFICER, JAPHETH'S WIVES (except ARABELLA)

ERNEST, *upstage.*

Let's go! Come on my sweethearts.

WIVES' CHORUS

It is extraordinary
And oh so arbitrary
To be taken suddenly
by the constabulary.

DEBORAH, *last out of the wagon, clothes disheveled, to Ernest.*

Monsieur, quit pushing me!

(*During the following discussion Ernest and the patrol officer chat upstage.*)

CLARY

What's the meaning of this?

DEBORAH

I don't understand any of this!

THE OTHERS

Neither do I! Neither do I!

DEBORAH

It's unacceptable. As soon as we got off the train in Paris, we lost Arabella and Monsieur Des Toupettes in the crowd. We were taken to the Four Nations Hotel hoping to find Japheth, our husband. We had barely settled in when two gentlemen came and asked us to leave. They piled us all into a coach without windows.

CLARY

And it was so hot! The coaches are so uncomfortable in Paris!

DEBORAH

So uncomfortable! We were loaded up and hauled here.

CLARY

Where is here? (*The wives look all around.*) It's nice . . .

REBECCA

Very elegant!

DEBORAH, *noticing the numbered cells.*

Wait, I see. Look at these numbered doors! It's another hotel!

ALL

A hotel?

DEBORAH

Obviously. They were probably overbooked in the other one so they had us brought here.

BEATRICE

We'll be better off here!

(*Ernest closes the door upstage.*)

DEBORAH

This hotel seems very comfortable. It must be expensive.

CLARY

We'll find out. (*Points to Ernest who is walking forward.*) There's the porter. (*To the wives.*) There's always a porter in big hotels.

DEBORAH

I'll ask! (*To Ernest.*) Excuse me, monsieur . . .

ERNEST

Call me Ernest.

DEBORAH

Very well. Monsieur Ernest, how much will it cost us to stay here?

ERNEST

How much will it cost?

DEBORAH

Yes, for everything including the tip?

ALL

Yes, yes!

ERNEST, *laughing.*

You know very well that you'll be housed and fed free of charge.

ALL

Free of charge?

DEBORAH

And they say Paris is expensive!

ERNEST

Come on! (*Aside.*) They must be joking. (*Aloud.*) You'll be staying here. (*He points to the cells.*)

CLARY

These are our rooms?

ERNEST

Yes, your small rooms. Let's go: half of you here, the others over there! (*The wives go into the cells on the right and the left.*)

DEBORAH

And where do I stay?

ERNEST, *opening the jail.*

You, pudgy, over here!

DEBORAH

With pleasure, monsieur. Oh, there's a piano. It's charming. (*Giving a coin to Ernest.*) This is for you, my friend.

ERNEST, *looking at the coin.*

Ten cents! She wants to corrupt me! I'm locking you in!

SCENE 9

ERNEST, BRIQUET, then BALIVEAU

BRIQUET, *a feather duster in hand.*

I'm here to tidy up.

ERNEST

Where's the commissioner?

BRIQUET

In there. He's signing reports.

ERNEST

The wagon arrived and all the cells are occupied.

BRIQUET

By women?

ERNEST

Call girls!

BRIQUET

Call girls? And are they pretty?

ERNEST

Smashing!

BRIQUET

And you didn't alert me! Selfish! (*The piano can be heard in the jail playing "Roses from the South" by Strauss.*) What's that?

ERNEST

It's the piano in the clink. A call girl is playing!

BRIQUET

"Roses from the South" . . . (*He sings while dancing.*)

Come with me and celebrate the spring!
Let's pick lilacs and roses!

Ah! What a cheerful police station! There's no time to get bored here.

BALIVEAU, *enters, a portfolio under his arm.*

You're dancing in my station now?

BRIQUET

Not my fault. Someone's playing the piano in the clink. I can't help myself!

BALIVEAU, *to Ernest.*

Oh, the wagon arrived? And?

ERNEST

Eleven call girls. They're here.

BALIVEAU

Good! I'll interrogate them. (*To Briquet, pointing at the table where the coffee service remains uncleared.*) What? You're dancing and you haven't cleared the table? Take the tray away!

BRIQUET

Yes, commissioner! (*He takes the tray and in his haste knocks the coffee pot against Baliveau's sleeve.*)

BALIVEAU, *backing up.*

Be careful, you animal! You stained my clothes with coffee.

BRIQUET

Oh no, monsieur. Coffee doesn't stain. It's a stain remover. (*He wipes Baliveau with a napkin taken from the tray.*)

BALIVEAU, *grabbing the napkin from Briquet.*

Not like that, you klutz! I'll wipe it off myself. Get rid of that!

BRIQUET

Yes, commissioner! (*He exits, waltzing and singing along with the piano.*)

Don't you want the half-opened flowers . . .

BALIVEAU, *to Ernest who is also waltzing.*

Time to earn my keep. Bring in the prisoners! (*He continues wiping his sleeve. Ernest opens all the cells. The wives enter. When he opens the jail, Deborah can be seen at the piano.*)

ERNEST

Step forward ladies!

BALIVEAU

What a surprise! They're charming! (*He instinctively puts the napkin under his arm.*)

DEBORAH

I was just finishing up my superb waltz! (*Pointing out Baliveau.*) It's the maître d'!

THE WIVES

Hello, monsieur!

DEBORAH

Delighted to meet you, monsieur. We're very comfortable here.

ALL

Yes! Yes!

BALIVEAU, *aside.*

What is she saying? (*Aloud.*) Come on. No more pleasantries. Sit down.

DEBORAH

I was just telling your porter how much we enjoy your place.

BALIVEAU

I told you to sit! (*The wives sit wherever they can.*)

DEBORAH

We're sitting down, monsieur. (*She sits down at the same table as Baliveau.*)

BALIVEAU, *to Deborah.*

Not here, over there!

DEBORAH

Pardon me. I didn't know. (*She goes and sits with the others.*) This maître d' is very handsome. A bit gruff, but handsome.

BALIVEAU

First, let's take care of formalities. Ernest, the book?

DEBORAH

What formalities?

CLARY

I know! I've traveled before. In hotels they take down the names of the guests.

DEBORAH

They're going to take our names?

CLARY

Of course.

BALIVEAU

All right, your names?

BEATRICE, *standing.*

Pardon me, monsieur. What time will dinner be served?

BALIVEAU, *sternly.*

We're not here to joke around. Sit down!

CLARY, *to the wives.*

He's unpleasant!

DEBORAH

You can tell right away that we're in a classy establishment.

BALIVEAU, *to Rebecca.*

Okay, you first. Your name?

REBECCA, *standing.*

Rebecca!

BALIVEAU, *writing.*

Rebecca. Your last name?

REBECCA

Paterson.

BALIVEAU, *writing.*

Paterson. Good. Sit down. (*To Clary.*) Number two, stand up. (*Clary stands.*) Your name?

CLARY

Clary.

BALIVEAU, *writing.*

Last name?

CLARY

Paterson.

BALIVEAU

Paterson! Are you her sister? (*He points at Rebecca.*)

CLARY

No monsieur.

BALIVEAU

Her cousin?

CLARY and REBECCA

No monsieur.

BALIVEAU

What do you mean?

CLARY

She has my husband's name.

BALIVEAU

I see, you're her sister-in-law.

CLARY

No monsieur.

BALIVEAU

She's your sister-in-law?

REBECCA

No monsieur.

CLARY

She married my husband!

BALIVEAU

I see. They divorced?

REBECCA

No monsieur! My husband is also her husband.

CLARY

We're colleagues!

REBECCA and CLARY

Voilà!

BALIVEAU

What are you saying? I don't understand a word.

DEBORAH, *standing and walking toward Baliveau.*

I'll explain everything. It's the law where we're from. The prophet said, "Be fruitful and multiply!"

BALIVEAU, *to Deborah.*

Are you done? Leave me in peace, and sit down.

DEBORAH

Yes monsieur. (*She sits in Baliveau's place.*)

BALIVEAU

Not there, go back to your place, and sit down!

BEATRICE, *standing.*

Pardon me, monsieur, what time is dinner?

BALIVEAU, *aside.*

She is annoying me with her dinner requests! (*Aloud.*) Sit down. This is no joke! (*To Zinna.*) Let's see. You, your name?

ZINNA

Zinna!

BALIVEAU

Last name?

ZINNA

Paterson!

BALIVEAU

Again?

ZINNA

Mr. Paterson is my husband.

BALIVEAU

Damn it! He's already married to two others?

DEBORAH, *standing.*

I'll explain everything, monsieur. The prophet said . . .

BALIVEAU, *getting angry.*

Listen you! You and your prophet need to leave me alone. Sit down! You'll speak when it's your turn! Now, the rest of you, quickly, your names?

ALL, *standing.*

Mrs. Paterson!

BALIVEAU

You too?

ALL

Indeed.

WIVES' CHORUS

We've just arrived from America
On a ship 'cross the Atlantic-a.
We've hurried here—we're a dozen—
To look for our little husband!

DEBORAH

I convinced Paterson to marry me.

CLARY

He selected me as his second wife.

BEATRICE

I am Mrs. Paterson number three.

REBECCA

I was the fourth great love of his life.

ELISA #1

But because the four were not all first-rate,

ELISA #2

He married wives five, six, seven, and eight!

THE OTHERS

We all seduced him without any fuss,
And now he's got a full dozen of us.

CHORUS

We've just arrived from America
On a ship 'cross the Atlantic-a.
We've hurried here—we're a dozen—
To look for our little husband!

CLARY

Now do you understand?

DEBORAH

Yes, do you understand?

BALIVEAU

I understand! I understand that you've been duping me for the last hour with fake names!

DEBORAH, *shouting.*

Fake names? Never! We have nothing to hide . . .

BALIVEAU

Listen, old lady, I order you not to yell! You've been identified as a dangerous troublemaker.

DEBORAH, *surprised.*

Me? Identified! By whom?

BALIVEAU

Don't deny it. It's useless. I won't buy your lies. You've already been sentenced to five years in prison for corruption of a minor!

DEBORAH

Me? (*Aside.*) What's wrong with this maître d'? (*Aloud.*) You're mistaken. You must be confusing me with another guest.

BALIVEAU

You're Nini Plumeau!

DEBORAH, *beside herself.*

Nini Plumeau . . . Not at all . . . I'm Deborah . . .

ALL

She's Deborah!

BALIVEAU

Another false name. You don't want to confess? That's fine. Back in. All of you! Go!

ALL

We'll leave!

DEBORAH, *very composed.*

Yes monsieur, we will leave. (*To the wives.*) I've had enough of this hotel. It must not have many clients!

ALL

Oh yes!

DEBORAH, *to Baliveau.*

We will take our suitcases and leave.

BALIVEAU

Leave! Good one! You'll leave when I say!

DEBORAH, *nobly to Ernest.*

Porter, please fetch the coach!

BALIVEAU

Calm down, you won't have to wait long!

DEBORAH

Good!

BEATRICE, *to Deborah.*

I really want to eat. (*To Baliveau.*) Pardon me, when will we dine?

BALIVEAU

You! Drop your dinner thing!

DEBORAH

Fine. We'll dine elsewhere!

CLARY

Yes, let's go fetch our bags!

ALL

Yes! Yes!

BALIVEAU

That's it. Ernest, Hector, lock this lot up.

DEBORAH, *to Ernest who is pushing her into the jail.*

Don't push! I'll complain to my consul!

(*They return to the cells.*)

SCENE 10

BALIVEAU, ERNEST, then BRIQUET

BALIVEAU

Dang! Those are some irritating prostitutes! I'll teach them not to mock me. (*To Ernest.*) Ernest, when the wagon returns send them all to the jail downtown! Give me the book. I'll tell my secretary to write up the charges. Most importantly, keep an eye on Nini Plumeau! (*He exits.*)

BRIQUET, *entering upstage, to Ernest.*

Ah! That was a good lunch. Your turn!

ERNEST

I'm off. You're on duty now. Guard the prostitutes that we have locked up here, and send them downtown when the wagon returns.

BRIQUET

Understood!

ERNEST

Most importantly, keep an eye on Nini Plumeau.

BRIQUET

What's Nini Plumeau?

ERNEST

A madam who was a big deal back in the Louis-Philippe era.[38]

BRIQUET

Gads. She's not young anymore.

ERNEST

I'm off to lunch.

BRIQUET

Bon appétit, Ernest.

ERNEST

Thank you! (*He exits.*)

SCENE II

BRIQUET, then DES TOUPETTES, ARABELLA

BRIQUET

Prostitutes! Here? I haven't seen them yet. I'm all alone. I'm tempted to take a peek. (*He goes to a cell and looks through the keyhole.*) What? She's packing up?

DES TOUPETTES, *entering upstage.*

The commissioner, please.

BRIQUET, *without turning around.*

Shh!

ARABELLA, *entering.*

So, are they here?

BRIQUET

Shh!

DES TOUPETTES

What's that officer doing? The commissioner, please!

BRIQUET

He's busy. What do you want from him? (*He turns around.*)

ARABELLA, *to Des Toupettes.*

Briquet!

DES TOUPETTES

Briquet!

BRIQUET

Monsieur Des Toupettes! Madame! In Paris?

DES TOUPETTES

You're a police officer?

BRIQUET

Since this morning. I'm on duty here.

ARABELLA

So you must know. Answer quickly. Are they here?

BRIQUET

Who do you mean by "they"?

DES TOUPETTES

The others.

ARABELLA

They left us at the train station.

DES TOUPETTES

To go to the hotel.

ARABELLA

And we lost them.

BRIQUET

But who?

DES TOUPETTES

Japheth's wives! They were arrested at the Four Nations Hotel.

ARABELLA

And brought to the station.

DES TOUPETTES

This is the sixth police station we've visited!

BRIQUET

The Four Nations Hotel? Yes, they're here.

ARABELLA

Finally!

BRIQUET

They're locked up. We thought they were prostitutes. They're about to be taken downtown.

DES TOUPETTES and ARABELLA

Downtown?

BRIQUET

It's procedure!

ARABELLA

Impossible. You have to let them out! Briquet, my good Briquet, let them out right now!

BRIQUET

I can't. You'll have to speak with the commissioner.

ARABELLA

Okay. So, go get him.

BRIQUET

I'm going, I'm going. (*Exiting and laughing.*) Ha! Ha! The nephew's wives locked up in the uncle's jail! (*He exits left.*)

ARABELLA

Hurry!

DES TOUPETTES, *sitting down.*

Finally. Whew.

ARABELLA

What are you doing?

DES TOUPETTES

I'm resting!

ARABELLA

I see that. But you've got to run.

DES TOUPETTES

Run?

ARABELLA

To the train station to get our luggage. Then take the bags to the Grand Hotel and book rooms for us.

DES TOUPETTES

But the commissioner . . .

ARABELLA

I'll take care of it.

DES TOUPETTES

But . . .

ARABELLA

You're going to complain again when you're the cause of this whole mess?

DES TOUPETTES

Me?

ARABELLA

Of course. Who told us our husband was cheating on us? Who got us riled up against him? Who brought us to Paris?

DES TOUPETTES

But I really only wanted to bring you.

ARABELLA

You think I could abandon my colleagues?

DES TOUPETTES

If only I could do it over!

ARABELLA

Well? Get going! (*Pushing him.*) Move it!

DES TOUPETTES

What a job! What a job . . . (*He exits. Arabella sits down.*)

SCENE 12

BRIQUET, BALIVEAU, ARABELLA

BRIQUET, *entering and announcing.*

The commissioner.

ARABELLA, *standing.*

Ah!

BALIVEAU, *entering.*

Who's asking for me?

ARABELLA

Me, monsieur. I've come to . . . (*Recognizing him.*) Baliveau!

BALIVEAU

Ernestine!

BRIQUET, *aside.*

They know each other! (*He exits discreetly.*)

ARABELLA

My first husband!

BALIVEAU

You? My good Ernestine. What a surprise.

ARABELLA

Indeed!

BALIVEAU

I'm so happy to see you again!

ARABELLA

Me too.

BALIVEAU

How have you been since we had the pleasure of divorcing?

ARABELLA

Fabulous. And you?

BALIVEAU

Perfectly fine! You know, you're charming.

ARABELLA

You think?

BALIVEAU

You look better than in my day . . . a little rounder.

ARABELLA

Marriage will do that.

BALIVEAU

What? You remarried?

ARABELLA

For the third time, yes!

BALIVEAU

Congratulations. And are you happy with number three?

ARABELLA

So-so.

BALIVEAU, *relaxing.*

Ah! Too bad. The exchange rate wasn't in your favor.

ARABELLA

Perhaps. But . . . You're a police commissioner now?

BALIVEAU

At your service.

ARABELLA

A happy accident! It so happens that . . . (*Cassoulet enters.*)

SCENE 13

The same, CASSOULET

CASSOULET

Don't stand up, it's just me.

BALIVEAU

Ah! My dear friend, you've come at the perfect time. I found our wife!

ARABELLA

Cassoulet!

CASSOULET

Ernestine!

BALIVEAU

Your second husband!

CASSOULET

How? What? You, here? What a surprise! Still in good health?

ARABELLA

Very good, thank you!

CASSOULET

My good Ernestine, I'm so happy to see you again.

BALIVEAU

That's what I said!

CASSOULET

You know, you're charming. A bit rounder . . .

BALIVEAU

That's what I said!

ARABELLA

You think?

CASSOULET

You look better than in my day.

BALIVEAU

And mine!

BOTH, *together.*

Much better! Much better!

ARABELLA

Gentlemen! You flatter me.

BALIVEAU

We're not exaggerating. My dear Ernestine . . . (*He leans in to kiss her.*) May I? (*To Cassoulet.*) May I?

CASSOULET

But of course!

ARABELLA, *resisting.*

But, Monsieur Baliveau!

BALIVEAU

Thank you! (*He kisses her.*)

CASSOULET, *following Baliveau's lead.*

My dear Ernestine . . . (*To Baliveau.*) May I?

BALIVEAU

But of course!

ARABELLA, *resisting.*

Monsieur Cassoulet!

CASSOULET

Thank you! (*He kisses her.*)

BALIVEAU

By the way, did you know she has remarried?

CASSOULET

Ah! And are you happy with your number three?

ARABELLA

I wouldn't tell you if I weren't.

CASSOULET

In other words, he's not up to our level.

BALIVEAU

He's not up to our level!

ARABELLA

Well, that's true.

BOTH

Ah! He's not up to our level!

SCENE 14

The same, JAPHETH

JAPHETH, entering.

No letters. The hotel was closed. (*He sees Baliveau.*) Uncle!

BALIVEAU

Ah! My friend, come here! (*To Arabella.*) Let me introduce you to my nephew.

JAPHETH, *aside.*

Arabella!

ARABELLA

My husband!

BALIVEAU

Your husband!

CASSOULET

Her husband!

ARABELLA, *aside.*

Triple husbands! Three of a kind!

JAPHETH, *aside.*

Arabella in Paris! What a mess!

BALIVEAU

What did she say? (*To Arabella.*) What did you say?

JAPHETH

Nothing, Uncle. I . . .

BALIVEAU

That's enough out of you! (*To Arabella.*) My nephew is your husband?

CASSOULET

Number three?

ARABELLA

Well, yes!

JAPHETH

But that's not true. Not on your life!

BALIVEAU

That's enough out of you. (*To Arabella.*) You married my nephew!

ARABELLA

In America, six months ago!

BALIVEAU, *to Japheth.*

What? You're married?

JAPHETH

Uncle, I can explain . . .

BALIVEAU

And with my wife, to boot!

JAPHETH

How could I have known? (*To Arabella.*) It's all your fault!

ARABELLA

My fault?

JAPHETH

Why didn't you tell me that you already had two husbands?

ARABELLA

I don't kiss and tell!

BALIVEAU, *to Japheth.*

You're missing the point. You disrespected me! You got married despite my prohibition! This just won't do!

JAPHETH

Uncle, I can explain . . .

BALIVEAU

That's enough out of you!

ERNEST

Commissioner, the police wagon is here.

BALIVEAU

Good! Open the cells!

ARABELLA, *aside.*

Oh! Shoot! I forgot about the others.

BALIVEAU

Give me the time to write up charges and we'll continue this discussion.

JAPHETH

Uncle!

BALIVEAU

That's enough out of you!

SCENE 15

The same, DEBORAH, then CLARY, then the OTHER WIVES, then BRIQUET

JAPHETH

Deborah!

DEBORAH, *throwing herself in Japheth's arms.*

Japheth!

BALIVEAU

What's going on?

CASSOULET

An old madam!

BALIVEAU, *to Deborah.*

You know my nephew?

DEBORAH

He's my husband!

BALIVEAU, *to Japheth.*

Come again? You have two wives?

JAPHETH

No, let me explain . . .

CLARY, *entering.*

Japheth!

JAPHETH

Clary!

CLARY

My husband!

BALIVEAU

Her too? You have three wives!

ALL THE WIVES, *entering.*

Japheth, our husband!

JAPHETH

My wives! Oof! That's that!

BALIVEAU

What's the meaning of this?

DEBORAH

He's a Mormon.

ARABELLA

He has twelve wives!

BALIVEAU

Twelve!

JAPHETH

I can explain . . . (*All the wives move upstage.*)

BALIVEAU

So one wife wasn't enough! You had to marry twelve! Everything is over between us. You're cut out of my will!

BRIQUET, *entering with tea service.*

Here's your five o'clock tea.

BALIVEAU and JAPHETH

Go to hell! (*They kick the tray, and it falls to the floor.*)

BRIQUET, *recognizing the wives.*

Oh! The gentleman's dozen!

(*Curtain.*)

ACT III

The stage represents the Family Union agency, a garishly luxurious salon decorated in poor taste. At left is the main entrance at an angle. Further back is a door leading to Cassoulet's apartment. At the front is another door. Upstage three doors open to other rooms. Here and there, on the walls, hang thank you notes from clients. At right, in the front is a table with registries, papers, etc. The set is completed with mismatched furniture.

SCENE I

CASSOULET, GODET, an OLDER CLIENT, five or six other clients

MEN'S CHORUS

We hope and pray—
And we will pay—

For wives from your agency.
We're of an age
To be engaged,
We'll love them faithfully.
Find us a bride,
We want to be tied!
Find us a bride,
Fill us each with pride!

(*They surround Cassoulet.*)

CASSOULET

Find you a bride? But that's why I'm here! And you can't find better than Monsieur Casabianca, of the Family Union. (*To clients.*) You're already signed in; who's first?

OLDER CLIENT

I am! (*He presents his card.*)

CASSOULET, *looking him over.*

Widower? Right?

OLDER CLIENT

How can you tell?

CASSOULET

Your odd look . . . and I'm a pro.

OLDER CLIENT

It's true. I'm a widower, and I'd like to remarry as soon as possible. I saw your ad in *Le Petit Journal* right below the ad for American suspenders where you advertise an heiress worth three million. That would suit me.

CASSOULET

You should have come in sooner. I placed her the day before yesterday. I'm sorry.

OLDER CLIENT

Not as sorry as I am.

CASSOULET

I have another worth three thousand francs.

OLDER CLIENT

I'll take her.

CASSOULET

Deal. (*Older Client goes upstage.*) Next!

GODET

I'm up, monsieur. I'm a stationmaster in Châtellerault.

CASSOULET

And you'd like to marry?

GODET

I've waited too long. I've never even sown my wild oats.

CASSOULET

And you want to get married to do so?

GODET

You said it. There aren't many women where I'm from.

CASSOULET

What? There aren't any prostitutes in Châtellerault?

GODET

Yes, there are two. But that's not enough for eighteen thousand inhabitants.

CASSOULET

Very well! I'll find you what you need. (*Closing his book.*) Now you're all registered. My guests will arrive soon. While waiting, let me invite you to move into the next room where a photographer is waiting to take flattering pictures of you.

GODET

You're going to photograph us?

OLDER CLIENT

Me too?

CASSOULET

Like all my clientele! I offer either twelve free portraits or a revolver. The women usually choose the revolver. Gentlemen! (*He points right.*) Forgive me for not coming with you. I dismissed my servant yesterday. (*The clients start walking out.*) One more thing! Tomorrow is the Paris Grand Prix.[39] If any of you would like to wager on the favorites, I can take your bets.

ALL

What?

CASSOULET

I'm a bookie. I've added a side business taking bets on races. You can wager on horses here just like at the track. But do keep it quiet. We're being monitored closely. In addition, I sell my expert picks for five francs a day or twenty francs for a six-day subscription.

OLDER CLIENT

And your tips are good?

CASSOULET

I picked four out of the five winners at the races in Auteuil.

OLDER CLIENT

Well then, I'm in.

GODET

I'm in too.

OTHER CLIENTS

Me too! Me too!

CASSOULET, *distributing envelopes.*

Here, take this. Look over the odds. Steel Wire is at five to one, Artemis is even. (*A client gives him his envelope.*) Thank you. (*And another.*) Thank you. (*Giving change.*) Here you are. Thank you.

GODET

Here are twenty francs. But that won't stop you from finding a wife for me?

CASSOULET

On the contrary.

THE OTHERS

Us too?

CASSOULET

Rest assured.

MEN'S CHORUS, *reprise.*

We hope and pray—
And we will pay—
For wives from your agency.
We're of an age
To be engaged.
We'll love them faithfully.
Find us a bride,
We want to be tied!
Find us a bride,
Fill us each with pride!

(*All the clients exit right. Cassoulet remains alone.*)

CASSOULET

Find us a bride! Find us a bride! The truth is that I don't have any more women to offer. I haven't arranged a marriage in two months! That's why I decided to add a new business—gambling—to my old one, marriages. Now I have two businesses! This way, if I can't make money from women, I can always make it from horses.

SCENE 2

CASSOULET, BRIQUET

BRIQUET, *dressed as a servant.*

Excuse me, Monsieur Casabianca!

CASSOULET

That's me! (*Aside.*) Another male client. (*Aloud.*) How can I help you?

BRIQUET

I'm Briquet. You don't recognize me?

CASSOULET

You do look familiar.

BRIQUET

Last week at Commissioner Baliveau's place?

CASSOULET

Right. You're a police officer?

BRIQUET

Not anymore. Monsieur Baliveau forced me to resign because he said I helped his nephew deceive him. (*He sits down.*) He threw me out.

CASSOULET

And you're here to get married?

BRIQUET

Yes. That would help me be more at ease.

CASSOULET

You have bad timing. I don't have any women for the moment.

BRIQUET

Really?

CASSOULET

Unfortunately. I always seem to have at least four men for every woman, and I can't marry her to all four.

BRIQUET

No, they would notice.

CASSOULET

So when I have a woman, I keep her for my serious clients.

BRIQUET

I see.

CASSOULET

Come back later. But in the meantime, if you want a good horse, I recommend Steel Wire.

BRIQUET

Steel Wire? Why? I don't know how to ride.

CASSOULET

Not to ride, to bet on!

BRIQUET

No thanks. I want a wife. Oh well. I guess I'll die a bachelor.[40] (*He begins to exit but stops and returns.*) Wait. I just had a thought. You wouldn't be interested in hiring me as a servant, would you?

CASSOULET

What? In fact . . . since I dismissed mine yesterday. Let me see. Turn around. Walk that way. (*Briquet obeys.*)

BRIQUET

(*Aside.*) He's inspecting me. (*Aloud.*) What do you think?

CASSOULET

Not bad. Very distinguished.

BRIQUET

I've been told.

CASSOULET

All right then, it's agreed. You're hired.

BRIQUET

Thank you, monsieur.

CASSOULET

You're hired as both a servant and a knight.

BRIQUET

A knight?

CASSOULET

Yes. In our profession it's good to have a bit of nobility in one's salon. So I trust my servant with this, um, delicate role.

BRIQUET, *standing tall.*

I'll try to be worthy of the task. But what do I do?

CASSOULET

It's simple. You speak with clients and do not use contractions. You avoid contractions when you speak, do you not?

BRIQUET

Contractions shouldn't e'er be used.

CASSOULET

Good. It's decided. Let me give you a couple lines that you can repeat.

BRIQUET

Go ahead, I'm ready for them.

CASSOULET

"I am the knight of the Old Domain. My ancestors fought in the Crusades."

BRIQUET

The Crusades? That doesn't make sense.

CASSOULET

That's not your concern!

BRIQUET

Perfect! But despite my natural elegance, I might not look exactly like a knight.

CASSOULET

Don't worry about that. You'll find the livery and the uniform of your predecessor over there. It will fit you like a glove.

BRIQUET

And what will my wages be?

CASSOULET

You'll get fifty francs for being a servant and fifteen for being a knight.

BRIQUET

But knights don't serve for money! Uh, where's the cloakroom?

CASSOULET, *pointing front left.*

Over here at the end of the hall.

BRIQUET

At the "endeth" of the hall. Good. (*Exiting.*) But knights don't serve for money! (*He exits stage left.*)

SCENE 3
CASSOULET

CASSOULET, *watches Briquet leave.*

A bit awkward. But he'll do. (*Looking at his watch.*) Damn! Already two o'clock and not a single woman has come in. The men will have to dance with each other like yesterday. (*Japheth enters upstage left.*)

SCENE 4
CASSOULET, JAPHETH

JAPHETH, *at the door.*

Excuse me! Monsieur Casabianca?

CASSOULET

Come in. This is the place.

JAPHETH

I'm here to . . . What? Cassoulet!

CASSOULET

Japheth! My successor!

JAPHETH, *aside.*

Ah . . . Will I ever stop running into Arabella's husbands? (*Aloud.*) So you're Monsieur Casabianca?

CASSOULET

Yes, I changed Cassoulet to Casabianca. It flows better!

JAPHETH

Indeed!

CASSOULET

And you've come to get married.

JAPHETH

Not at all. I'm already far too married as it is.

CASSOULET

I was wondering . . . You're not lacking wives. Are you here for my second business?

JAPHETH

What business?

CASSOULET

Here's the start list for tomorrow's race: Steel Wire, Judith, Miss Blankett, Artemis . . .

JAPHETH

I see! My friend, if you want to see a man in a pickle, here I am.

CASSOULET

In a pickle! Why?

JAPHETH

You remember the awful scene at my uncle Baliveau's place?

CASSOULET

Eugene was furious!

JAPHETH

I tried to plead my case, but he was having none of it. He threw my twelve wives and me out on the street.

CASSOULET

Must've been heavy!

JAPHETH

At eight o'clock at night with nowhere to go, I took eight carriages—an entire station—and, towing my wives behind, I went to the Grand Hotel. The manager told me he wasn't willing to let a harem stay there and that I needed to go somewhere else. We got back in our eight carriages—we looked like an entire wedding party—and went to the Continental Hotel. I spell out my credentials. I explain that I'm a Mormon traveling with my twelve wives. They tell me, "You've made a wrong turn. This isn't the zoo." We ended up spending the night in our eight carriages!

CASSOULET

No way!

JAPHETH

The next day I rented a furnished apartment and moved in.

CASSOULET

And you're settling in?

JAPHETH

Not at all. Things were so good in America. But life's not bearable here. My wives are rebelling, and they won't obey me anymore.

CASSOULET

Oh!

JAPHETH

They don't even consider me their husband.

CASSOULET

Oh no!

JAPHETH

They force me to sleep alone!

CASSOULET

Oh no! Take them back to America.

JAPHETH

But they don't want to go. They've tasted life in Europe and insist on staying. Guess where I found them the other night? At the Folies Bergère. And the next day the Moulin-Rouge![41] They were painting the town red! Deborah was hitting on a soldier. Not a pleasant sight for a husband. So I made a decision.

CASSOULET

What did you decide?

JAPHETH

Answer me this. Could you find twelve husbands right away?

CASSOULET

You want to marry off your wives?

JAPHETH

As soon as possible.

CASSOULET

But you can't if your marriages aren't dissolved.

JAPHETH

They will be soon. I just sent a telegram to Reverend John Smith requesting twelve divorces. He's a friend. He wouldn't turn me down. So can you take care of my order?

CASSOULET

I'd be happy to. I've been short on wives.

JAPHETH

Excellent!

CASSOULET

Do you know my terms? It's one hundred francs to register and one hundred francs once the item is delivered. I'll offer you a discount given the quantity of the stock.

JAPHETH

Oh, I'll pay full price. But please, find good husbands for them. Be selective when choosing my successors. I want to marry my wives off, but I do want them to be happy.

CASSOULET

Oh, they will be. What's more, these ladies will be able to choose their husbands themselves. From two to four P.M. every day I hold a dance, a marriage party . . . People dance and flirt! I arrange them into friendly groups. Something always works out.

JAPHETH

Perfect. Here's the list of my wives with their age, hair color, and distinctive characteristics. I'm off to the hotel to have them get ready and I'll bring them to you. Cassoulet, you're my savior.

CASSOULET

And you're mine! (*Japheth exits.*)

SCENE 5

CASSOULET, then BRIQUET

CASSOULET, *dancing.*

Twelve wives. What luck! (*Singing.*)

Ah! Such joy!
Such exhilaration![42]

(*Arriving at his desk.*) I'll get them signed up. (*Picking up a registry.*) Oops. Wrong one. It's my betting book, my racing registry. (*He picks up the other book.*) Here's my marriage registry.

(*Briquet enters left wearing a red jacket, black leggings, black stockings, shiny shoes with large buckles, white wig and mustache, white boutonniere, and a monocle attached by a thick silk ribbon.*)

BRIQUET

Here I am. How do I look?

CASSOULET

Ah, it's you . . . Not bad. Turn around.

BRIQUET

I'm looking sharp!

CASSOULET

I'm going to my office to register my new clients. If anyone comes, remember your lines. You know them?

BRIQUET

Perfectly. I practiced them while I was dressing.

CASSOULET

All right, we'll see how it goes. (*He exits right.*)

SCENE 6

BRIQUET, then DES TOUPETTES

BRIQUET, *alone, looking at himself in a mirror.*

Without a doubt. I'm seriously chic. If I were a woman, I'd love me.

DES TOUPETTES, *entering.*

Excuse me, are you Monsieur Casabianca?

BRIQUET

Monsieur Des Toupettes!

DES TOUPETTES, *surprised.*

You know my name, monsieur? I'm sorry . . . Do I know you?

BRIQUET

I'm disguised as a gentleman. It's Briquet.

DES TOUPETTES

Briquet! Wow. You change careers every week.

BRIQUET

I'm looking for my dream job. This week I'm representing the nobility for Monsieur Casabianca.

DES TOUPETTES

I'm here to see him, in fact. I've already come twice without meeting him. Is he for real?

BRIQUET

I don't know. I've only been working for him for an hour.

DES TOUPETTES

I saw his ad in *Le Figaro* a couple days ago, and it got me thinking I should get married. It's still the best way to make a fortune. Plus, I've had enough of bachelorhood. It's not all it's cracked up to be.

BRIQUET

Tell me about it!

DES TOUPETTES

I just did! After what happened with Japheth's wives I've given up on Ernestine. I'd like a wife of my own. Do you think I'll find what I'm looking for here?

BRIQUET

I don't know. I've heard wives are a scarce commodity. (*Noticing the registry on the table.*) Oh! Wait. We'll find out right away. Here's the boss's book.

DES TOUPETTES

His marriage book?

BRIQUET

Yep. It's his registry of women who are payable and receivable. (*He opens the book.*)

DES TOUPETTES

Let's have a look!

BRIQUET

Okay. First we have, "Number one Judith."

DES TOUPETTES

Pretty name!

BRIQUET

Now for her condition: "Weight: fifty-six and a half kilos."[43]

DES TOUPETTES

It lists the weight?

BRIQUET

Everything's here! (*Reading.*) "Daughter of Lord Palmerston and of Lady Saxifrage." (*Interrupting his reading.*) She's an illegitimate daughter.

DES TOUPETTES

Thanks, I'd rather avoid that.

BRIQUET, *reading.*

"Grignolet."

DES TOUPETTES

No . . . not a man.

BRIQUET

Understood. (*Reading.*) "Odette. Weight: fifty-two and a half kilos."

DES TOUPETTES

She weighs less than the first.

BRIQUET

She must be thinner.

DES TOUPETTES

Next?

BRIQUET

"Miss Blankett."

DES TOUPETTES, *with emphasis.*

Oh no . . . no Americans. I've had enough of America!

BRIQUET

Okay! Aha! Here's a deal for you! "Artemis."

DES TOUPETTES

Artemis?

BRIQUET

There's a note in the margin: "Sure thing, presents well, especially recommended."

DES TOUPETTES

Ah! Artemis would suit me fine. Is she from a good family?

BRIQUET

Oh, excellent! "Daughter of Lady Catherine and Château-Lansac"!

DES TOUPETTES

Nobility?

BRIQUET

High nobility! (*Cassoulet enters at right, a registry under his arm.*) You can get all the details you want. Here's the boss!

SCENE 7

The same, CASSOULET

CASSOULET, *to Briquet.*

A client? (*He puts down his registry.*) Monsieur.

BRIQUET, *whispering to Cassoulet.*

He's here for Artemis.

CASSOULET

Ah! Very well! Go get the service tray ready.

BRIQUET

All right. I'm going to get back in my service uniform. (*To Des Toupettes.*) Good day, monsieur. (*He exits.*)

CASSOULET, *offering a seat to Des Toupettes.*

You're familiar with my agency, monsieur?

DES TOUPETTES

Just by chance, really. I'm in a rut and would like a fresh start.

CASSOULET

This is the best way. With a bit of luck . . .

DES TOUPETTES

I'd take this Artemis that Briquet told me about.

CASSOULET

Ah! (*Aside.*) He's not as dumb as I thought.

DES TOUPETTES

But before committing, I'd like a bit more information.

CASSOULET

That's perfectly normal. You didn't see her last Sunday at Longchamp?

DES TOUPETTES

At Longchamp? I never go there . . . Is she good?

CASSOULET

Oh, superb. She has magnificent form.

DES TOUPETTES

That sounds great!

CASSOULET

A pretty head and a good pedigree, good blood!

DES TOUPETTES

The blood of Château-Lansac!

CASSOULET

Precisely! And what legs, monsieur. Very fine legs.

DES TOUPETTES, *surprised.*

You've seen them?

CASSOULET

Everyone can see them.

DES TOUPETTES, *aside.*

That's troubling.

CASSOULET

And I won't even mention her hindquarters.

DES TOUPETTES, *surprised.*

Her hindquarters?

CASSOULET

Anyway, she presents well, and you can take her without a second thought.

DES TOUPETTES

Really?

CASSOULET

She only has one flaw. She's skittish, and when she's startled she jumps.

DES TOUPETTES

She jumps?

CASSOULET

A mild inconvenience. You'd be missing out if you didn't take her for twenty-five louis.[44]

DES TOUPETTES

Twenty-five louis?

CASSOULET

For less if you'd like. But be quick. She's very hot.

DES TOUPETTES

Well, thank you, but you can keep her. A woman who jumps . . . who knows what she'll jump on!

CASSOULET

A woman? Who said anything about a woman?

DES TOUPETTES

Well, you!

CASSOULET

Me? I'm talking about Artemis.

DES TOUPETTES

Artemis isn't a woman?

CASSOULET

Not at all. It's one of the favorites at the Grand Prix.

DES TOUPETTES, *aside.*

A bookie! (*Aloud.*) I see. I'm sorry, I've come to the wrong floor. I thought I was at a marriage agency!

CASSOULET

You're on the right floor. Bookmaking is my second business. I also arrange marriages.

DES TOUPETTES

That's why I'm here.

CASSOULET

Oh, excellent, monsieur, no problem! You've come at the right time, I'm expecting a delivery of a nice stock of beautiful women.

DES TOUPETTES

Great news!

CASSOULET

Let me get you registered. Age?

DES TOUPETTES

Twenty-eight.

CASSOULET

Profession?

DES TOUPETTES

Bachelor . . . I don't have an inheritance but I have a distinguished name.

CASSOULET

Excellent. Nobility is highly sought after. What's your name?

DES TOUPETTES

Hector . . . Hector Des Toupettes!

CASSOULET

Des Toupettes! Ernestine's seducer! It's you! You scoundrel! (*He attacks him.*)

DES TOUPETTES, *struggling.*

But monsieur! I don't . . .

CASSOULET

I'm Cassoulet!

DES TOUPETTES

Cassoulet . . . Damn!

CASSOULET

I've finally got you!

DES TOUPETTES

I accept your challenge, monsieur!

CASSOULET

A duel? Oh no, you wouldn't want that.

DES TOUPETTES

What then?

CASSOULET

I have a much better way to get revenge.

DES TOUPETTES, *frightened.*

What, murder?

CASSOULET

No . . . Marriage! You came here to get married and I'll marry you. That's how I fight. Marriage is my weapon!

DES TOUPETTES

I prefer that!

CASSOULET

I'll find you a lovely wife!

DES TOUPETTES

Good!

CASSOULET

Who will cheat on you like mine cheated on me.

DES TOUPETTES

Oh no, I'm not as dumb as you!

CASSOULET

We shall see!

DES TOUPETTES, *trying to leave.*

Well, I'll be back.

CASSOULET, *stopping him.*

Oh no, no, no! I'm not letting you go. You'll only leave here once you're good and married.

DES TOUPETTES

But I don't have a tuxedo!

CASSOULET

I'll lend you one. I dress all my clients. I have everything you'll need over here. Let me show you. (*He pushes him to the right.*)

DES TOUPETTES, *resisting.*

But, but . . .

CASSOULET

Go ahead. (*Des Toupettes exits. Japheth enters left.*)

JAPHETH

Here I am with my wives!

CASSOULET

Come in. I'll be with you right away. (*He follows Des Toupettes out.*)

JAPHETH

Come in, ladies!

SCENE 8

JAPHETH, DEBORAH, ARABELLA, CLARY, the OTHER WIVES

WIVES' CHORUS

Since we're invited to the ball,
We arrive on time, one and all.
We will come quickly, all wide-eyed,
With our sweet husband at our side.

BEATRICE

Charming pleasure, the stuff of dreams.
At a ball the women are queens.
With a wry smile we play our parts,
Seducing men and charming hearts.

CHORUS

Since we're invited to the ball,
We arrive on time, one and all.

We will come quickly, all wide-eyed,
With our sweet husband at our side.

JAPHETH

Here we are! My dear wives, it goes without saying that I expect a good attitude and distinguished manners.

ALL, *murmuring.*

Another speech!

JAPHETH, *continuing.*

Don't stand out! Remember that we're in polite society where restraint is de rigueur.

ARABELLA

What is this place?

JAPHETH

It belongs to a good friend . . . Cassoulet de Casabianca.

ARABELLA

Cassoulet?

JAPHETH

Yes, one of your exes who agreed to invite us to a dance.

DEBORAH

We're going to dance! Hot dog!

JAPHETH

C'mon Deborah . . . Watch what you say!

DEBORAH

What's wrong? People say it at the Moulin Rouge.

JAPHETH

At the Moulin Rouge, but not here.

DEBORAH

We know how to behave in high society, don't we ladies?

THE OTHERS

Darn tootin'!

JAPHETH

"Darn tootin'" . . . Now don't make a scene!

ARABELLA

But what are you thinking bringing us to Cassoulet's place?

JAPHETH, *uncomfortable.*

What am I thinking? Um . . . It's to entertain you, to make you happy. You're always wanting to get out of the apartment.

ALL

Yes! Yes!

JAPHETH

So . . . I . . . As a good husband I look for appropriate entertainment.

DEBORAH

And then you tell us we're behaving badly . . .

ALL

Yes, that's what you said.

JAPHETH

I didn't say that, but . . .

ARABELLA

Just because we went to the roller coaster in Belleville two or three times.

DEBORAH

It's a very nice place.

JAPHETH

It may be, but it's not a place for respectable women, especially without their husbands or their lovers.

DEBORAH

Don't preach to us!

ALL

No! No!

CLARY

We've had enough.

BEATRICE

It's always the same sermon.

REBECCA

The same criticisms.

JAPHETH

Mrs. Japheths . . .

CLARY

We're not in America anymore, buddy.

JAPHETH

She dares call me "buddy"!

DEBORAH

In Paris women are free.

ARABELLA

And we intend to take advantage of our freedom.

ALL

Yes! Yes!

JAPHETH

But . . .

DEBORAH

Yes monsieur, we're going to enjoy it. I've suffered in silence too long. Now I'm letting my emotions flow.

ALL

Us too!

JAPHETH

Deborah!

DEBORAH

Go to hell!

JAPHETH

Go to hell? What? And things were going so well in America.

ARABELLA

What do you expect? She's right.

To tell the truth it's not much fun
To share a husband twelve to one.
A twelfth of a man is too small,
And jealousy infects us all.
No! Life can't continue like this!
Such a budget prevents our bliss.
We will no longer be content
With a small fraction of our gent.
No, no, no! We all vow
To stop this nonsense now!
Now's the time to get real!
Sharing is not our deal.

ALL WIVES

No, no, no! We all vow
To stop this nonsense now!
Now's the time to get real!
Sharing is not our deal.

ARABELLA

Here is a proverb I obey:
"Do what you must and come what may."
You, Monsieur, are never alone;
Your sheets stay warm, your wives stay prone.
We all feel cheated and ignored.
Of hugs and kisses you get more
Than anyone in Christendom
While we lack the bare minimum.

ALL

No, no, no! We all vow
To stop this nonsense now!
Now's the time to get real!
Sharing is not our deal.

JAPHETH, *aside.*

Well, at least I'll soon be rid of them. (*Cassoulet enters. Aloud.*) Here is the master of the house. A bit of decorum, ladies.

SCENE 9

The same, CASSOULET, then BRIQUET, guests

JAPHETH

My dear agent! (*Correcting himself.*) My dear friend, let me introduce you to the Japheth wives.

CASSOULET

Aha! It's my delivery! Ladies . . .

ALL

Monsieur . . .

CASSOULET

Charming! Thank you all for accepting my invitation.

ARABELLA

Hello Cassoulet.

CASSOULET

My ex-wife! (*Aside.*) It will be strange to arrange her marriage. (*Aloud.*) How are you?

ARABELLA

Very well. We're here for your little shindig.

CASSOULET

It's nice of you to come.

JAPHETH, *whispering to Cassoulet.*

Well, what do you think? Can you place them easily?

CASSOULET, *whispering.*

Leave it to me.

DEBORAH, *to Cassoulet.*

Are we going to dance soon? I have ants in my pants!

CASSOULET, *aside.*

She's mature, this one. (*Aloud.*) Right away. I'll introduce you to my guests. They're in the other room. (*He opens the doors upstage.*) Enter, gentlemen! (*The guests enter.*) Ladies, I present your dance partners. They are all fine dancers.

THE WIVES

Gentlemen!

THE MEN

Ladies!

JAPHETH, *to Cassoulet.*

This is your assortment?

CASSOULET

Yes!

JAPHETH

Introduce me.

CASSOULET

With pleasure. (*To the men.*) Gentlemen, let me introduce you to Monsieur Japheth Paterson, a good friend with an interest in your future.

JAPHETH

More than you can know. I'm delighted to meet you. (*He shakes hands with several of them.*)

GODET, *to Cassoulet.*

These are our future brides?

CASSOULET

Yes. Ask them to dance. (*To the others.*) You too, gentlemen.

DEBORAH, *looking at Godet as he walks toward her.*

What a handsome man! (*Godet invites Clary to dance.*) Oh well, he chose Clary.

CLARY, *to Godet.*

With pleasure, monsieur.

(*The men invite the women to dance. They all have partners except Deborah.*)

DEBORAH, *furious, to Japheth.*

What about me?

JAPHETH

What about you?

DEBORAH

No one wants to dance with me.

JAPHETH

What do you want me to do about it?

DEBORAH

Dance with me!

JAPHETH

Oh, I'd rather not dance.

CASSOULET

Ladies and gentlemen, it's time for the quadrille.

Now gentlemen, the time has come,
The orchestra begins to hum.
Let each man take a lady's waist,
Blonde or brunette, select with haste.
First greet your adored,
Let each take a bow.
Here's the happy chord.

The contradance now.

(*They keep dancing to the music. As the quadrille ends, Briquet enters at left and goes among the dancers while shouting.*)

BRIQUET, *dressed as a servant.*

The police are here!

ALL, *screaming.*

Ah!

(*In a flash all the characters disappear. Only Briquet and Cassoulet remain on stage.*)

BRIQUET

Everyone split?

CASSOULET

What did you say? The police?

BRIQUET

Yes, monsieur, there are two agents at the door.

CASSOULET

Damn! It must be because of my bookmaking.

BRIQUET

You're nabbed!

CASSOULET

Not yet. Go close the door.

BALIVEAU, *entering.*

Too late! Don't move! (*He motions to the officers outside.*) Stay in the hall. Monsieur Casabianca?

SCENE 10

The same, BALIVEAU

CASSOULET, *recognizing Baliveau.*

Eugene!

BALIVEAU, *recognizing Cassoulet.*

Gustave!

BRIQUET

It's Monsieur Baliveau!

BALIVEAU, *to Briquet.*

Leave us, my boy.

BRIQUET, *aside.*

I'll reassure our guests. (*He exits.*)

CASSOULET, *aside.*

Bad luck.

BALIVEAU

So you're running an illegal gambling ring?

CASSOULET

Not at all, not at all . . . Who told you that?

BALIVEAU

I have my sources.

CASSOULET

It's not true! I arrange marriages. I'm the head of the Family Union marriage agency.

BALIVEAU

But you're not uniting anyone.

CASSOULET

Who told you that?

BALIVEAU

I have my sources.

CASSOULET

Well, they're not telling the truth. And the proof is that right now I have twelve marriages in the works.

BALIVEAU

Come now. You're bluffing.

CASSOULET

Bluffing? No! I'm marrying off your nephew's twelve wives.

BALIVEAU

My nephew's wives? That's impossible.

CASSOULET, *trying to sneak away.*

He's here. Do you want to see him? I'll go get him.

BALIVEAU, *restraining him.*

That's okay. Leave him alone. I've ended my relationship with him.

CASSOULET

You'll forgive him sooner or later.

BALIVEAU

Never!

CASSOULET, *still trying to escape.*

I'll go get him.

BALIVEAU, *restraining Cassoulet again.*

No. Don't move! Don't change the subject. We've been notified that your agency has been running a clandestine bookmaking operation. I'm sorry, but I know my duty. I have to search your place.

CASSOULET

Search? Come now, Eugene. You wouldn't.

BALIVEAU

Don't call me Eugene now.

CASSOULET

I swear there's nothing to find.

BALIVEAU

Don't swear and tell the truth. It's going to be a one-thousand-franc fine.

CASSOULET

That's steep! Ah! Such bad luck. And the day before the Grand Prix. You couldn't have waited till Monday?

BALIVEAU

Monday? Why Monday?

CASSOULET

I had a sure bet tomorrow.

BALIVEAU

Right. Every gambler says that. "It's a sure bet." Then they lose.

CASSOULET

But this time I have insider information.

BALIVEAU

Insider information?

CASSOULET

Absolutely. A jockey told me who would win the Grand Prix.

BALIVEAU

Don't tell me. It's Artemis.

CASSOULET

Not at all . . . It's Volapuck!

BALIVEAU

Volapuck! Come on . . . He isn't even a long shot.

CASSOULET

That's on purpose. Artemis has a hitch in her hind leg.

BALIVEAU

She has a hitch?

CASSOULET

Yes, she has a hitch. Volapuck will be first to the pole.

BALIVEAU

But he's at sixty to one.

CASSOULET

Exactly.

BALIVEAU

And I already bet on Artemis.

CASSOULET

You should cover that bet by wagering on Volapuck!

BALIVEAU

Right away! (*He takes out his billfold.*) Dang. I don't have the cash!

CASSOULET

I trust you! You're good for it.

BALIVEAU

Thank you, Gustave! But business is business. I'm going to get the money. I'll be right back. (*He exits.*)

SCENE II

CASSOULET, then ARABELLA

CASSOULET

Got it! (*Writing.*) Twenty louis on Volapuck. (*Arabella enters right.*)

ARABELLA

Ah! This is too much!

CASSOULET, *aside.*

My ex-wife! (*Aloud.*) What's the matter, my dear friend?

ARABELLA

Oh, Cassoulet, it's you. I'm furious! Our husband, Japheth, just told us why he brought us here. It's to marry us off!

CASSOULET

And that makes you mad?

ARABELLA

Me? On the contrary. I'm used to change. But I don't want to trade in my one-eyed horse for a blind one.

CASSOULET

None of my bachelors are blind!

ARABELLA

No, but they're all impossible.

CASSOULET

You're not finding anything that suits you?

ARABELLA

Not at all. And if that's all you have on offer, I'd rather just keep Japheth.

CASSOULET

Oh no, no . . . Don't do that. I promised to place the whole dozen. I'll look myself. I might be able to find something.

ARABELLA

You won't find anything. I've looked.

SCENE 12

The same, DES TOUPETTES

DES TOUPETTES, *entering downstage.*

Here I am. Dressed up and ready for the sacrifice.

CASSOULET, *aside.*

Des Toupettes! There's an idea.

ARABELLA

Des Toupettes!

DES TOUPETTES

Ernestine!

CASSOULET

My friends, my dear friends . . . I'm needed in the next room. Make yourselves at home.

DES TOUPETTES

You're leaving us?

CASSOULET

Yes. Keep her company. Chat a bit.

ARABELLA

But . . .

CASSOULET

I'll be back. (*Aside, exiting.*) There's hope!

DES TOUPETTES

Ernestine! You're here!

ARABELLA

Yes, with all the others. Monsieur Japheth has decided to marry us off lock, stock, and barrel.

DES TOUPETTES

What?

ARABELLA

And you?

DES TOUPETTES

Me too. I'm here to get married.

ARABELLA, *laughing.*

Oh! There's a funny thought!

DES TOUPETTES

What?

ARABELLA

Do you still love me?

DES TOUPETTES

More than ever. You're my ideal.

ARABELLA

Well then, marry me.

DES TOUPETTES

I'd like that. Cassoulet and Japheth couldn't criticize me since I'd be making things right.

ARABELLA

So we can kiss without regret!

DES TOUPETTES

Wow! (*He kisses her.*) Oh, Ernestine!

ARABELLA

Oh, Hector!

SCENE 13

The same, JAPHETH

JAPHETH

Aha! There you are. And I find you kissing my wife! You'll pay for that!

DES TOUPETTES

Yes, but this time it's for the right reasons.

JAPHETH

What do you mean?

DES TOUPETTES

We're getting married.

JAPHETH

You're going to marry her? Ah, my friend, how kind! She's yours!

DES TOUPETTES

Ah, my friend . . . How can I ever thank you?

JAPHETH

I'm the one who should thank you. (*He corrects himself.*) I mean, make her happy!

DES TOUPETTES

I'll try. (*Aside.*) Am I making a huge mistake?

SCENE 14

The same, DEBORAH, CASSOULET, then BRIQUET

CASSOULET, *following Deborah who enters in tears.*

Come now, Madame, calm down.

DEBORAH

No!

JAPHETH

What's wrong?

DEBORAH

Nobody wants me!

JAPHETH

What?

CASSOULET

Don't cry. I'm telling you I have someone for you.

DEBORAH

No, everyone's taken.

CASSOULET

He's on his way.

DEBORAH

Is he nice?

CASSOULET

Charming! You'll see . . . (*To Japheth.*) What will you give me if I place her?

JAPHETH

Fifty-thousand francs for a dowry, and I'll double your commission.

CASSOULET

Good, consider it done. (*To Deborah.*) Come now, put yourself together, hide as much as you can.

BRIQUET, *dressed as a knight.*

Here I am, dagnabit!

CASSOULET, *to Deborah.*

Here he is!

DEBORAH

Oh, what a handsome man!

JAPHETH, *aside.*

He seems to have a good head on his shoulders.

CASSOULET

Step forward, good knight.

DEBORAH, *aside.*

He's a knight! (*She greets him with exaggerated bows.*)

CASSOULET, *directing Briquet to Deborah.*

Pay your respects . . .

BRIQUET, *bowing.*

Ladies and gentlemen of the company.

CASSOULET, *whispering to Briquet.*

Use your lines now.

BRIQUET

Okay, here I go. (*To the others.*) I am the Knight of the Old-Shack!

CASSOULET, *whispering to Briquet.*

Old Domain, you numbskull!

BRIQUET

Domain or shack . . . (*Starting again.*) My ancestors fought in the Cascades.

CASSOULET, *whispering.*

The Crusades, you idiot!

BRIQUET

Well, what? Crusade or cascade, it's the same. These ladies and gentlemen aren't so stupid as to not understand.

DEBORAH

This knight has a strange way of speaking.

CASSOULET, *to Deborah.*

Pay it no mind. He's an eccentric. (*Whispering to Briquet.*) I found you a wife.

BRIQUET, *whispering.*

A real one?

CASSOULET, *whispering.*

A great bargain. (*Pointing to Deborah.*) It's her.

BRIQUET

What? (*Aside.*) The old lady! (*Aloud.*) I'm not interested.

CASSOULET, *whispering.*

Her dowry is fifty-thousand francs.

BRIQUET, *whispering.*

It's not enough!

JAPHETH, *to Cassoulet.*

Well?

CASSOULET, *whispering.*

He says no.

JAPHETH, *aside.*

Dang! (*Aloud.*) I'll make it sixty thousand!

BRIQUET

No!

JAPHETH, *to Cassoulet.*

Seventy thousand!

CASSOULET, *to Briquet.*

Seventy thousand!

JAPHETH

Seventy-five thousand!

CASSOULET

Seventy-five thousand!

DEBORAH, *hyperventilating.*

You're auctioning me off!

CASSOULET, *pushing her away.*

Will you be quiet? It's not your concern. (*To Briquet.*) Seventy-five thousand!

BRIQUET, *after looking Deborah over.*

Oh . . . no . . . no . . .

JAPHETH, *to Cassoulet.*

Eighty thousand!

CASSOULET, *to Briquet.*

He says eighty!

BRIQUET, *tempted.*

Damn!

JAPHETH, *shouting.*

Ninety!

CASSOULET, *speaking like an auctioneer.*

Ninety thousand!

DES TOUPETTES and ARABELLA

Ninety thousand! He said ninety thousand!

DEBORAH

But . . . gentlemen . . . this isn't right!

CASSOULET

Will you be quiet! Ninety thousand!

BRIQUET

Oh!

JAPHETH

One hundred thousand!

DES TOUPETTES

We have one hundred thousand!

ARABELLA

We have one hundred thousand!

CASSOULET

One hundred thousand! One hundred thousand! Once . . . twice . . . Look at the object . . . You don't want it? You've looked it over? You'll regret it. Once . . .

BRIQUET, *energetically after a long struggle.*

I accept!

CASSOULET

Sold! Whew!

JAPHETH

That's it?

DEBORAH

Oh! I have a husband! (*She kisses Briquet.*)

BRIQUET, *pulling himself away.*

Madame . . . (*Aside.*) Being kissed by her is an experience!

SCENE 15

The same, ALL THE WIVES, ALL THE HUSBANDS, then, at the end, BALIVEAU

CASSOULET

Now for the others! (*Everyone enters.*) Gentlemen, here is your fiancées' husband. You must ask him for their hands. Stationmaster! Step forward and speak for all the others.

GODET

Oh no, I'm not very eloquent.

CASSOULET

Then you, Des Toupettes. It falls to you.

DES TOUPETTES

With pleasure. (*To the men.*) Put on your white gloves. (*They put them on.*)

JAPHETH

I'm listing with benevolence.

DES TOUPETTES

My friend, you know me well. You don't know these other gentlemen, but that doesn't matter. It is my honor to ask you, on their behalf and mine, for the hands of your twelve wives.

JAPHETH

Gentlemen, and if I may, my dear friends, you can't imagine how pleased I am, and I happily grant you their hands!

ALL THE MEN

Thank you!

BALIVEAU, *entering.*

What a crowd!

JAPHETH, *recognizing him.*

My dear uncle, come in. You'll be pleased with me. I married off all my wives.

BALIVEAU

Congratulations, my friend. (*Smiling.*) I'm happy to announce that I'm getting married.

JAPHETH

What! You have a wife?

BALIVEAU

No. But I've decided to take one, and I'm tasking Cassoulet with finding one for me right away. (*To Cassoulet.*) Here are your twenty louis.

CASSOULET

Thank you, Eugene! Business is picking up.

JAPHETH, *to his uncle.*

And my inheritance?

BALIVEAU

I'm saving it for my future children.

JAPHETH

If you have any!

ARABELLA

Finally we each have a husband to ourselves.

CLARY

It's better like this!

DEBORAH

Oh yes. (*She kisses Briquet.*) Oh, my little husband.

BRIQUET

I'm happy to be your husband, but I'm honest and don't want to deceive you about the merchandise. (*He takes off his wig.*) I'm Briquet.

JAPHETH

It's Briquet!

DEBORAH

A servant!

ALL

What?

DEBORAH

And I was going to marry him. Ah, Japheth, I'm still with you. (*She throws herself into Japheth's arms.*)

JAPHETH

What? You're with me? I'd rather not.

CASSOULET, *to Japheth.*

Don't worry. I'll place her!

JAPHETH

Well, I'm finally single . . . there's always that!

FINAL CHORUS

Let's not go back to America
On a ship 'cross the Atlantic-a.
We'll stay right here, we are a dozen
Each with our own sweet little husband!

(*Curtain.*)

STEPHANA'S JEWEL

ARTHUR BERNÈDE AND ALBERT DUBARRY

Vaudeville Folly in Three Acts
Premiered at the Théâtre Cluny, July 1892

In a study on love and marriage in nineteenth-century France, Adeline Daumard writes, "At the end of the century, the practice of spending family vacations in cities near the sea or in ocean resorts became popular for the upper classes. . . . Relationships between young men and young women staying in the same hotels or brought together by excursions or games took on a new air of freedom."[1] The action of *Stephana's Jewel* begins near the beach in Honfleur at an ocean resort where young (and old) men and women meet (or sometimes avoid meeting). These relationships start in the cultural moment described by Daumard and spiral out of control until finally resolving in a handful of marriage arrangements in the final act.

Stephana's Jewel opened in early July 1892 and had an initial run of approximately two months. It was then published in December of the same year for potential performances outside of Paris.[2] Contemporary reviewers called the play "a success" and praised the Théâtre Cluny for daring to launch a new play in the summer.[3] The pseudonymous Willy calls the play a "contagious folly" that "launched the spectators of Cluny into fits of malevolent gaiety causing, even among the most serious, very grave accidents."[4] The one negative review of the play is only negative enough to allow the critic, Hippolyte Lemaire, to maintain his reputation as a defender of good and proper middle-class morality. Lemaire writes that he cannot condone *Stephana's Jewel*, given that many of the play's laughs stem from "smutty double-entendres or obscenities."[5] But Lemaire ends up losing to his own worst demons, acknowledging that the most vulgar witticisms were also the most hilarious and that "frankly, the play [was] a success."[6]

The title of the play in French, *Le Bijou de Stéphana*, begins with a common epithet for female genitalia: *bijou*, or "jewel." The vulgar connotation of the title is implicitly confirmed by the action of the play, which revolves around Stephana and her many lovers and admirers. However, it is explicitly confirmed through a direct reference to Denis Diderot's 1748 libertine novel, *Les Bijoux indiscrets*, in which a sultan receives a magic ring that makes women's genitals—their "jewels"—speak to recount their sexual history. A contemporary review of *Stephana* begins: "Like *The Indiscreet Jewels* by Diderot, that grandiloquent swine, *Stephana's Jewel* also reveals things, my dear!"[7] Stephana, like Diderot's princess, is at once the keeper of all the secrets in the Rubineau family and the object of desire for all the men in the play. In short, what her *bijou* says matters. And since she has co-opted a real jewel that buzzes when true love is declared from the Mormon, Sir Gaveston, she is the ultimate master of minds, hearts, and, well, the rest.

CAST:	ROLE CREATED BY:
Stephana	Marguerite Gallayx[8]
Madame Rubineau	Adèle Cuinet
Charlotte Rubineau, daughter	Delaval
Corpulencia Gaveston	Andrée Canti
Aunt Flora	Bilhaut
Sir Gaveston's six daughters:	
Nelly	Giverny
Lucy	Chanoz
Betty	Dastie
Jenny	Marzac
Pretty	Fredorff
Baby	Berney
Maid	
Rubineau	P. Véret
Auguste Rubineau, son	Gustave Hamilton

Oscar de Pompignac	Pierre Numas
Sir Gaveston, Mormon	Adrien Lureau[9]
De Longuefugue	Allart
Jules, hotel server	Leroux
Waiter	
Police Sergeant	
Police officers	
Bathers	Cernay, Berthay, Lopez

ACT I

The action takes place in Honfleur. The stage represents the terrace of a seaside resort with the sea upstage. The curtain rises on guests, some holding spyglasses while standing with their backs to the audience looking out at bathers upstage. Rubineau, Madame Rubineau, Oscar, Charlotte, and Auguste are seated at a table.

SCENE I

RUBINEAU, MADAME RUBINEAU,
CHARLOTTE, OSCAR, AUGUSTE, BATHERS,
and then DE LONGUEFUGUE

MADAME RUBINEAU

Shall we go visit the ports? They say that they are among the most fascinating sites in Honfleur!

CHARLOTTE

Oh yes, Mother. Will you join us, Monsieur Oscar?

OSCAR

How could I stand even a moment apart from my ravishing fiancée! (*Aside.*) She is so clingy!

MADAME RUBINEAU

I am happy to have such a witty and generous man for a future son-in-law, Monsieur de Pompignac. What do you think, Rubineau?

RUBINEAU

I completely agree, my pet.

OSCAR, *aside.*

His pet!

AUGUSTE, *standing up.*

Well then, let's go!

MADAME RUBINEAU

We're off!

(*They stand and walk upstage toward the sea.*)

CHARLOTTE, *taking Oscar's arm.*

What an absolutely delicious boat trip that was from Trouville to Honfleur this morning. I wasn't sick even once.

OSCAR, *aside.*

She's already talking about morning sickness![10]

RUBINEAU, *to his wife.*

Walk a little slower, my dear . . . You know that too rapid a pace always gives me palpitations! Come along, Auguste!

(*They exit.*)

AUGUSTE

There are some lovely little ladies here! Time to ditch the parents!

(*He exits on the other side.*)

FIRST BATHER (female)

What in the world is that?

A BATHER (male)

Some good middle-class Parisians escaping their apartments.

THIRD BATHER (female)

More like monkeys escaped from the zoo.

FIRST BATHER (female)

Or some princes hiding out in odd disguises.

SECOND BATHER (female)

Or a roving band of actors.

FIRST BATHER (female)

Do you think they're from the Comédie Française?[11]

THIRD BATHER (female), *upstage.*

Countess, look at that! Six identically dressed women all swimming together.

FIRST BATHER (female)

Yes I see, baroness. And they're being supervised by that large woman there and a man who looks to be either American or English!

SECOND BATHER (female)

Aren't they just so ordinary, my dear?

ALL THE WOMEN

Completely ordinary.

THIRD BATHER (female)

And common.

FIRST BATHER (female)

Oh yes, baroness. Life preservers, everyone! The tide is coming in.

(*They return to the fore and sit at different tables.*)

SECOND BATHER (female), *looking to the right.*

Here comes Monsieur de Longuefugue.

THIRD BATHER (female)

The editor of *High Life in Honfleur.*

FIRST BATHER

That crackpot mixes everything up—people and things, names and places.

A BATHER (male)

Get this, marquise. Naturally, he came to interview me for his society page when I arrived two weeks ago. I introduced myself: Count Robert de Ligny le Châtel, residing at Brignolles in the Var. Do you know what he turned that into in his paper? Monsieur de Brignolles, residing at Brie-Comte-Robert-au-Châtel.

(*They laugh.*)

DE LONGUEFUGUE, *greeting them.*

Ladies. Gentlemen. What are we laughing at?

FIRST BATHER (female)

At those six young women swimming over there. You're always so well informed. Tell us who they are.

DE LONGUEFUGUE

Let's see, countess, let's see. I can't tell until they come out of the water. It helps if I can see their shapes.

FIRST BATHER (female)

What about the man and woman watching them? They're not in the water.

DE LONGUEFUGUE

Let's see. Yes, I just interviewed them. That's Sir Gaveston.

FIRST BATHER (female)

I know him.

DE LONGUEFUGUE

Really, countess, you've met him?

FIRST BATHER (female)

At the Opéra-Comique, in *La Dame blanche*.[12]

(*They laugh.*)

DE LONGUEFUGUE

It's not the same one.

SECOND BATHER (female)

Maybe they're related?

DE LONGUEFUGUE

No. This one is a Mormon from Utah. (*Reading his notes.*) He has six lawful wives.

ALL

How awful!

DE LONGUEFUGUE

Not at all. Polygamy is the rule in that religion. (*Reading.*) Six wives who have given him six daughters.

FIRST BATHER (female)

One per wife.

DE LONGUEFUGUE

He only brought one of his wives to France, the most recent one, to keep an eye on his six daughters. His six wives are all from different countries. One is Russian.

THIRD BATHER (female)

Does she sing him the national anthem?

DE LONGUEFUGUE

Probably. A Chinese wife, an English one, a Swiss one, a French one, and an Auvergnese one.[13]

A BATHER (male)

And they manage to communicate with each other?

DE LONGUEFUGUE

So it seems. All of their languages merge into his.

SECOND BATHER (female)

Sounds like he's holding court.

DE LONGUEFUGUE

In the tower of Babel!

(*They laugh.*)

SCENE 2

The same, STEPHANA, AUNT FLORA

STEPHANA, *entering from the left.*

Nothing!

AUNT FLORA, *from left.*

Empty-handed!

STEPHANA

What now, Aunt Flora?

AUNT FLORA

No sign of Oscar anywhere.

STEPHANA

What a monster! Maybe he saw me . . . He's probably hiding, but I'll find him!

AUNT FLORA

Fine, but find him yourself. I'm fading fast . . . I'm beat!

(*She sits at a table on the left.*)

STEPHANA

You know, this terrace is the hub of everything that happens in Honfleur. Maybe we'll catch him passing through.

DE LONGUEFUGUE

Ah! New arrivals! (*Approaching and greeting them.*) Ladies, I am the Viscount De Longuefugue.

STEPHANA

And what's that to us?

DE LONGUEFUGUE

The editor of *High Life in Honfleur.*

AUNT FLORA, *rising from her chair.*

A member of the press . . . (*She greets him.*)

DE LONGUEFUGUE

Might I be so bold as to ask your names and occupations for my newspaper?

AUNT FLORA

What's that, monsieur? . . . I'm . . .

STEPHANA, *sharply.*

You can call my aunt Mistress Anna Lardball.

AUNT FLORA

But . . .

STEPHANA, *whispering.*

Shut up! I don't want our names to appear in his newspaper. The last thing we need is for Rubineau to read it and find out we've come to Honfleur. I can't have that!

DE LONGUEFUGUE, *writing.*

Lardball, is that a foreign name?

STEPHANA

American.

AUNT FLORA, *affecting an American accent.*

Oh! Yes! . . . Good morning, sir! Old England!

DE LONGUEFUGUE

And you, miss?

STEPHANA

Her niece, Miss Catapult Charleston, native of Bougival . . . in Mexico.[14]

DE LONGUEFUGUE

Really! You have a Bougival in Mexico?

STEPHANA

Why not? There are tons of Bougivals. Now tell me, you who stay so well informed, you wouldn't happen to have a certain Oscar de Pompignac on your list of visitors, would you?

DE LONGUEFUGUE

Monsieur de Pompignac, let me see . . . Yes! . . . Arrived in Honfleur a week ago. Isn't that him, the young man talking to the woman over there? (*He points to a bather.*)

STEPHANA

Him? No, not at all!

DE LONGUEFUGUE

No, of course not . . . let me see . . . Ah yes! I have it. Monsieur Oscar de Pompadour . . .

AUNT FLORA

De Pompignac.

DE LONGUEFUGUE

De Pompignac! Yes, yes! (*Reading his notes.*) Arrived a week ago with Monsieur and Madame Rubineau . . .

STEPHANA, *stupefied.*

Rubineau!

DE LONGUEFUGUE

Precisely! Mademoiselle Rubineau is the daughter of a broker living on rue du Sentier.

AUNT FLORA

That's the one!

DE LONGUEFUGUE

A wedding is even in the works between Mademoiselle Rubineau and Monsieur Oscar de Pompignac.

STEPHANA, *startled.*

A wedding?

DE LONGUEFUGUE

Precisely!

(*They part company.*)

STEPHANA, *passing to the left.*

A wedding!

AUNT FLORA

Well, he really pulled one over on us!

STEPHANA

And here I was about to fall in love with him. What a scoundrel!

AUNT FLORA

Oh, he'll pay for this!

STEPHANA

And how! First of all, this wedding won't happen unless I let it, since I just happen to have . . . shall we say, a friendly relationship with his future father-in-law.

AUNT FLORA

You have Rubineau wrapped around your little finger.

STEPHANA

Oh, Monsieur Oscar thinks he can get married without my consent, does he?

AUNT FLORA

He could have at least given you the customary notice.

STEPHANA

Oh, just wait until I have him in my clutches. Then we'll have a good laugh.

AUNT FLORA

But, unless I'm mistaken . . . that's him coming our way!

SCENE 3

The same, OSCAR

OSCAR

Finally rid of my clingy little fiancée.

STEPHANA

Oscar!

OSCAR, *noticing Stephana.*

Stephana! How the hell . . . ?

STEPHANA

Finally!

AUNT FLORA

Here he is!

OSCAR

How . . . My dearest Stephana, it's you! You're here!

STEPHANA

In the flesh!

OSCAR

How long have you been here, my sweet?

STEPHANA

I arrived by train this morning! You told me that you were going to Asnières.

OSCAR

Yes, well . . . you see, I was going there . . . but I fell asleep and missed the stop . . . and I didn't wake up until we got here to Honfleur . . .

STEPHANA

Remarkable! That's quite the story! Sounds like something Jules Verne might have written! I, however, got bored in Paris without you, my Oscar.

OSCAR

Aren't you the sensitive soul! And how did you learn I was in Honfleur?

STEPHANA

Your concierge.

OSCAR

What a lout!

AUNT FLORA

No! He's a good guy. He told me: "Monsieur Oscar left for Asnières, but he usually falls asleep and ends up in Honfleur."

OSCAR

Very funny! And why exactly did you chase me all this way?

STEPHANA

Chase? Now that's not very nice, my dear.

OSCAR

No! I meant to say . . .

STEPHANA

You meant to say chase! And you said it.

AUNT FLORA, *singing.*

"Yes! You said it! Yes! You said it!" Just like in *La Favorite.*[15]

STEPHANA

No, it's in *Robert.*[16] Nonetheless, my darling, you know that one cannot live on love and water alone.

OSCAR

On water, no! But love . . . I know some for whom it is their specialty.

STEPHANA

Don't insult me, Oscar!

AUNT FLORA

Oh! Never insult a wounded woman!

STEPHANA

I've learned quite a bit about you, Oscar.

OSCAR

About me?

STEPHANA

Look me in the eyes and tell me that you're not getting married.

OSCAR

Me?

STEPHANA

You! You! You!

OSCAR

Well . . . you see . . . Someone proposed it to me . . . but I haven't yet said yes!

STEPHANA

But it's coming.

OSCAR

It's coming . . . Who told you about it? My concierge?

STEPHANA

No. A little bird told me.

OSCAR

Imagine that. A little bird. That's convenient, a little bird.

STEPHANA

I even know who you're marrying.

OSCAR

Really? A little bird again?

STEPHANA

No. A big one.

OSCAR

Oh, a big one this time?

STEPHANA

You're marrying Mademoiselle Rubineau, the young daughter of Rubineau. Impressed?

OSCAR

I admit it!

STEPHANA

And you thought I'd just let things roll merrily along like that? You think I'm just going to accept this unusual situation?

AUNT FLORA

You're going to blow a gasket, as they say, my friend.

STEPHANA

I'll cause a scene . . . at your wedding!

OSCAR

Stephana! My dear Stephana!

STEPHANA

I'll hire a little kid and set him on the counter in front of the justice marrying you, and I'll say: "Look at what this joker left me with."

OSCAR

Stephana, I swear, if you do that, I'll blow my brains out right in front of you!

STEPHANA

Brains? Wouldn't you need some to be able to blow them out? And you have no more heart than brains! To have taken advantage of a poor, frail little woman . . .

OSCAR

Poor?

STEPHANA

Yes! Poor and frail! I feel it, a shrinking within my breast.

OSCAR

It doesn't show.

AUNT FLORA

Are you making fun, monsieur?

STEPHANA

He's making fun! After all I've given him!

OSCAR

But you had nothing!

STEPHANA

Shut up, you! You're becoming discourteous.

OSCAR

I'm shutting up. And I'm leaving tonight for Paris.

STEPHANA

With Mademoiselle Rubineau?

OSCAR

And her father.

STEPHANA

What, her father is here?

OSCAR

Of course. Since last night.

AUNT FLORA, *whispering.*

Golly! Let's hope he doesn't see us.

STEPHANA, *whispering.*

I couldn't care less! (*Aloud.*) Listen, Oscar, there is one thing that could assuage my anger.

OSCAR

Do tell, what is it?

STEPHANA

Your generosity. Until now my love was free.

OSCAR

Five hundred francs a month is free?[17]

STEPHANA

As good as free! How can I be expected to live on that, in this world of horse-riding lessons and Chinese Bezique?[18] It's sheer misery. I'm only asking for a little money to properly care for my aunt.

AUNT FLORA

What a thoughtful child!

OSCAR

A little money?

STEPHANA

Or a lot, if you like. I'll leave it up to you.

OSCAR

Oh, we'll see when I send it to you . . .

STEPHANA

No! We'll agree first, then you'll send it to me once we've settled on the amount.

OSCAR

Got it. I'll see you later, then, Stephana. All I'm asking is that you stay calm!

STEPHANA

It's a bit hard to swallow, after all. To see the only man you've ever loved leave for a little cutie pie who doesn't know her head from her tail.

OSCAR

Well, that can be learned, thank God! Goodbye forever.

STEPHANA

No. Goodbye for now.

AUNT FLORA

You're lucky you ran into her. If you'd run into me, things would have turned out differently.

OSCAR

Yes, well, fortunately I didn't run into you. At least there's that. (*While exiting.*) Goodbye, Auntie!

SCENE 4

STEPHANA, AUNT FLORA

AUNT FLORA

So, are you just going to let him go?

STEPHANA

That depends on the money.

AUNT FLORA

Ah, all in good time . . . Say, niece?

STEPHANA

What, Aunt?

AUNT FLORA

I'm hungry!

STEPHANA

Well then, go to the resort café!

AUNT FLORA

Right! I'll leave you to yourself for a moment. (*She exits.*)

STEPHANA, *alone.*

So, Monsieur Rubineau is here! The old scoundrel didn't tell me that he was coming to spend his Sunday in Honfleur either. And he's marrying his daughter off to Oscar!

That's rich! Me, pseudo-mother-in-law to my deranged lover![19]

SCENE 5

STEPHANA, SIR GAVESTON, the WAITER, then DE LONGUEFUGUE

SIR GAVESTON, *entering and sitting at a table.*

Garçon!

WAITER

What can I get you, sir?

SIR GAVESTON

I'm thirsty!

WAITER

Bock, kirsch, orgeat, absinthe, Pernod . . .

SIR GAVESTON

Beer.

WAITER

Excellent, sir. One strong bock.

STEPHANA

Now there's a handsome man!

SIR GAVESTON

This is so upsetting! How could I have lost my wife, Corpulencia, and my six daughters: Lucy, Nelly, Betty, Pretty, Jenny, and Baby?

WAITER

Here you are, sir!

SIR GAVESTON

You haven't seen my wife, have you?

WAITER

I don't know her.

SIR GAVESTON

Mistress Gaveston! Distinguishing features: American, forceful personality, intimidating, ample bosom . . .

WAITER

There are many . . . ample women in Honfleur right now.

SIR GAVESTON

Straw hat, red coat, white skirt, with six daughters.

WAITER

No sir . . . (*He exits.*)

STEPHANA, *aside.*

Six daughters! He must be an American plantation owner!

SIR GAVESTON

This is troubling. I was hoping to take the return boat back to Le Havre.

STEPHANA, *reading a newspaper.*

The boat doesn't leave until five o'clock, sir.

SIR GAVESTON

Thank you, madame. (*Aside.*) Well, isn't she a lovely lady.

STEPHANA, *standing, aside.*

A wealthy foreigner. (*Aloud.*) Monsieur is foreign?

SIR GAVESTON

No! I'm American! I have six wives whom I love!

STEPHANA

Six wives?

SIR GAVESTON

Yes! I'm a Mormon, and we can have up to twelve wives.

STEPHANA

My heavens!

SIR GAVESTON

My six wives have each given me one daughter.

STEPHANA

Quite the brood!

SIR GAVESTON

And I've just lost my sixth wife and my six daughters.

STEPHANA

Don't worry, you'll find them.

SIR GAVESTON

I hope so. Where could they have wandered off to! (*Aside.*) In the meantime, this little lady seems like nice company. (*Aloud.*) I'm Sir Gaveston!

STEPHANA

Oh, so you're Sir Gaveston! I had no idea . . .

SIR GAVESTON

Yes. I came to France to market one of my inventions.

STEPHANA

And what is this invention?

SIR GAVESTON

A little buzzer.

STEPHANA

And what does this little buzzer do?

SIR GAVESTON

It's an instrument for measuring love in women and men.

STEPHANA

A love meter?

SIR GAVESTON

Yes! It consists of an electronic apparatus with a bell encased in a tinplate box. This very sensitive instrument, placed in a person's pocket, instantly senses changes in heart rate. The bell rings as soon as the wearer's heart starts beating faster for his or her interlocutor.

(*He shows it to her.*)

STEPHANA

Isn't that marvelous! It just looks like a tin of sardines!

SIR GAVESTON

Yes! But with this little instrument, deception is impossible! If a woman tells you that she loves you, just put it in her pocket. If she's lying, it doesn't ring.

STEPHANA

That could be damned irritating!

SIR GAVESTON

In America, women are faithful. No one would buy it there. But I expect I'll make a fortune in France!

STEPHANA

Every husband will want one! How much will your little buzzer cost?

SIR GAVESTON

One hundred francs.

STEPHANA

That's pricey.

SIR GAVESTON

Not for what it does.

DE LONGUEFUGUE, *enters running.*

Excuse me, monsieur, I saw you from over there, and I would very much like to find out your name and profession for my newspaper *High Life in Honfleur.*

SIR GAVESTON

I already gave you my information.

DE LONGUEFUGUE

Oh, really? And you, madame?

STEPHANA

So did I.

DE LONGUEFUGUE

Oh, very well, very well. I was just saying to myself, those people look familiar. (*He begins to leave.*)

SIR GAVESTON

May I ask you something, sir?

DE LONGUEFUGUE

A subscription?

SIR GAVESTON, *pulling him aside.*

Do you know this young lady?

DE LONGUEFUGUE

Oh yes, very well!

SIR GAVESTON

Who is she?

DE LONGUEFUGUE

Who is she? . . . let's see . . . (*He takes out his notebook and flips through it.*) She is . . . she is . . . Oh yes, here she is! Mademoiselle Rubineau!

SIR GAVESTON

Rubineau?

DE LONGUEFUGUE

Yes, Charlotte Rubineau, daughter of Sosthène Rubineau, broker from Paris, rue du Sentier.

SIR GAVESTON

Charlotte Rubineau!

DE LONGUEFUGUE

I must ask you to excuse me, monsieur, but I'm on my way to the station to catch a train. I must go to Paris for some important business. (*He exits.*)

SIR GAVESTON, *returning to Stephana, who has gone back to reading her newspaper.*

So you're Miss Rubineau?

STEPHANA

Me? (*Aside.*) What is he talking about?

SIR GAVESTON

Yes! You! I know. Mr. Chatterbox told me.

STEPHANA, *confused.*

He told you, eh? (*Aside.*) He knows Rubineau.

SIR GAVESTON

Well, miss, you are my niece.

STEPHANA, *standing up.*

Your niece? (*Aside.*) He's crazy.

SIR GAVESTON

Of course! My fourth wife is the sister of Sosthène Rubineau, broker residing on rue du Sentier in Paris.

STEPHANA, *aside.*

Well, you don't say! (*Aloud.*) Yes, you're right! You astound me, sir!

SIR GAVESTON

I find you charming.

STEPHANA

That shows you've got taste.

SIR GAVESTON

How is your father?

STEPHANA

My father, never met him!

SIR GAVESTON

Of course you have! Monsieur Rubineau . . .

STEPHANA, *aside.*

He really thinks I'm Rubineau's daughter . . .

SIR GAVESTON

Is your father like you?

STEPHANA

Not so much.

SIR GAVESTON

Too bad! That's a shame because you're absolutely *delightful*!

SCENE 6

The same, CORPULENCIA, NELLY, LUCY, BETTY, JENNY, PRETTY, then BABY

CORPULENCIA

Napoleon! Napoleon! I've finally found you.

SIR GAVESTON

Corpulencia . . . I'm so happy to see you again!

CORPULENCIA

What happened to you, Napoleon?

SIR GAVESTON

Me? What about you?

CORPULENCIA

I confused the hotels when I went for a swim.

SIR GAVESTON

I forgive you. All of you come here so I can introduce you to Miss Rubineau, my niece from France.

ALL.

Miss Rubineau!

STEPHANA, *aside.*

This Mormon won't let it go. Why disabuse him?

NELLY.

So mademoiselle is our cousin?

SIR GAVESTON

Yes!

STEPHANA, *aside.*

I suppose I should play the part. (*Aloud.*) Madame, Mesdemoiselles, it's an honor to meet you.

SIR GAVESTON

This is my sixth wife, Corpulencia Battington . . . She's good and fertile. And these are my six daughters.

CORPULENCIA

Introduce yourselves, girls.

NELLY

I'm Nelly.

PRETTY

I'm Pretty.

LUCY

I'm Lucy.

JENNY.

I'm Jenny.

BETTY

I'm Betty.

CORPULENCIA

Greet her, girls.

(*They all greet her.*)

STEPHANA

But that's only five.

SIR GAVESTON

What, five? (*He counts them.*) One, two, three, four, five. Yes, there's one missing, but which?

NELLY

It's Baby. She's not lost, Daddy. She stayed behind to . . .

(*She stops herself.*)

SIR GAVESTON

To do what?

CORPULENCIA

It's too scandalous to mention!

SIR GAVESTON

Well . . . okay then.

BABY, *entering.*

Here I am, Daddy.

SIR GAVESTON

You're straggling, miss.

BABY

Yes, Daddy. It's because when I was swimming . . .

STEPHANA, *interrupting.*

I'm delighted to make your acquaintance! Won't Papa Rubineau be thrilled!

BETTY

You're getting married soon, aren't you, Cousin?

STEPHANA

Married?

NELLY

We received the announcement . . . to Monsieur Oscar de . . . de . . .

THE OTHER FIVE

Pompignac!

STEPHANA

Oh . . . yes, of course! (*Aside.*) And now I'm marrying Oscar! Wouldn't be the first time![20]

JENNY

Are we invited to the wedding?

BETTY

We'll dance!

LUCY

And how!

BABY, *kicking her legs.*

We'll whoop it up!

SIR GAVESTON, *sternly.*

Miss Baby . . .

STEPHANA, *apologizing for her.*

Blame the swimming incident.

CORPULENCIA

Napoleon! Napoleon! It's time to catch the return boat to Le Havre.

SIR GAVESTON

Oh! Yes, Corpulencia Battington!

STEPHANA

But, Uncle, if you're returning to Paris, why not take the train instead of the boat?

CORPULENCIA

Because our luggage is in Le Havre.

SIR GAVESTON

And we don't take the train on Sundays.

STEPHANA

For religious reasons?

SIR GAVESTON

No, because of impactions.

STEPHANA

Impactions? Oh, you mean train wrecks.

SIR GAVESTON

Yes, that's it. There are extra trains on Sundays, and there's a risk of impactions. In America, we expect them . . . we're prepared. But they're rare in France. No one is prepared, and getting impacted when you don't expect it would be humiliating. We won't leave for Paris until tomorrow morning. And as soon as we get there, we'll go see my brother-in-law Sosthène Rubineau at 92, rue du Sentier.

STEPHANA, *aside.*

Oh, he'll be thrilled! (*Aloud.*) But before that, Uncle . . . (*Aside.*) Too bad I have to call him uncle! (*Aloud.*) I want to ask a favor of you.

SIR GAVESTON

What is it? Tell me, Miss . . . Charlotte, that's it, right?

STEPHANA, *aside.*

Charlotte? Who is she? (*Aloud.*) Yes! Charlotte!

SIR GAVESTON

Charlotte Rubineau, lovely name.

STEPHANA

Yes, yes! Would you mind giving me that little jewel of a buzzer?

SIR GAVESTON

Gladly, for one hundred francs.

STEPHANA

My father, Rubineau, will pay you in Paris.

SIR GAVESTON

Very well, then! Here's the jewel.

STEPHANA

Thank you!

SIR GAVESTON

Goodbye, Charlotte.

ALL

Goodbye, Charlotte.

SCENE 7

STEPHANA, then RUBINEAU, MADAME RUBINEAU, CHARLOTTE

STEPHANA

That was exhausting! . . . It's curious, that dumb Mormon's invention. I wouldn't have called it a little buzzer though. I would have called it a tomcat detector. (*We hear a terrible racket. Someone screaming: "Help!"*) What in the world? . . . Rubineau, his wife, and his daughter. I'd better make myself scarce!

(*Rubineau, Madame Rubineau, and Charlotte enter flabbergasted. Stephana recedes upstage.*)

MADAME RUBINEAU

How do they put up with that? Herds of cattle in the streets! Why did we ever leave Paris?

RUBINEAU

One of those horned herbivores almost killed me!

CHARLOTTE

Daddy, I was so scared!

RUBINEAU

It's your mother's fault!

MADAME RUBINEAU

My fault?

RUBINEAU

Certainly! With all the red you wear, it's no wonder those creatures came after us.

MADAME RUBINEAU

Well, would you prefer I wear yellow?

RUBINEAU

I don't prefer anything. But I was almost gored because of you.

MADAME RUBINEAU

Because of me? Because of me? A bit of an exaggeration, don't you think? The livestock wanted nothing to do with me!

RUBINEAU

They wanted nothing to do with you because you were raised in the country—so you're accustomed to those kinds of horned beasts.[21]

MADAME RUBINEAU

No need to remind me of that. We have been married twenty-one years, after all . . .

STEPHANA, *on the left, aside.*

Oof! Right in the gut!

CHARLOTTE

Say, Daddy, are we going for a swim? You said that Trouville was too crowded but that here in Honfleur we could relax.

RUBINEAU

Charlotte, give me a moment.

CHARLOTTE

So there was no point in taking the boat to Honfleur to swim in peace.

MADAME RUBINEAU

Sosthène, are we just going to wait around here?

STEPHANA, *aside.*

Sosthène! He told me his name was Alcibiades.[22]

RUBINEAU

Just a moment! First we have to find Auguste. He wandered off with Oscar, our future son-in-law, and didn't say where they were going. I'm exhausted from running around. Two times now you've made me walk all the way around the harbor in this sun.

MADAME RUBINEAU

Poor thing, would you like us to carry you? I'm going to go look for him. Come with me, Charlotte.

CHARLOTTE

Yes, mother.

MADAME RUBINEAU

We'll come back here to pick you up when we've found Auguste and Monsieur Oscar.

CHARLOTTE

See you in a bit, Daddy.

RUBINEAU

Yes, in a bit! In a bit!

(*They exit to the right.*)

SCENE 8

RUBINEAU, STEPHANA, still off to the side.

RUBINEAU

I am exhausted though! Leaving Paris on the 5 A.M. seaside express train . . . carrying a melon. And they're so heavy! You shouldn't travel with melons at this time of year, anyway . . . but my wife writes me to come and bring her one. Then, as soon as I get to Trouville, they decide to spend the day in Honfleur.

STEPHANA, *approaching and whispering.*

Hello, Sosthène . . .

RUBINEAU, *stupefied, stands up.*

Huh? What? What the . . . ? Stephana, in Honfleur!

STEPHANA

Why yes, Sosthène! Why did you tell me that your name was Alcibiades?

RUBINEAU

I'm done for . . . Go away . . . go away . . . my wife will come back any moment . . . Don't speak to me . . . (*With dignity.*) I don't know you, madame! I don't know you!

STEPHANA

You don't know me at the seaside! Oh! The big scoundrel! The vile scoundrel! *I* know *you* all too well . . . whether in Honfleur or rue Clauzel.

RUBINEAU, *aside.*

She's going to cause a scandal. (*Aloud.*) Fine, yes, yes! I know you! But how did you find me here, my dear?

STEPHANA

I came here on a stroll, like you . . . by gosh!

RUBINEAU

Excuse me! I came here to meet up with my wife!

STEPHANA

Well, I came here to meet up with my lover.

RUBINEAU

Quiet! Quiet! Let me get you something to drink?

STEPHANA

No, thank you. I'm not thirsty. We need to chat, Sosthène!

RUBINEAU

No! Call me Alcibiades! (*Aside.*) My wife and my daughter and my son-in-law are all coming back! (*Aloud.*) Fine! What do you want? Quickly, my Stephana!

STEPHANA

Alcibiades, your little Stephana is in a real pickle!

RUBINEAU

In a pickle?

STEPHANA

Yes! Your Stephana needs some bread!

RUBINEAU

Waiter, bring some bread for the lady!

STEPHANA

Go on, Sosthène, don't play dumb with me. (*Caressing him.*) My goodness, you look handsome today.

RUBINEAU

Really? You think so?

STEPHANA

Yes! You're fresh and rosy. You look hale and hearty.

RUBINEAU

In truth, things are going well.

STEPHANA

Come on, baby, I just need twenty-five louis![23]

RUBINEAU

Oh, I get it! Bread, pickle, it means money. It means twenty-five louis!

STEPHANA

Why, yes, I suppose.

RUBINEAU, *aside.*

If my wife heard this! (*Aloud.*) So, you need twenty-five louis?

STEPHANA

You said it, dearest. And quickly, if you please!

RUBINEAU

Well, I don't have it on me.

STEPHANA

You say that, but a refined man always has fifty louis on him. And you are a refined man, Alcibiades, aren't you?

RUBINEAU

Refined without the fineries, more like!

STEPHANA

Come on, don't be silly! (*Caressing him.*) It's for a good cause. My poor aunt is sick.

RUBINEAU

Oh, your aunt is sick?

STEPHANA

Yes! She needs a big operation, and the surgeon is asking for twenty-five louis in advance.

SCENE 9

The same, AUNT FLORA

AUNT FLORA

I'm back, and I am parched!

STEPHANA, *aside.*

Perfect timing!

RUBINEAU

The aunt! How was your operation?

AUNT FLORA

My operation?

STEPHANA

Yes, your operation!

AUNT FLORA

Oh! It went well! I ate nine sandwiches, and boy were they salty!

RUBINEAU

Well?

STEPHANA

That's just it. It's her condition. She has an oversized stomach. She needs it clamped off.

RUBINEAU

A clamp in the stomach?

STEPHANA

Yes! Isn't that right, Aunt?

AUNT FLORA

Oh! Clamp here, clip there.

STEPHANA

You don't believe me, Alcibiades?

RUBINEAU

Oh no, I do.

STEPHANA

Then kiss me!

RUBINEAU

But people can see us!

STEPHANA

The whole world could see us for all I care! It's worth it for one of your kisses!

RUBINEAU

She can't get enough of me!

(*They kiss.*)

SCENE 10

The same, MADAME RUBINEAU, AUGUSTE, CHARLOTTE

MADAME RUBINEAU

What is going on, Sosthène?

RUBINEAU

My wife! Oh . . . no . . . no . . . no . . . I'm doomed . . .

MADAME RUBINEAU

Just what is the meaning of this, Monsieur Rubineau?

AUGUSTE

No doubt about it, Dad is busted!

MADAME RUBINEAU

Who is this woman?

RUBINEAU

This woman? . . . This woman? . . . it's a young woman . . . a young woman . . .

AUGUSTE

Oh boy! Is Dad going to lose it?

MADAME RUBINEAU

Well, who is this young woman?

RUBINEAU

Hold on a minute . . . you should have a seat! It must have been hot out there on the beach. Do you want to cool off?

AUGUSTE

Looks like the beach wasn't the only place where things were heating up!

MADAME RUBINEAU

Will you answer me? Who is this creature?

STEPHANA

Creature? Take a look at yourself!

RUBINEAU

Indeed, I forgot to introduce her . . . it's funny actually . . . a remarkable coincidence! How we met up . . . it's funny . . . ha ha ha!

MADAME RUBINEAU, *imitating him.*

Ha ha ha! Have you quite finished your ha ha ha's?

RUBINEAU

The mademoiselle that you see here . . . well . . . she's . . . no, it will surprise you when you hear it . . .

SCENE II

The same, DE LONGUEFUGUE

DE LONGUEFUGUE, *seeing Stephana.*

There you are, miss! Finally I've found you!

STEPHANA

What's going on?

DE LONGUEFUGUE

The boat is about to leave. And your father noticed that he had once again lost one of his six daughters.

MADAME RUBINEAU

The girl's a lost soul! I was right!

DE LONGUEFUGUE

No! She's a found girl!

MADAME RUBINEAU

Monsieur, whose daughter is this "foundling"?

DE LONGUEFUGUE

Why, Sir Gaveston's.

MADAME RUBINEAU

My brother-in-law?

RUBINEAU

Yes! That's exactly what I was just about to tell you! (*Aside.*) Phew! I thought it was all over!

(*A bell sounds.*)

DE LONGUEFUGUE

That's the last bell. Come along! They're going to raise the gangplank!

STEPHANA, *aside.*

For us both, Monsieur Rubineau. (*Aloud.*) No, monsieur, tell Sir Gaveston that I'm afraid of getting seasick and that I would rather return to Paris with Monsieur and Madame Rubineau.

MADAME RUBINEAU

Even so . . .

STEPHANA, *throwing her arms around Madame Rubineau's neck.*

But, Aunt, don't deny me the pleasure of your company!

DE LONGUEFUGUE

Okay. Sir Gaveston is sure to be disappointed . . . (*He exits.*)

SCENE 12

The same, without DE LONGUEFUGUE

CHARLOTTE

So, mademoiselle, you're my cousin?

STEPHANA

Come again?

MADAME RUBINEAU

Excuse me?

RUBINEAU

It's an American expression.

AUGUSTE

This cousin of mine is absolutely intoxicating!

MADAME RUBINEAU

But won't your father be worried?

STEPHANA

Not at all! He knows that I'm with my governess.

RUBINEAU

Yes! Mademoiselle is with her governess . . . Aunt Flora.

MADAME RUBINEAU

What did you say?

RUBINEAU

Me? Nothing at all!

MADAME RUBINEAU

Well . . . where is this governess?

STEPHANA

Here she is! Come over here ma'am . . . Mrs. Piddle!

AUNT FLORA

Huh? Piddle? Where?

STEPHANA

Yes, come here! She's a bit shy.

MADAME RUBINEAU

Don't be afraid, Mrs. Poodle . . .

AUNT FLORA, *aside.*

It's Poodle now? Just watch, next she's going to make me sleep on the floor!

STEPHANA

So you see, it's as though I was all alone . . . then all of a sudden I hear someone say the name Monsieur Rubineau, and I cried out: "That's my uncle!"

RUBINEAU

Dear child. (*Aside.*) May the devil take her!

AUGUSTE, *aside.*

She seems a bit rough around the edges, this little American. Perhaps I can help polish her up a bit!

MADAME RUBINEAU

And you just abandoned your father like that?

STEPHANA

Why not? In America . . .

RUBINEAU

Yes, yes, American ways. American parenting, you know, very hands-off . . .

AUGUSTE

My cousin, I'm Auguste, mother and father's son, brother of my sister, your cousin. How I've already taken to you!

CHARLOTTE

Me too!

STEPHANA

You're too kind!

MADAME RUBINEAU

Here comes our future son-in-law.

STEPHANA, *under her breath.*

Oscar! What the devil? This'll complicate things!

SCENE 13

The same, OSCAR, then DE LONGUEFUGUE

OSCAR

My dear madame, monsieur, Mademoiselle Charlotte, Auguste . . . (*Noticing Stephana, aside.*) Huh? Stephana is with them? What's the meaning of this?

STEPHANA, *aside.*

Here we go!

RUBINEAU

My friend, it's good to see you. Let me introduce you to my niece, Miss Gaveston, a young American.

OSCAR, *aside.*

His niece! An American! What nerve! (*Aloud.*) A pleasure, mademoiselle, a pleasure.

STEPHANA

Charmed to make your acquaintance!

MADAME RUBINEAU

And this is her governess, Mrs. Poodle.

OSCAR, *aside.*

The aunt, a governess?!

STEPHANA

She's the one who watches out for my . . . respectability.

OSCAR, *aside.*

I'll be hanged if I understand anything here.

CHARLOTTE

Come back with us, Cousin.

STEPHANA

All the way to Paris, yes! Once we arrive I'll rejoin Daddy at his hotel.

AUGUSTE

But no! You'll stay at the house with us. We'll take good care of you! You'll see.

RUBINEAU, *aside.*

Now there's an idea! Auguste has no idea what he's saying!

MADAME RUBINEAU

Auguste is right! Come home with us. You'll be more comfortable than in a hotel. And tomorrow you can go find your father.

RUBINEAU, *aside.*

Oh no! I'm going to faint!

STEPHANA

I gratefully accept! (*Aside.*) I'll catch you, Sosthène!

MADAME RUBINEAU

Speaking of your family, how is my husband's sister?

STEPHANA

Your husband's sister . . .

MADAME RUBINEAU

Yes, your father's wife?

STEPHANA

Oh, well, you know, Daddy has six wives.

MADAME RUBINEAU

Six wives!

STEPHANA

It's permitted in the Mormon religion.

AUGUSTE

Six wives! I think I'm going to become a Mormon!

MADAME RUBINEAU

His sister is named Enguerrande.

STEPHANA

Enguerrande? I know that name! Yes! She's number four. She's well. Like the rest, they're all well!

RUBINEAU, *aside.*

That was close!

OSCAR

What a pretty picture you paint!

CHARLOTTE

Let me kiss you, my cousin!

RUBINEAU

No, no, in America women don't kiss each other.

AUGUSTE, *advancing toward her.*

Do they kiss men?

MADAME RUBINEAU

Auguste! You're frightening her!

AUGUSTE

No, she's not bothered! Isn't that right, you're not bothered?

MADAME RUBINEAU

Auguste!

AUGUSTE

All right already! I'll stop.

DE LONGUEFUGUE, *enters pulling out his watch.*

Ladies, we'll have to hurry if you don't want to miss your train.

RUBINEAU, *whispering to Stephana.*

Get lost along the way and fifty louis are yours.

STEPHANA

Never! I want to experience the joys of family life for myself.

DE LONGUEFUGUE

Let's go! Hurry!

STEPHANA, *taking hold of Rubineau.*

You can't lose me that easily! Your arm please, my little uncle!

(*They all go upstage.*)

DE LONGUEFUGUE, *to Aunt Flora.*

Aren't you the Marquise de Noisy-le-Sec?

AUNT FLORA

Why not?

DE LONGUEFUGUE

Your husband just fell in the oyster tank!

ACT II

The action takes place in a salon in the home of Monsieur Rubineau. There are doors upstage and on the sides. The furnishings are bourgeois and include a piano.

SCENE I

STEPHANA

STEPHANA, *entering from the back, she struts triumphantly downstage.*

I'm here, and I'm staying! This little Stephana has a head on her shoulders! And when she gets something into her head, it's like when you put some coins in a vending machine: it might not work, but it never gives back the coins! This time, though, it will work. (*She sits.*) I rather like it here.

SCENE 2

STEPHANA, the MAID, then AUGUSTE

MAID, *entering.*

Would mademoiselle like some tea, coffee, or hot chocolate this morning?

STEPHANA

I'll take a vermouth.

MAID, *dumbstruck.*

Uh . . . Well . . . We don't actually have any.

AUGUSTE, *entering.*

Well then, go get some.

MAID

Of course. On my way.

(*She exits.*)

STEPHANA, *standing.*

I beg your pardon, monsieur.

AUGUSTE

Monsieur? But I'm your cousin. Call me "my cousin."

STEPHANA

I wouldn't dare, my cousin.

AUGUSTE

You Americans are so prudish! Fine, call me Auguste.

STEPHANA

Auguste? It's a pretty name.

AUGUSTE

Now that depends on who has the name. For example, if Father were called Auguste, it would suit him like a delicate rosebud on an elephant's lapel. Me, however, I don't think myself so ridiculous going by it.

STEPHANA

Not at all!

AUGUSTE

And I'm comfortable telling you that I love you.

STEPHANA

Really? You love me?

AUGUSTE

Oh yes! I love you, my darling Stephana!

STEPHANA

Auguste, my sweet, please don't be so familiar.[24] We hardly know each other.

AUGUSTE

Well then, let's get to know each other. Oh, my cousin, if only you knew what I feel for you in my heart . . .

STEPHANA

Just since yesterday? You'll never convince me of that.

AUGUSTE

Time doesn't matter when it comes to love!

STEPHANA

Well, let's find out. (*She pulls Gaveston's little box from her pocket.*) Do you see this?

AUGUSTE

Yes, it's a tin of sardines.

STEPHANA

No! It's Sir Gaveston's . . . that is, my father's invention. The tomcat detector.

AUGUSTE

Your father hunts tomcats?

STEPHANA

No! That's just what I call his invention.

AUGUSTE

I don't see what that . . .

STEPHANA

Patience! You say that you have feelings for little old me?

AUGUSTE

I believe I do!

STEPHANA

Really?

AUGUSTE

Excuse me! I give you my word . . . and there's plenty more where that came from! I'm always good for a laugh, you know.

STEPHANA

Okay, put this little tin box in your pocket.

AUGUSTE

Done! (*He puts the box in his pocket.*)

STEPHANA

Now, tell me that you love me!

AUGUSTE

My cousin! I love you! (*The buzzer sounds.*) What? Well, that's funny!

STEPHANA

It means you're telling the truth.

AUGUSTE

Amazing!

STEPHANA

All right, I believe you, my love! Please return my little jewel.

AUGUSTE, *returning the box.*

Here you go! So Sir Gaveston really invented this marvelous little device?

STEPHANA

Yes! At first I didn't believe in this marvel, but now I believe in it wholeheartedly.

AUGUSTE

And in my love?

STEPHANA

Golly! I guess I have to.

AUGUSTE

Well then, may I . . . ?

STEPHANA

Scandalous! We need to get to know each other better.

AUGUSTE

Since you insist that we get to know each other better before we get to *know* each other, let's get to know each other better.

(*We hear Rubineau's voice outside.*)

STEPHANA

I hear Alcibiades's, I mean, Monsieur Rubineau's voice.

AUGUSTE

Father's voice? I'm going to tell him that I'm madly in love with you and ask his permission to marry.

STEPHANA

Not so fast! He mustn't even see us together yet.

AUGUSTE

Come on, my dearest little cousin.

STEPHANA

I just can't say no to you, my cousin.

(*They exit to the right.*)

SCENE 3
RUBINEAU

RUBINEAU, *entering from the left.*

And what a fine mess I've gotten myself into! Stephana, my mistress, here in the family home! And no way to get rid of her! I'm dying here! What if my wife finds out? I don't want to think about what will happen! And my son-in-law, what would he say? He's such a levelheaded, reserved, thoughtful young man! He might call the whole thing off!

SCENE 4
RUBINEAU, MADAME RUBINEAU, CHARLOTTE, then the MAID

CHARLOTTE, *entering.*

Good morning, Daddy, how are you? Did you sleep well? (*She kisses him.*)

RUBINEAU

Yes, very well.

MADAME RUBINEAU

But I heard noise coming from your bedroom last night. I thought you might be sick. I was about to get up to bring you a tea.

RUBINEAU, *standing.*

That's the last thing I would have wanted!

MADAME RUBINEAU

Why?

RUBINEAU, *sheepishly.*

Because . . . because . . . What I mean is that I would have felt terrible for having troubled you.

MAID, *entering with a bottle and two glasses on a tray.*

Here's the vermouth.

MADAME RUBINEAU

The vermouth? Did you ask for vermouth?

RUBINEAU

Me? . . . (*To Charlotte.*) Did you ask for vermouth?

CHARLOTTE

Daddy, I don't even know what that is!

MADAME RUBINEAU

Well then, who?

MAID

Your niece.

RUBINEAU

My niece?

MADAME RUBINEAU

It would seem she's quite a drinker! Get a load of that! These Americans!

MAID

Yes, madame. (*She exits upstage.*)

MADAME RUBINEAU

What an odd niece you have, Monsieur Rubineau!

RUBINEAU

An American niece. (*Emphatically to Charlotte.*) And you, are you still excited to get married, my little Charlotte?

CHARLOTTE

Oh yes, Daddy! Monsieur de Pompignac is just so . . . !

MADAME RUBINEAU

A very serious young man! (*Whispering to her husband.*) We should prepare her gently for her marital responsibilities.

RUBINEAU

Yes, yes. Listen my child. Your mother and I have to speak to you seriously.

CHARLOTTE, *coming forward.*

About what, Daddy?

RUBINEAU

About . . . your marital . . . obligations . . . to your husband. You're getting married in eight days!

CHARLOTTE

Eight days! What an eternity!

RUBINEAU

You won't always say that!

MADAME RUBINEAU

Quiet, Sosthène! You're going to say something stupid. Listen to me, Charlotte . . . (*She comes around and sits her down.*) I don't need to remind you to be submissive to your husband, to accept his desires without reticence.

CHARLOTTE

Of course, Mother.

RUBINEAU, *sitting to the side.*

All his desires.

CHARLOTTE

Yes, Daddy.

MADAME RUBINEAU

It might seem unusual at first . . . but you'll quickly get used to it! Isn't that right, Monsieur Rubineau?

RUBINEAU

Yes, my dear.

CHARLOTTE

Oh, I plan on spoiling my husband! I'll make him a nice little bedroom next to mine!

RUBINEAU, *standing.*

Next to? Oh no!

MADAME RUBINEAU

You will only have one bedroom for you both.

RUBINEAU

Two chambers? That's the wrong kind of congress!

CHARLOTTE

But, Daddy, you each have your own bedroom, you and mother.

RUBINEAU

Yes, but we . . . it's . . . it's because we've known each other for a very long time.

MADAME RUBINEAU

And your father snores like a bear. It was the only way I could get any sleep.

CHARLOTTE

But, Mother, what if Monsieur Oscar snores?

RUBINEAU

Then you'll whistle him a little tune. Whistling stops snoring, you'll see.

CHARLOTTE

Then why don't you just whistle to quiet Daddy, Mother? That would have saved a bedroom.

RUBINEAU

Your mother never learned to whistle!

CHARLOTTE

Me either.

RUBINEAU

I'll teach you. You purse your lips, like this . . .

CHARLOTTE

I can't.

RUBINEAU

It'll come.

SCENE 5

The same, AUGUSTE

AUGUSTE

Can I come in?

MADAME RUBINEAU

Of course, Auguste, come in.

RUBINEAU

Your mother and I have finished.

AUGUSTE

I have something that I want to ask you.

RUBINEAU

Go ahead, but quickly.

AUGUSTE

Dad, I'm bored with women!

RUBINEAU

You? You're only twenty!

AUGUSTE

I mean, of women who are . . . shall we say *accommodating*.

CHARLOTTE

Mother, what does he mean by women who are accommodating?

MADAME RUBINEAU, *embarrassed.*

He means . . . he means . . .

RUBINEAU

He means women with their own apartments! You know, accommodations. (*Whispering to Auguste.*) Get out of here, you animal!

MADAME RUBINEAU

Charlotte, go check on lunch. Monsieur Oscar is coming to eat with us.

CHARLOTTE

He's coming to lunch! Wonderful!

(*Charlotte exits.*)

AUGUSTE

It's just that I've had enough of single life . . . I want to dive into wedded bliss.

RUBINEAU

You?

AUGUSTE

Yes, me! So, since Uncle Gaveston is coming over, I would like you to talk to him on behalf of yours truly.

MADAME RUBINEAU

How's that? Uncle Gaveston . . . coming here . . . I don't understand.

AUGUSTE

What is there to understand? I have a thing for his daughter.

RUBINEAU

Which one? He has six.

AUGUSTE

The one who's been here since night before last. My darling cousin Stephana!

RUBINEAU, *leaping.*

Stephana!

MADAME RUBINEAU

She is charming, if a bit unrestrained.

RUBINEAU

Too unrestrained.

AUGUSTE

Like America where she's from! At any rate, she's the one I want!

RUBINEAU

Right . . . no!

MADAME RUBINEAU

Why? Miss Gaveston is very rich. It might not be such a terrible idea!

RUBINEAU, *aside*.

That's all I need! (*Aloud.*) You can't marry your cousin! The daughter of a Mormon! Think about it.

MADAME RUBINEAU

What's so bad about that, being the daughter of a Mormon?

RUBINEAU

A man with six wives! That would give you six mothers-in-law!

AUGUSTE

Maybe that is too much for one man.

RUBINEAU

And Miss Gaveston seems too excitable!

AUGUSTE

Exactly! I've always dreamt of having an excitable wife!

RUBINEAU

You said it, you're dreaming. So you're not serious.

AUGUSTE

Must I swear to you that I am?

RUBINEAU

Quiet, Auguste!

MADAME RUBINEAU

After all, Sosthène, you have to realize that this child can't remain . . . like he said . . . his whole life.

AUGUSTE

If you only knew, Dad, how much I love her! Get this, she has a little jewel.

RUBINEAU

A little jewel?

AUGUSTE

An indiscreet jewel!

RUBINEAU, *agitated.*

She's read Diderot! Can't be!

AUGUSTE

She showed it to me. I put it in my pocket, and it buzzed.

RUBINEAU

What is he talking about?

AUGUSTE

This jewel proves that I adore her and she adores me.

RUBINEAU

You adore her? She adores you? Well, you shouldn't adore each other! First of all, marriages between cousins don't work! Look it up!

AUGUSTE

Why's that?

RUBINEAU

You'll see that it interferes with repopulation. And then there's . . . well, that's enough!

AUGUSTE

That might be true, Dad, but it's nothing to you. You already have what you need . . .

RUBINEAU

Leave me in peace!

MADAME RUBINEAU

I'll take care of it. Come along, Auguste.

AUGUSTE

No! Say what you want, but a father responding to his son like that, it's not right! Not right at all!

(*Madame Rubineau exits with Auguste.*)

SCENE 6

RUBINEAU alone, then STEPHANA

RUBINEAU

Can you imagine my son married to Stephana! That would be too much! You wouldn't see anything more twisted than that in a Greek tragedy! I mean, you may as well go see *Phèdre* at the Odéon! Now there's a play the censors should have taken their scissors to![25]

STEPHANA, *entering.*

Hello, my darling little uncle, are you well?

RUBINEAU

Stephana! I'm begging you! This farce has gone on long enough! You've got to leave!

STEPHANA

Leave? You wouldn't want that, by Jupiter! I'm actually quite comfortable here. Plus, it's in your interest to have me here where you can keep an eye on me!

RUBINEAU

Keep your voice down, you wretch!

STEPHANA

Why should I? Haven't you heard? Your son is in love with me. He just made his declaration of love. In fact, he wants to marry me! He's a sweet kid, so you'd better watch out if you leave me!

RUBINEAU

And there you have it, Phèdre in the flesh! That's the icing on the cake!

STEPHANA

You know, Sosthène, you have quite the peculiar family!

RUBINEAU

How so?

STEPHANA

Your daughter is cute, that goes without saying. But your wife . . . ooh la la! (*She laughs.*)

RUBINEAU

Stephana, be nice.

STEPHANA

Tell me I'm wrong! (*Stretching out on the couch.*) It really is nice here! Come sit beside me. I want to run my fingers through your curls.

RUBINEAU, *sitting close to her.*

Come now, my darling, will you please leave?

STEPHANA

I will for five thousand francs.

RUBINEAU, *leaping up.*

Five thousand francs!

STEPHANA

I won't leave for a penny less! I want to become an honest woman, and to do that I need to be independent rather than still at the mercy of silly old men. (*She lies down on the couch.*)

RUBINEAU

Oh, Stephana! I thought you loved me, but here you are demanding money before I even have a chance to offer it.

STEPHANA

I would be waiting an awfully long time, old boy. You don't love me anymore, do you?

RUBINEAU

Of course I do!

STEPHANA

Let's see! (*Giving him the buzzer.*) Here, put this in your pocket.

RUBINEAU

That? Okay, why not? (*He puts it in his pocket.*)

STEPHANA

Now tell me that you love me.

RUBINEAU, *half-heartedly.*

I love you! I love you! I love you! . . .

STEPHANA

You see, it didn't buzz.

RUBINEAU

What didn't buzz?

STEPHANA

The detector. Give it back!

RUBINEAU, *handing it back to her.*

Here!

STEPHANA

It's surprising, in any case.

RUBINEAU

Stephana, this can't go on. You pretend to have seen Sir Gaveston at Honfleur.

STEPHANA

Golly! Maybe I did, maybe I didn't!

RUBINEAU

How come you never mentioned Sir Gaveston before?

STEPHANA

You never asked about my genealogy.

RUBINEAU

I beg you, leave before he gets here. My wife will eventually figure everything out . . .

STEPHANA

Your wife . . . she's too dumb to figure it out.

RUBINEAU

Dumb? Not half as much as you think! You know, she heard noises coming from my bedroom last night!

STEPHANA, *laughing.*

Ha ha ha! That's hilarious!

RUBINEAU

She almost got up to make me some tea.

STEPHANA

She is so devoted, that sweet Madame Rubineau. And you're cheating on her! It's not right.

RUBINEAU, *getting closer to her.*

Stephana, you know how much I love you. Prove your love for me by leaving!

STEPHANA

I would very much like to, but not for less than ten thousand francs.

RUBINEAU

The price has gone up! Stephana, don't make me do something I'll regret!

STEPHANA

What is this? A revolution? Monsieur is rebelling against me. Come give your sweet little Stephana a kiss! Here! Now! At my feet! This is how you handle rebellion when you have the upper hand! Kiss me!

(*They kiss.*)

SCENE 7

The same, MADAME RUBINEAU

MADAME RUBINEAU

What's going on here?

RUBINEAU, *aside and revealing himself.*

Oh no! My wife!

STEPHANA

Hello, Auntie.

MADAME RUBINEAU

Monsieur Rubineau, you're being awfully familiar with your niece.

RUBINEAU

My niece? What niece? . . . Oh! Stephana . . . I mean Miss Gaveston . . . she's just so lovable, the dear child.

MADAME RUBINEAU

I don't deny it, but still . . .

STEPHANA

Auntie, Monsieur Rubineau was simply filling in for my father. I love him like a guardian angel!

RUBINEAU

Yes! That's it! I'm her angel . . . and I was just enveloping her in my wings.

MADAME RUBINEAU

Your wings or your lips?

RUBINEAU

My winged lips.

MADAME RUBINEAU

A bit much, don't you think! At any rate, I need you right this instant. Excuse us for a moment, my niece. Come with me, Sosthène.

RUBINEAU

Coming, my love! (*Aside to Stephana.*) Scram!

STEPHANA

Twenty thousand!

RUBINEAU

What? Twenty! No!

(*He exits with his wife.*)

SCENE 8

STEPHANA

STEPHANA

With twenty thousand from him and twenty thousand from Oscar, I'll have a nice little dowry. One that would permit me to marry an honest man. Oh, how I crave honesty! They're nice here, but a bit stupid. Except the son, he's not bad at all . . . There's something about the way he says, "I love you" . . . Now where is Aunt Flora? Did she fall asleep at the buffet in Lisieux?

SCENE 9

STEPHANA, OSCAR

OSCAR, *a bouquet in hand.*

My dear fiancée, please permit me to offer you . . .

STEPHANA

Thank you, Oscar!

OSCAR

Stephana!

STEPHANA

In the flesh!

OSCAR

What are you doing here?

STEPHANA

What about you?

OSCAR

I'm here to . . .

STEPHANA, *mockingly.*

To shower your little snookum of a fiancée with flowers . . .

OSCAR

It's my right.

STEPHANA

No!

OSCAR

Nonetheless . . .

STEPHANA

So long as a woman hasn't told her man, "Go ahead and get married to someone else!" that man doesn't have the right to shower another girl with flowers. Give me that bouquet!

OSCAR

Listen, Stephana.

STEPHANA

Did I give you permission to go marry someone else?

OSCAR

I didn't think I needed your permission.

STEPHANA

That's men for you! You love them, and they mock you.

OSCAR

Not at all! Me, mock you? God as my witness, Stephana, I'm going to tell you the truth. I was drowning. Someone threw me a line, and I grabbed it.

STEPHANA

And the line is little Charlotte?

OSCAR

Exactly.

STEPHANA

Poor Oscar, how did you get here? Has your funding completely dried up?

OSCAR

The Sahara's got nothing on my finances.

STEPHANA

And here I was counting on you for twenty thousand.

OSCAR

A misplaced hope it was! (*Singing the line from* L'Africaine.)[26]

STEPHANA

Yes, but there's your little snookum's dowry.

OSCAR

Fortunately, my "snookum" . . . yeah, that word kind of leaves a bad taste . . .

STEPHANA

Don't you know that I could jeopardize your marriage if I wanted?

OSCAR

How so?

STEPHANA

My goodness! I guess I can tell you since we've come to this point. I have Monsieur Rubineau wrapped around my little finger.

OSCAR

You?

STEPHANA

Me!

OSCAR

That old Cupid!

STEPHANA

His arrow flies true.

OSCAR

You were cheating on me with that oaf of a broker?

STEPHANA

No, I was cheating on him with you!

OSCAR

A fine distinction, indeed; indefensible nonetheless. My dear Stephana, you will not take advantage of the situation. You will permit this marriage to take place.

STEPHANA

You don't deserve it, you scoundrel.

OSCAR

True, but you're a romantic! And a romantic would never jeopardize the future of the young man she once loved . . . and maybe still loves!

STEPHANA

It's true . . . what you say. You think you're over someone . . . free of them, but not at all. Then you find out that the scoundrel has moved on, and pow! It all comes crashing back.

OSCAR

My Stephana!

STEPHANA

My Oscar!

(*The buzzer rings.*)

OSCAR

What was that?

STEPHANA

Ignore it! It's just Love tugging at the bell cord. Kiss me one last time.

OSCAR

One for the road!

SCENE 10

The same, RUBINEAU

RUBINEAU, *watching them stunned.*

What's going on here?

STEPHANA

Sosthène!

OSCAR

Oof . . . the jig is up!

RUBINEAU, *indignant.*

Young man, on the eve of your marriage to my daughter, how could you allow yourself to perpetrate such immoral acts on this young woman?

STEPHANA

There's no law against it.

OSCAR

My dear father-in-law . . .

RUBINEAU

Don't "dear father-in-law" me, you cad! You've taken advantage of this young woman . . . Miss Gaveston . . . my niece! You've defiled my home! Get out! And take her with you!

OSCAR

I don't want her, thanks anyway! Monsieur Rubineau, if a man wants to keep his home undefiled, he should start by not introducing his own little weaknesses . . . charming though they may be.

RUBINEAU

Monsieur!

OSCAR

Oh, I've known her for a long time . . . your niece! Darling Stephana.

RUBINEAU

Good heavens!

OSCAR

My dear father-in-law . . . we all experience an occasional resurgence of youthful indiscretion . . . (*Patting Rubineau's belly.*) You know what I mean, you old Romeo!

RUBINEAU

Old Romeo! . . . you know . . .

STEPHANA

Forgive me, Alcibiades! I let it slip!

RUBINEAU

I'm done for! Ruined! (*He falls into a chair.*)

OSCAR

Calm yourself, my dear . . . (*Aside.*) You know, I don't know what to call him anymore . . . (*Aloud.*) My dear . . . associate! You have nothing to fear from me.

RUBINEAU

Cruel Stephana, she was cheating on me, and with whom?

OSCAR

Do we need to spell it out for you? It was me she loved.

RUBINEAU

At the same time as me?

OSCAR

She's quite capable of loving two men at the same time.

RUBINEAU

You cheated on me like that, mademoiselle, and you have the audacity to demand twenty thousand francs from me?

STEPHANA

No, twenty-five.

RUBINEAU

Twenty-five? Never!

STEPHANA

We'll see.

OSCAR

Come on, Alcibiades, you were cheating on your wife. Why would you think you could stop our . . . your sweet friend from cheating on us both, at least a little?

STEPHANA

Just a tiny bit.

RUBINEAU

It's all a bit hard to digest! You must understand, monsieur, I can't let you marry my daughter now.

OSCAR

No, I don't understand.

RUBINEAU

Regardless . . . a son-in-law sharing a mistress with his father-in-law. That puts an end to things.

OSCAR

No, it just complicates them.

STEPHANA

Come on, Sosthène, be reasonable!

SCENE II

The same, AUGUSTE

AUGUSTE, *entering.*

Papa, Uncle Gaveston is here.

RUBINEAU

My brother-in-law!

AUGUSTE

With his wife and Mademoiselle Stephana's sisters.

STEPHANA

Damn!

RUBINEAU, *stunned.*

Stephana's sisters! This is going to get ugly! I am going to lose my mind! My head is killing me! I need some time to compose myself. Welcome them for me. Go get your mother! I need an icepack for my head! (*He exits*, *agitated.*)

AUGUSTE

What's wrong with Papa? Is he losing it?

OSCAR

Ignore him. He's just having an attack.

STEPHANA

Yes! He has a toothache.

AUGUSTE

Good! Serves him right!

OSCAR

Serves him right? For what?

AUGUSTE

I asked his permission to marry my cousin, Stephana, and he sent me packing.

OSCAR

He was right, young man!

AUGUSTE

Why?

OSCAR

Because . . . because Miss Stephana is engaged to someone else.

AUGUSTE

Engaged to someone else! What a disappointment! What a blow!

STEPHANA, *whispering.*

You stay out if it!

OSCAR, *whispering.*

Oh no! (*Humming.*) The father, the son, and the son-in-law, that's too much! A little modesty, my dear!

SCENE 12

The same, SIR GAVESTON, his wife and six daughters, without RUBINEAU

SIR GAVESTON

Hello! I'm Sir Gaveston.

OSCAR, *greeting him.*

I'm the son-in-law, sir.

SIR GAVESTON

Perfect!

AUGUSTE

And I'm the son.

SIR GAVESTON, *pointing to Stephana.*

And this must be the daughter?

AUGUSTE, *to Gaveston.*

Of her father.

SIR GAVESTON

Come give me a kiss, miss.

STEPHANA

Gladly! (*She kisses him.*)

SIR GAVESTON

She is charming.

CORPULENCIA

Come give me a kiss as well, miss.

STEPHANA

Of course!

THE SIX DAUGHTERS

Us, too!

STEPHANA

Looks like I'm making the rounds again!

AUGUSTE, *to Oscar.*

Look how close they are! Oh, how I long to be a part of that family!

OSCAR

I already told you, Stephana is engaged to someone else.

AUGUSTE

Maybe she is, but what about the other six! I'm going to get Mom to help me choose a different one.

OSCAR

And your sister?

AUGUSTE

She'll be happy to see you. Come with me. (*To Stephana.*) Miss, make Sir Gaveston comfortable. I'll go get my parents. (*He exits.*)

OSCAR, *greeting them.*

Madame, Sir, Miss . . . (*Whispering to Stephana.*) Watch it!

STEPHANA, *whispering.*

No worries.

SCENE 13

SIR GAVESTON, CORPULENCIA, their six daughters, STEPHANA

STEPHANA

So, Uncle, have you seen much of Paris since you arrived?

SIR GAVESTON

Oh yes! We saw the Eiffel Tower.

CORPULENCIA

The Grévin wax museum.

NELLY

Miss Helyett.[27]

SIR GAVESTON

And the slaughterhouses!

STEPHANA

You visited slaughterhouses?

SIR GAVESTON

For science. I wanted to see if the blood of French cattle contains as much potassium chloride as the blood of American cattle.

STEPHANA

How charming.

CORPULENCIA

And Sir Gaveston discovered that it contains three hundred fifty-nine thousandths, compared to three hundred thirty-six.

JENNY

With a lot of hypoxanthine.

LUCY

And a fair amount of creatine.

MARY

And some cholesterine.

BABY

And a certain quantity of margarine.

STEPHANA

This is all so enlightening. People just don't visit slaughterhouses enough.

SIR GAVESTON

I'm going to write a report on it for the Academy of Rocky Mountain Butchers.

STEPHANA

Most curious. (*She shivers.*) And where are you staying?

SIR GAVESTON

We're staying at the Hôtel Modèle.

STEPHANA

I'm afraid I don't know it.

CORPULENCIA

It's in the big square with the bronze statue of a pudgy woman.

STEPHANA

Place de la République!

SIR GAVESTON

I see. So that's the Republic, that pudgy woman?

STEPHANA

Yes.

SIR GAVESTON

She seems sturdy.

STEPHANA

Does she? How do you like your hotel?

SIR GAVESTON

It's very nice! Very posh!

CORPULENCIA

Last night we went to the Moulin Rouge.

STEPHANA

The Moulin Rouge?

SIR GAVESTON

For science!

STEPHANA

Of course, for science! And what did you observe?

JENNY

We observed that people have a lot of fun there.

CORPULENCIA

Oh yes! A fat man pinched me.

SIR GAVESTON

Corpulencia!

CORPULENCIA

I didn't say where, dear.

STEPHANA

I know where . . .

SIR GAVESTON

Really, you know?

STEPHANA

Yes, it's a custom.

SIR GAVESTON

Have you been to the Moulin Rouge?

STEPHANA

Only once, with Mother and Daddy . . . How about those young women!

BETTY

Do you know how to dance like that?

STEPHANA

A little.

ALL

Teach us, Cousin!

STEPHANA

I don't know if I should . . .

CORPULENCIA

Let me join in, Niece.

SIR GAVESTON

Me, too.

STEPHANA

It's just that I need accompaniment . . . even just a piano.

SIR GAVESTON

Go play the piano, Corpulencia.

CORPULENCIA

Gladly, dear.

STEPHANA

I.

I know a spot by Place Pigalle,
A marvelous establishment.
The gayest in the capital!
Every evening there's well spent,
Rubbing elbows with the who's whos,
M'sieur Joie-de-vivre and Old Man Booze.

Chorus

You'll have a grand time *au Moulin*,
Drink and dance and schmooze
At the Moulin Rouge!
You'll have a grand time *au Moulin*,
So move your feet, shuffle, shuffle off and dance.

(*All repeat the chorus.*)

II.

Then in the garden full of light,
We'll ride white mules and put on airs.
Can you imagine such a sight?
Passers-by giving looks and stares
As we trot them 'round so joyfully,
Galloping, jumping gracefully.
(Chorus)

III.

We'll visit the pretty almehs,[28]
Who dance from th' elephant's belly,[29]
Then from the poshest balcony
Listen to the elephant sing.

He puffs his . . . cheeks in serenades
And that's what turns the windmill's blades.
(Chorus)

SCENE 14

The same, MADAME RUBINEAU, AUGSUTE, CHARLOTTE, then RUBINEAU

MADAME RUBINEAU
What is going on here?

STEPHANA
Uh oh!

MADAME RUBINEAU
Has my salon become a cabaret?

SIR GAVESTON
A cabaret? What's that?

MADAME RUBINEAU, *calling.*
Rubineau! Rubineau!

RUBINEAU, *running in.*
What are you yelling about? What's wrong?

MADAME RUBINEAU
These lunatics were dancing around like this! (*She flails her arms and legs.*)

STEPHANA, *introducing them.*
Monsieur and Madame Rubineau!

CORPULENCIA
The sister-in-law.

ALL THE GIRLS, *running to Madame Rubineau.*
Auntie! Dear Auntie!

RUBINEAU
What do you mean, Auntie?

SIR GAVESTON
I am Sir Gaveston. Hello.

RUBINEAU
Gaveston! . . . Damn!

(*Gaveston steps forward and places his daughters to the left. Auguste moves to the far right.*)

MADAME RUBINEAU

But why were they doing this? (*She gesticulates.*)

RUBINEAU

They were praying. Yes! That's how Mormons pray. Muslims raise their arms, Mormons raise their feet.

MADAME RUBINEAU

Really? How charming! I certainly didn't expect that . . .

SIR GAVESTON

Let me introduce one of my six wives, Corpulencia, number six. She may be fat, but she's good and fertile.

MADAME RUBINEAU

So she is wife number six?

RUBINEAU, *out of sorts.*

This is my wife. She's skinny . . . well, no, she's fat . . . and fertile . . . by which I mean . . . oh, forget it! This is my wife.

SIR GAVESTON

Hello.

MADAME RUBINEAU

Madame, you're a mother, and so am I. We understand each other. Come, let us embrace.

CORPULENCIA

Of course. (*They embrace.*)

AUGUSTE, *looking at them.*

Well, isn't that a pretty picture!

SIR GAVESTON

And these are my six daughters: Nelly, Lucy, Betty, Jenny, Pretty, and Baby.

MADAME RUBINEAU

You're forgetting the seventh.

ALL

The seventh?

MADAME RUBINEAU

Yes, the one who was singing over there.

RUBINEAU, *yelling and holding his jaw.*

Oh, my tooth! (*He crosses up to the left.*)

SIR GAVESTON

This young lady is not my daughter.

MADAME RUBINEAU

Not your daughter!

SIR GAVESTON

Isn't she yours?

RUBINEAU, *yelling.*

Oh no! (*He sits on the table.*)

CORPULENCIA

What's wrong with him?

SIR GAVESTON

A toothache. He doesn't know what to do.

AUGUSTE

Say, Uncle, that's quite the brood you've got there.

SIR GAVESTON

My brood?

AUGUSTE

Yes, these seven young women.

SIR GAVESTON

I only have six daughters.

AUGUSTE

Come on, you joker, don't tease me.

MADAME RUBINEAU, *whispering.*

How strange that Sir Gaveston doesn't recognize his own daughter, Stephana!

RUBINEAU

She must be illegitimate . . .

SCENE 15

The same, OSCAR

OSCAR

My dear father-in-law, you called for me?

MADAME RUBINEAU

Ah! Here's my son-in-law.

SIR GAVESTON

Your son-in-law? (*To Stephana.*) You're getting married, mademoiselle?

STEPHANA

Me? Not on your life! You're thinking of my sister, Charlotte. I'm Stephana.

RUBINEAU, *whispering to Oscar.*

My good friend, I'll add ten thousand francs to my daughter's dowry if you get me out of this!

OSCAR, *whispering.*

Ten thousand! Count on me! Keep him busy for a minute. (*He exits.*)

RUBINEAU, *aside.*

Keep him busy? How? I can't exactly invite them to skip rope with me. (*Whispering to his wife.*) Keep him busy for a moment.

MADAME RUBINEAU, *whispering.*

Me? Why?

RUBINEAU, *whispering.*

He seems bored! Entertain him.

MADAME RUBINEAU, *whispering.*

I'd be happy to. (*Aloud.*) So, Sir Gaveston, you've come to France to launch your little invention.

SIR GAVESTON

Yes! And to find a seventh wife.

AUGUSTE

A seventh wife! Ooh la la!

MADAME RUBINEAU, *admiringly.*

Seven wives! What a man!

SIR GAVESTON

Yes, and your daughter has caught my eye.

CHARLOTTE.

Me?

STEPHANA

No, me! (*Aside.*) Now that could be a nice setup!

AUGUSTE

So you're still pretending that Miss Stephana isn't your daughter?

SIR GAVESTON

I am, because she's your sister.

AUGUSTE

I can prove she's not my sister! I wanted to marry her!

SIR GAVESTON

Well, she's not my daughter! In fact, I'm sorely tempted to make her my seventh wife!

STEPHANA

Milord, milord!

MADAME RUBINEAU, *whispering to Rubineau.*

Well then, monsieur, might she be *your* illegitimate child?

RUBINEAU

How can you think that, my dear? (*Aside.*) Where is Oscar?

MADAME RUBINEAU, *aside.*

This all seems a bit fishy!

RUBINEAU

I'll show them around the house.

SIR GAVESTON

The house?

RUBINEAU

Yes, it's most curious! From a scientific point of view. It contains a remarkable variety of microbes.

MADAME RUBINEAU

Microbes? But, Sosthène . . .

RUBINEAU, *whispering.*

Leave me to it; it'll entertain him. (*Aloud.*) Come with me, brother-in-law.

SIR GAVESTON

Gladly. Are you coming, Corpulencia?

CORPULENCIA

Gladly! Come along, misses.

THE SIX GIRLS

Yes, mother.

RUBINEAU, *leading them to the right.*

Come through here. After you. Won't you go! (*He shoves them out to the right and closes the door on them once they've gone through.*) And there you are!

AUGUSTE

What are you doing, Papa?

RUBINEAU

I'm locking them up.

STEPHANA

You're locking them up?

MADAME RUBINEAU

Sosthène!

STEPHANA

But you're holding them against their will.

RUBINEAU

I'm locking them up because I suspect these Americans of being devious pickpockets.

MADAME RUBINEAU and CHARLOTTE

Oh my heavens!

STEPHANA

It's not true! He's lying!

OSCAR, *returning.*

There, it's done. Where are they?

RUBINEAU

They're looking for microbes.

OSCAR, *whispering.*

Okay . . . I just sent a note to the police station asking them to send someone to check on this suspicious American family.

STEPHANA

That's too much!

RUBINEAU

Perfect! Oscar, my daughter is yours!

OSCAR

And the extra ten thousand francs?

RUBINEAU

We'll talk about that later.

OSCAR

Seriously?

SCENE 16

The same, AUNT FLORA

AUNT FLORA

Hello . . . ladies and gentlemen!

STEPHANA, *aside.*

My aunt! What the devil?

RUBINEAU, *aside.*

Mother Flora! I shudder to think . . .

OSCAR, *whispering.*

The aunt . . . well, that's ruined!

AUNT FLORA

I'm looking for Stephana. How's it going, Oscar sweetie?

MADAME RUBINEAU

Oscar sweetie? What's that supposed to mean?

AUNT FLORA

So you know my old pal Rubineau, too?

MADAME RUBINEAU

Her old pal Rubineau?

RUBINEAU

Yes! It's an American expression.

MADAME RUBINEAU

Ah . . . madame is American!

AUNT FLORA

Me? I'm from rue du Plâtre in Paris. Stephana wrote me saying that she was staying here. So I said to myself: "Old girl, gather up your knicks and your knacks and go buddy up to your niece and your old pal Rubineau."

AUGUSTE, *to Oscar.*

Papa is busted!

OSCAR

Yeah, I do believe that's all she wrote!

RUBINEAU, *aside.*

I think I'm going to be sick.

MADAME RUBINEAU

What's that supposed to mean? Do you know this woman?

RUBINEAU

I met her once . . . by chance . . . in the Vendôme column.

AUNT FLORA

You don't know me? Go on! You think you're better than me, lover boy? I'm the one who answers the door when you come to see your sweet little Stephana.

MADAME RUBINEAU

What is this I'm hearing?

OSCAR

No, can't be! Madame is mistaken! She's confusing him with someone else.

AUNT FLORA

Don't you be a smart aleck, Oscar! Are you going to say that you don't know me either? Who brings you cocoa in bed each morning?

OSCAR

Madame!

AUGUSTE

Cocoa, not too shabby!

CHARLOTTE, *crying.*

Cocoa! Do you hear this, mother?

MADAME RUBINEAU

All right, that's it! Just who is this Stephana?

STEPHANA

You really want to know? She's independent! She's a modern woman! Too long a victim of men! A repentant Magdalene who wants nothing more than to join respectable society.

AUNT FLORA

Yeah! She just wants to get her act together, that brave little thing, so she can care for her dear Aunt Flora! After having been the mistress of those two dummies!

MADAME RUBINEAU

Dummies? Their mistress?

CHARLOTTE

Both of them?

AUGUSTE

At the same time?

STEPHANA

I've had enough of these greedy old peacocks!

AUNT FLORA

Me too!

STEPHANA

Everything is ruined, but it's your own fault, Sosthène! I forgive the sixty thousand francs you owe me. Good riddance! Come along, Auntie! (*She exits with Aunt Flora.*)

AUGUSTE

She's abandoning me! Stephana! Stephana! (*He exits after her.*)

OSCAR

Well, you got what you asked for! And then some!

RUBINEAU

Too much!

MADAME RUBINEAU

Sosthène, Sosthène, you're nothing but a dirty cheater! And you, Monsieur de Pompignac, get out! Get out!

OSCAR

Please let me explain, madame . . .

CHARLOTTE, *crying.*

Mommy! What a mess!

MADAME RUBINEAU

Quiet, you! I understand everything now! My home has become a modern Sodom!

OSCAR

That's a bit of an exaggeration, don't you think?

MADAME RUBINEAU, *glassy-eyed as though hallucinating.*

Everything is becoming clear . . . And I was going to make you some tea last night! And bring it to you there in our wedding bed, (*Sobbing.*) where you first kissed me softly on my virginal forehead . . . Get out, you shameless monster! You make me sick! As for us, my daughter and me, we're going to enter a convent!

CHARLOTTE

Mother, no!

OSCAR, *to Rubineau.*

This is all your fault! If you had just given Stephana what she wanted . . .

RUBINEAU, *aside.*

Oh no . . . I'm thoroughly enjoying my wife's tantrum.

(*We hear knocking from the right.*)

OSCAR

Who's that knocking over there?

RUBINEAU

That's just the others . . . I locked them up.

CHARLOTTE

Oh, Daddy! Oh, Mother! Oh, Oscar! What a mess! What a mess!

(*She collapses.*)

OSCAR

Mademoiselle!

MADAME RUBINEAU

Stand back, you cad! (*To her husband.*) Look what you've done to your child!

RUBINEAU

Our child!

MADAME RUBINEAU

And she'll be the last! I'm closing up shop!

RUBINEAU

I couldn't care less about that! You should've closed up shop on me a long time ago! When someone keeps serving you swill, madame, eventually you end up looking elsewhere for the good wine!

MADAME RUBINEAU

That's enough, monsieur! We are finished! Someone else will appreciate this swill that you turn up your nose at!

RUBINEAU

Someone else? I pity him!

MADAME RUBINEAU

Yes, someone else! You can go rot at your depraved orgies! I'm divorcing you! I'll go become someone's mistress. Come, Charlotte!

SCENE 17

The same, a POLICE SERGEANT followed by two officers, then AUGUSTE

POLICE SERGEANT, *upstage.*

Nobody's going anywhere.

MADAME RUBINEAU

But . . .

POLICE SERGEANT

I'm telling you, even if you were the emperor Napoleon himself, no one is getting through.

OSCAR

Allow me, sergeant . . .

POLICE SERGEANT

I don't allow anything.

RUBINEAU

Yes, but . . .

POLICE SERGEANT

Least of all that! (*To Madame Rubineau.*) So are you the suspicious American?

MADAME RUBINEAU, *revolted.*

Me, an American . . .

AUGUSTE

No, that's Mother!

POLICE SERGEANT

That doesn't prove anything!

OSCAR

Sergeant, I'm the one . . .

POLICE SERGEANT

Oh, so you're the one! Cuff this suspicious American!

OSCAR

No! I'm the one who wrote to the station alerting you of the presence of this . . . shady American.

POLICE SERGEANT

So where is this shady American?

(*We hear knocking from the door on the right.*)

OSCAR

He's holed up in there with his family, and he won't leave. (*We see Auguste enter upstage.*)

POLICE SERGEANT, *toward the door on the right.*

Open up, in the name of the law!

SIR GAVESTON, *offstage.*

Open it yourself! The key is on your side.

POLICE SERGEANT

Well, what do you know? They were locked in from the outside. (*He opens the door.*)

SCENE 18

The same, SIR GAVESTON, CORPULENCIA, and their six daughters

SIR GAVESTON

What kind of a sick joke is this?

POLICE SERGEANT

So you're the American?

SIR GAVESTON

Yes! I'm Sir Gaveston, and this is my wife and my six daughters.

POLICE SERGEANT

Look me in the eyes.

SIR GAVESTON

I'm looking.

POLICE SERGEANT, *to Oscar.*

Why did you tell me he was shady? He's not shady at all!

OSCAR

I, well . . .

POLICE SERGEANT

Your letter to the station did indeed say "suspicious."

SIR GAVESTON

Me, suspicious?

CORPULENCIA

Suspicious!

THE SIX DAUGHTERS

Suspicious!

POLICE SERGEANT, *to the officers.*

All right, now I see it! Seize the whole family! I'm going to search them. (*The officers grab Sir Gaveston.*)

SIR GAVESTON

Search me?

CORPULENCIA and the GIRLS, *screaming.*

You're going to search Daddy? That's terrible! That's not right!

POLICE SERGEANT

Resist and I'll knock your block off!

SIR GAVESTON

My block? I'd prefer to keep it. Go ahead and search.

POLICE SERGEANT, *finding one of his buzzers.*

A tin of sardines. Looks like we've got a live one, boys!

SIR GAVESTON

A what?

POLICE SERGEANT

Quiet you! I'll ask the questions here! What is this box?

SIR GAVESTON

It's my invention.

POLICE SERGEANT

Probably got a little spring-loaded something or other in it, eh?

SIR GAVESTON

Yes.

POLICE SERGEANT

He admits it! Search the women!

THE SIX GIRLS and CORPULENCIA

Help! Help us!

SIR GAVESTON

Well, my brother-in-law Rubineau certainly has a special way of welcoming us!

POLICE SERGEANT, *to the officers.*

What'd you find on the women?

FIRST OFFICER

Three little Eiffel Towers.

SECOND OFFICER

Twenty-five matchbooks and two tops.

POLICE SERGEANT

I get the picture! These dolls are just a bunch of shoplifters.

THE WOMEN

Dolls?

POLICE SERGEANT

Let's go, everyone to the station!

ALL, *yelling.*

To the station!

SIR GAVESTON

Dolls! My daughters! You're taking *me* to the station? Never! You can't arrest me!

CORPULENCIA

Me either!

AUGUSTE

Oh boy!

POLICE SERGEANT

Let's go! Come on! Move it!

SIR GAVESTON

I refuse! I'm American.

POLICE SERGEANT, *to one of his officers.*

You seize the old man! I'll take care of the woman and the girls!

SIR GAVESTON

I must protest!

CORPULENCIA

Napoleon! Napoleon!

POLICE SERGEANT

No politics here! Let's go!

(*The officers drag them by force, all yelling and struggling.*)

POLICE SERGEANT, *pointing to Madame Rubineau.*

And that fat one there, too!

MADAME RUBINEAU

Me?

CHARLOTTE

Mommy?

POLICE SERGEANT

The girl, too! Get 'em all! The whole gang!

OSCAR

You're letting them arrest your wife?

RUBINEAU

She'll be back soon enough, like always!

ACT III

The action takes place in a suite in the Hôtel Modèle. There are doors upstage on the right and the left. A table on the right is covered with newspapers, an overnight bag, and a small handbell. There is a sofa next to the table and several chairs. Upstage a trunk is placed on a folding stand.

SCENE I

JULES, RUBINEAU, OSCAR

(*They enter upstage, led by Jules.*)

JULES

Come in, gentlemen. Here we are, room 33.

RUBINEAU

Room 33, and this is Sir Gaveston's room?

JULES

Yes, Sir Gaveston's room. But we just call it room 33.

OSCAR

The guests staying here just arrived from Le Havre, right?

JULES

Two days ago. I'm sure about that!

RUBINEAU

With six girls and a large woman?

JULES

That describes them perfectly. The gentleman returned late last night and asked the clerk not to wake him before noon.

OSCAR

Excellent! Thank you, my friend. You can go.

JULES

If you gentlemen need me, I'll be in the corridor.

SCENE 2

RUBINEAU, OSCAR

OSCAR

In the *corridor*? How Parisian! Say, you never thanked me for getting you your daughter and wife back.

RUBINEAU

Thank you for my daughter . . . How do you think Gaveston will react when he sees us?

OSCAR

Badly at first. But he'll warm up to us once he finds out he was released thanks to us.

RUBINEAU

I'm surprised Auguste isn't already here. You know, I don't want any trouble with Sir Gaveston.

OSCAR

I believe it! A relative as rich as him . . .

RUBINEAU

And whose six daughters my son is in love with.

OSCAR

Wait a minute. I thought he was in love with Stephana.

RUBINEAU

Friend, don't say that name in front of me.

OSCAR

Can you believe the little tart was cheating on us both?

RUBINEAU

Excuse me, she was cheating on you with me.

OSCAR

You think . . .

RUBINEAU

She told me so.

OSCAR

She said the same to me!

RUBINEAU, *extending a hand.*

So we have no reason to be angry with each other.

OSCAR

Not at all! Now, let's wake Sir Gaveston.

RUBINEAU

Yes! But which room is his? This one or that one?

OSCAR

It's one of the two!

RUBINEAU

Unless there's a third.

OSCAR

That's just it, I don't want to risk walking in on the six girls.

RUBINEAU

I'm with you! Americans are so prudish. Is there no bell? Ah, there's one!

(*Oscar sees the bell on the table and rings it.*)

OSCAR

That'll get their attention.

RUBINEAU

Let's give him a minute to wake up. Oh, my friend, what a disaster, regardless! And we're in this together, you know. The fortune belongs to my wife. If she divorces me, the money goes with her. I'll be poor as a pauper, naked as a jaybird! You get the picture, right?

OSCAR

Yeah, I get it. It's not pretty!

RUBINEAU

If I have nothing, what kind of a dowry can I give my daughter? Besides, Madame Rubineau would never let Charlotte marry you!

OSCAR

Pshaw. Mademoiselle Charlotte is in love with me. She'll forgive me and convince her mother to forgive me, too.

RUBINEAU

You, maybe. But not me. What a mess!

OSCAR

Is the Mormon ever going to wake up?

RUBINEAU

Gosh! He's going to be furious after a night in the clink! I'm scared.

OSCAR

I'm the one taking all the blame!

RUBINEAU

You messed everything up in the first place! It's only right that you should fix it.

OSCAR

Should I ring again?

RUBINEAU

Go ahead.

(*Oscar rings the bell again.*)

OSCAR

If that doesn't wake him, then he's dead.

SCENE 3

The same, SIR GAVESTON, CORPULENCIA, their six daughters, AUGUSTE

SIR GAVESTON, *arriving from upstage.*

Finally! Here we are!

OSCAR

And look! Their bedroom was back there.

RUBINEAU, *running to Sir Gaveston.*

A thousand apologies, my dear cousin!

SIR GAVESTON

Get back!

ALL THE WOMEN

Get back!

RUBINEAU

That's what I was afraid of.

SIR GAVESTON

Monsieur, from a scientific point of view, there is not one cousin in a hundred thousand who would have acted as you did!

OSCAR

If I may, Monsieur Rubineau was misled by an anonymous letter.

SIR GAVESTON

Really?

RUBINEAU

In which I was led to believe that the Brotherhood of the Trowel was going to pay me a visit.

CORPULENCIA

The Brotherhood of the Trowel?

OSCAR

Yes! A troop of pranksters who act out their farces in people's homes.

RUBINEAU

My goodness, you must understand . . . I'm a father . . . like you, you're a father, too . . . We are both fathers . . . Anyway, I apologize.

AUGUSTE

After all, it was Father who got you released. Let's let bygones be bygones and embrace once again! (*He moves to embrace Sir Gaveston's daughters.*)

CORPULENCIA

How scandalous!

THE SIX GIRLS

Oh no! Not scandalous at all!

SIR GAVESTON

I accept your apology. My wife and daughters do as well! Still, spending the night in the police station is hardly comfortable.

CORPULENCIA

And when I asked what we were doing there, that one officer replied: "You're waiting for the police wagon."

THE SIX GIRLS

The police wagon!

RUBINEAU

My poor cousin! What did you do all night at the police station?

CORPULENCIA

Me, I slept.

THE SIX GIRLS

Not us!

SIR GAVESTON

Me either. I was thinking about your daughter!

RUBINEAU

About Charlotte?

SIR GAVESTON

No! Stephana!

OSCAR, *to Rubineau.*

He still thinks she's your daughter!

RUBINEAU

But, my dear friend, my wife already told you that Stephana is not our daughter.

SIR GAVESTON

I know . . . but your wife seems a bit batty.

RUBINEAU

Batty?

SIR GAVESTON

Due to marital problems . . . But that makes no difference. I find your daughter charming.

CORPULENCIA

Charming!

AUGUSTE, *to the girls who now surround him.*

So, my cousins, is everything better now?

NELLY

Oh yes, Cousin.

JENNY

We talked about you all night.

NELLY

We knew that you were convinced of our innocence, Cousin.

AUGUSTE

Your innocence! Yes, of course, you're all so innocent! And did the officers treat you well?

JENNY

Not at all!

BABY

They jostled us around!

LUCY

Because we're women . . .

MARY

If we were men . . .

AUGUSTE

Then they would have knocked you out!

RUBINEAU

Were you at least able to rest a bit?

SIR GAVESTON

No, I just got back from the station.

OSCAR

That's odd. The bellhop told us not to wake room 33 since they were out cold.

CORPULENCIA

Room 33, that's us!

OSCAR

I even rang you like this! (*He rings the bell.*)

RUBINEAU

And you came immediately.

SCENE 4

The same, DE LONGUEFUGUE

DE LONGUEFUGUE

Who in the world is ringing a bell in my apartment? (*He enters in boxer shorts and shirt sleeves, his boots in hand.*)

ALL THE GIRLS

How scandalous! (*They all run to the right.*)

SIR GAVESTON

A man in my abode!

DE LONGUEFUGUE

In your abode? Well, you have some nerve! What are you doing here, monsieur?

RUBINEAU

What about you?

(*Corpulencia covers her eyes.*)

OSCAR

Why, that's the editor of *High Life in Honfleur*!

RUBINEAU

He's the one who interviewed me.

DE LONGUEFUGUE

Yes, I recognize you! You're the Marquis de La Rochebrune.

RUBINEAU

Me? No, I'm Rubineau, of rue du Sentier.

DE LONGUEFUGUE

Ah, yes! The Mormon with six daughters! Of course!

SIR GAVESTON

No, I'm the one with six daughters.

DE LONGUEFUGUE

Very well, but what are you doing in my home?

SIR GAVESTON

But you're the one in my sitting room!

DE LONGUEFUGUE

Your sitting room?

AUGUSTE

Goodness, yes, in room 33.

DE LONGUEFUGUE

But 33, the two hunchbacks, that's me, isn't it?

SIR GAVESTON

You're mistaken. It's us.

JULES, *entering.*

A letter for room 33.

SIR GAVESTON and DE LONGUEFUGUE

Give it here!

JULES, *looking at De Longuefugue.*

What are you wearing? You're going to ruin the hotel's good name!

RUBINEAU

There, young man, is this monsieur staying in room 33?

JULES

Him? No, he's in room 22.

DE LONGUEFUGUE

Room 22!

ALL

Ah!

JULES

You even said when they gave you your room number: "22, the two hens. That'll be easy to remember!"

RUBINEAU

But you remembered 33, the two hunchbacks!

DE LONGUEFUGUE

I've made a terrible mistake! A thousand apologies!

CORPULENCIA

Have you been sleeping in my bed?

DE LONGUEFUGUE, *to Jules.*

We'll change the sheets. Here, hold my boots.

JULES, *taking the boots.*

Right away, sir, we'll change the sheets. Travelers come and go quickly, don't they! (*He exits carrying the boots.*)

DE LONGUEFUGUE

Permit me to finish dressing.

AUGUSTE

How are you still not dressed?

DE LONGUEFUGUE

How absentminded of me! I apologize again! This has never happened to me before. (*He exits to the left.*)

SCENE 5

RUBINEAU, SIR GAVESTON, OSCAR, CORPULENCIA, AUGUSTE

AUGUSTE

Now there's a spectacular idiot!

CORPULENCIA

What's that letter, dear?

SIR GAVESTON

Oh yes! (*To Rubineau.*) Look at that, it's from your wife!

RUBINEAU

From my wife?

SIR GAVESTON

Yes! (*He reads.*) "If you are as kind as you are handsome, you will hear the grievances of a poor, suffering soul. I will be at your hotel at two o'clock." Signed "Hortense, the former Madame Rubineau."

RUBINEAU

"The former"? She's crazy!

SIR GAVESTON

Marital problems. What did you do to her?

RUBINEAU

Me? Why, my heart is purer than mother's milk!

AUGUSTE

You shouldn't say such things, Father.

RUBINEAU

That's enough from you, imp!

OSCAR

My dear father-in-law, we need to get close to Madame Rubineau to bring her around to our side . . . and that will be no small task!

RUBINEAU

It's going to take everything we've got!

AUGUSTE

I'm staying to speak with Cousin Gaveston.

RUBINEAU

Stay if you want. Goodbye, my dear Gaveston. I stand before you a man afflicted.

SIR GAVESTON

Indeed!

RUBINEAU

Yes, and you have six wives. Astounding!

SIR GAVESTON

I have the right to twelve.

OSCAR

Twelve! What a marvel! Goodbye, good sir and madame. Come, father-in-law.

RUBINEAU, *exiting.*

Twelve wives for one man! How do they remember who's who?

(*They exit.*)

SCENE 6

SIR GAVESTON, AUGUSTE, CORPULENCIA

SIR GAVESTON

Shall we sit?

CORPULENCIA

Yes, please!

(*They sit.*)

AUGUSTE

Uncle, I have, like Saint Paul, found my road to Damascus.

SIR GAVESTON

Saint Paul? We have a Hotel Saint Paul in Quebec.

CORPULENCIA

It's very nice.

AUGUSTE

It's not the same thing. I mean that I want to become a Mormon. Is it difficult?

SIR GAVESTON

You, a Mormon? What do you think, Corpulencia?

CORPULENCIA

He's a bit delicate . . .

AUGUSTE

That doesn't matter! I have the right mindset. You say a man can have up to twelve wives in your community?

SIR GAVESTON

No more!

CORPULENCIA

If he's in good health!

SIR GAVESTON

Our doctors determine that.

AUGUSTE

Your doctors?

SIR GAVESTON

Yes! They interview the current wives and decide whether the household can increase based on the reports.

AUGUSTE

A question: Can you marry all twelve at once?

SIR GAVESTON

No! You need some time in between each marriage.

CORPULENCIA

Yes, you have to wait two weeks.

SIR GAVESTON

So that each new wife has time to get used to the household routines.

AUGUSTE

Two weeks! You don't think that in a week she might be able to . . .

CORPULENCIA

Oh no!

SIR GAVESTON

We may be Mormons, but we're still just men.

AUGUSTE

I understand. Well, Uncle, I come to you a catechumen.

CORPULENCIA

A catechumen?

AUGUSTE

Yes, your Mormon catechism has seduced me. And I come to ask you for the hands of your six daughters en bloc.

SIR GAVESTON

En bloc?

AUGUSTE

Yes, it's a parliamentary expression. Please note that, while I am asking for them en bloc, I will marry them one at a time after the appropriate interval, as you explained.

SIR GAVESTON

One every two weeks?

AUGUSTE

Yes.

SIR GAVESTON, *rising.*

It's an acceptable offer, but keep in mind that I'm not officially accepting your request.

AUGUSTE

But why?

CORPULENCIA

That has to be made by your mother and father.

SIR GAVESTON

With two witnesses.

AUGUSTE

Two witnesses!

SIR GAVESTON

Yes, to testify in case of withdrawal.

AUGUSTE

Okay, wait! And if there's a withdrawal?

CORPULENCIA

An indemnity must be paid to the girls.

AUGUSTE

So, a penalty?

SIR GAVESTON

Yes, a penalty.

AUGUSTE

You're very pragmatic, you Mormons.

SIR GAVESTON

And we don't give dowries.

AUGUSTE

Understood. I'll return with Dad, Mom, and two witnesses. (*He stands.*) Would you permit me to go kiss my cousins?

CORPULENCIA

No! After the wedding, not before!

AUGUSTE

Not even just a little sample?

SIR GAVESTON

Never!

AUGUSTE

Well, then, see you soon! Tell the girls that I love them all!

SIR GAVESTON

En bloc?

AUGUSTE

Yes, en bloc! Look at me, I'm a Mormon! Papa's going to be so surprised!

SCENE 7
SIR GAVESTON, CORPULENCIA, then DE LONGUEFUGUE

SIR GAVESTON

Now I can get comfortable! (*He takes his slippers from the trunk on the folding stand.*)

CORPULENCIA

You need it, my dear.

SIR GAVESTON, *upstage.*

Yes, yes. Much needed. (*He sits to take off his boots.*)

CORPULENCIA

Let me help you. (*She kneels before him and helps remove his boots.*)

SIR GAVESTON

He's not bad for a Frenchman, that little cousin of ours.

CORPULENCIA

Is his father rich?

SIR GAVESTON

Yes . . . he could make my six daughters very happy. (*He places his boots on the floor upstage, puts on his slippers, and comes to the fore.*) Corpulencia, I need to speak to you about something serious.

CORPULENCIA

I'm listening, my love.

SIR GAVESTON

Corpulencia, my dear wife, I am in love.

CORPULENCIA, *lowering her eyes.*

Oh, my love!

SIR GAVESTON

No! Not with you!

CORPULENCIA

Oh . . . I thought . . . I'm sorry.

SIR GAVESTON

I'm in love with someone else.

CORPULENCIA

It's your right, my dear husband!

SIR GAVESTON

Corpulencia, when we left America, your companions, my five other wives, delegated their powers to you.

CORPULENCIA

That's not saying much.

SIR GAVESTON

It is what it is. I want to know what you would say to our doctor when I ask him for the right to take a seventh wife.

CORPULENCIA

Speaking for all of your wives, I would answer that you could rise to the occasion.

SIR GAVESTON

Thank you! I expected no less from you.

CORPULENCIA

And who did you fall in love with, my dear?

SIR GAVESTON

The charming Stephana. What do you think of her?

CORPULENCIA

Very nice.

SIR GAVESTON

So, you think you could get along with her?

CORPULENCIA

Perfectly, yes.

DE LONGUEFUGUE, *entering now wearing pants.*

Excuse me . . . I don't have any soap. You wouldn't by chance have a bar you could lend me?

CORPULENCIA, *covering her eyes with her hands.*

Oh!

SIR GAVESTON

When you are more appropriately dressed, yes.

DE LONGUEFUGUE

But to appropriately dress, I need to wash myself.

SIR GAVESTON

Well then, go wash yourself!

DE LONGUEFUGUE

But I can't without soap.

SIR GAVESTON, *going to search in the trunk.*

Fine, I'll loan you mine. It's Mormon soap, so be careful. Here.

DE LONGUEFUGUE

Thank you! Ah, there are my boots! (*He takes Gaveston's boots and exits left.*)

SIR GAVESTON

He's gone, Corpulencia, you can open your eyes.

CORPULENCIA

He's just shameless!

SCENE 8

The same, JULES

JULES, *entering upstage with boots in hand.*

There's a lady downstairs who claims to have written to room 33.

SIR GAVESTON

It's Madame Rubineau.

JULES, *having set the boots down.*

She says she's here to speak with you, monsieur.

SIR GAVESTON

I'm aware.

CORPULENCIA

Would you like me to leave, darling?

SIR GAVESTON

Yes, leave us alone, Corpulencia.

CORPULENCIA

Gladly, my love. (*She exits to the right.*)

SIR GAVESTON, *to Jules.*

Show the lady in.

JULES, *exiting.*

Room 33 is going to welcome another lady! Lucky bastard!

SIR GAVESTON, *alone.*

I can't receive a lady in my slippers. (*He goes to put on De Longuefugue's boots.*) They won't go on! . . . My feet must be swollen from standing too long. There we go! Done! (*He can hardly walk.*)

JULES, *upstage.*

You may enter . . . (*He presents Madame Rubineau and exits.*)

SCENE 9

SIR GAVESTON, MADAME RUBINEAU

MADAME RUBINEAU

Ah, here you are, Cousin Gaveston.

SIR GAVESTON

Madame Rubineau!

MADAME RUBINEAU

How are you this morning?

SIR GAVESTON

Not bad! Apart from my health, which is not very good.

MADAME RUBINEAU

You're unwell?

SIR GAVESTON

Yes, from a night spent in the police station.

MADAME RUBINEAU

I can't express how sorry I am for what happened! To see you, Sir Gaveston, you and your wife and your six daughters, victims of one of these far-too-frequent miscarriages of justice, and taken down to the station!

SIR GAVESTON

You were, too.

MADAME RUBINEAU

Yes, but only for a moment. The peacekeepers realized their error in my case.

SIR GAVESTON

Yes, well, they keep the peace a little too well if you ask me!

MADAME RUBINEAU

I was afraid that you'd never forgive me. But you *are* as kind as you are handsome!

SIR GAVESTON

Madame?

MADAME RUBINEAU

I feel I already know you well. I'm fond of you. I . . . I admire you! I think that we would make a lovely couple, you and I! I always dreamed I'd marry an elegant man like you . . . a distinguished man!

SIR GAVESTON

Yes . . . Would you care to sit down? (*Aside.*) I cannot stay on my feet!

MADAME RUBINEAU, *aside as she sits on the sofa, and Sir Gaveston sits in a chair.*

Is that all he has to say? (*Aloud.*) As lovable as you are, and still young at heart!

SIR GAVESTON

Cousin Rubineau!

MADAME RUBINEAU

Cousin Gaveston!

SIR GAVESTON

How is your second daughter?

MADAME RUBINEAU

But, my dear, I don't have a second daughter.

SIR GAVESTON, *agitatedly standing.*

Good Lord, this hurts! (*He walks in visible pain.*)

MADAME RUBINEAU, *aside.*

Oh no! This is really getting to him! (*Aloud.*) Wait, yes, I do have a second daughter in fact. Now why don't you sit down?

SIR GAVESTON, *sitting down.*

Why don't I ever see her with you?

MADAME RUBINEAU, *uncertain.*

Why? Because . . . because I pensioned her off.

SIR GAVESTON

Pension? At her age?

MADAME RUBINEAU

Yes, well, it's a . . . bourgeois pension. Rue des Martyrs. But let's not talk about her. Come sit a little closer to me. (*Sir Gaveston sits on the sofa.*) I can tell you this, Cousin Gaveston, because I know you . . . I have great affection for you . . . Monsieur Rubineau made me very unhappy! He was unfaithful to me! Have your wives ever been unfaithful to you?

SIR GAVESTON

How's that?

MADAME RUBINEAU

I mean, your six wives have never given you cause to . . . doubt their affections?

SIR GAVESTON

My six wives have never given me anything but my six daughters.

MADAME RUBINEAU, *aside.*

He must not understand French well . . . (*Aloud.*) At any rate, I've decided to divorce him.

SIR GAVESTON

Divorce? You? Oh, you mustn't do that!

MADAME RUBINEAU

I had thought to become a courtesan . . . but someone talked me out of that. And I do want to remain an honest woman.

SIR GAVESTON

You're right to do so! (*Aside.*) I can't stand it anymore!

(*He runs to the back and rips off his boots.*)

MADAME RUBINEAU, *to herself.*

What is he doing? He's taking off his boots! In front of me! Maybe it's an American thing.

SIR GAVESTON, *returning.*

That's better! (*He puts on his slippers.*) Please forgive me, my feet have swollen too large for my shoes.

MADAME RUBINEAU

In my case, it's the heart that's become too large for my bosom.

SIR GAVESTON

Oh. Your heart?

MADAME RUBINEAU

Gaveston, do you find me beautiful?

SIR GAVESTON

I find you attractive . . . for your age.

MADAME RUBINEAU

For my age! Didn't you come to France with the intention of finding a seventh wife?

SIR GAVESTON

Yes.

MADAME RUBINEAU

Well, I'm offering myself to you.

SIR GAVESTON, *taken aback.*

What?

MADAME RUBINEAU

Yes, and as soon as my divorce from that scoundrel is final, I promise to give myself completely to you, Gaveston! Will you have me? Well, answer! I'm waiting!

SIR GAVESTON, *coldly.*

No, I think I'll pass.

MADAME RUBINEAU, *stupefied.*

Why?

SIR GAVESTON

Because I'm only marrying for a seventh time for scientific reasons . . . for repopulation.

MADAME RUBINEAU

For repopulation? Haven't I already proven myself capable of that?

SIR GAVESTON

Excessively! Your capacity might already be spent.

MADAME RUBINEAU, *simpering.*

But think about it; I'm only thirty-nine years old. And besides, it seems to me that it would make a perfect study for a man of science, to discover whether a woman of thirty-nine is as capable as a nineteen-year-old of producing new defenders of the faith.

SIR GAVESTON

I'd rather leave that research to someone else.

MADAME RUBINEAU

So, monsieur would rather have a little tart who doesn't know anything?

SIR GAVESTON

Yes, in fact. I prefer to educate my wives myself.

MADAME RUBINEAU, *vexed.*

I understand. I don't meet your standards.

SIR GAVESTON

I advise you not to divorce.

MADAME RUBINEAU, *coldly.*

Monsieur, you can keep your advice. I respected you! I thought you were different from other men. I thought you were superior. I thought you were worthy of sharing my bed in good times and bad. Clearly I was mistaken. I'll leave you to your shallow ways and depart while I still have my dignity.

SIR GAVESTON

Yes, very good. Take your dignity and go back to your husband. You're not going to do better than him.

MADAME RUBINEAU

We'll see about that.

(*There's a knock upstage.*)

SIR GAVESTON

Come in!

MADAME RUBINEAU, *crying.*

No, don't come in! (*To Gaveston.*) At least wait until we've a little space between us. No need to compromise my reputation.

SIR GAVESTON, *distancing himself from her.*

Fine! You can come in now!

SCENE 10

The same, STEPHANA, AUNT FLORA

STEPHANA

Is this number 33?

SIR GAVESTON

Her! That's her! Your daughter!

MADAME RUBINEAU

That, my daughter?

STEPHANA

That? Well, look at you, Madame Angot![30]

AUNT FLORA

Let me take care of this, niece.

STEPHANA

Be my guest!

AUNT FLORA

Madame, shall we take this outside?

MADAME RUBINEAU

Outside? With you? What for?

AUNT FLORA

Your husband brought disgrace upon my dear child. You contributed in your own way to this moral degradation. So much so, in fact, that in the eyes of this honorable Englishman . . .

SIR GAVESTON

No! American!

AUNT FLORA

It's the same thing. (*Continuing.*) So much so, that in the eyes of Sir Gravestone here, my niece must look like a real strumpet!

SIR GAVESTON

No, not at all!

STEPHANA

Thank you, my dear!

MADAME RUBINEAU

What are you getting at, madame?

AUNT FLORA

At this: that some compensation is in order! Your husband owes it to us, but you hold the purse strings. You and I must come to an agreement on the amount.

MADAME RUBINEAU

Come to an agreement?

STEPHANA

Not here, Aunt! You know how I hate discussing money. Go talk about this somewhere else, you two.

MADAME RUBINEAU, *passing by her.*

And this is the creature that chases me out! So be it! I'm leaving, and you will never hear from me again! (*She exits.*)

STEPHANA

Suits me!

AUNT FLORA

Excuse me, *I* want to hear from her again! She's not getting off that easy! (*She exits upstage.*)

SCENE II

SIR GAVESTON, STEPHANA, then DE LONGUEFUGUE

SIR GAVESTON

So, you definitely are not Madame Rubineau's daughter.

STEPHANA

Madame Rubineau? No! But I might be Monsieur Rubineau's daughter.

SIR GAVESTON

How so?

STEPHANA

My birth has always been shrouded in mystery.

SIR GAVESTON

Mystery?

STEPHANA

Yes! I was found at the foot of the Obelisk just two hours old with an academic medal on my chest.[31]

SIR GAVESTON

Wow! What an honor for such a young a child! (*Aside.*) That was a joke!

STEPHANA

It was obviously my father's medal. It was wrapped in paper on which someone had written: "Stephana, born two hours ago, boulevard Bineau." A little later, when I learned to read, I searched in the *Who's Who of Paris* for all the recipients of the medal who might have lived on that boulevard at the time of my birth. There was only one! Later, I met Monsieur Rubineau and I thought: "*boulevard Bineau* on the one hand, and *rue Bineau* on the other!" A strange coincidence, don't you think? He must be my father!

SIR GAVESTON

My cousin Rubineau was never awarded an academic medal.

STEPHANA

No, but his father was!

SIR GAVESTON

Then he'd be your brother?

STEPHANA

A mystery!

SIR GAVESTON

It is most curious!

DE LONGUEFUGUE, *entering and now wearing a vest and boots.*

Excuse me for interrupting.

SIR GAVESTON

Again?

DE LONGUEFUGUE

You wouldn't by chance have a comb that you could lend me?

SIR GAVESTON

No!

DE LONGUEFUGUE

But I can't go out without combing my hair!

SIR GAVESTON, *aside.*

He is so frustrating! (*He goes to the trunk.*)

DE LONGUEFUGUE, *to himself.*

My boots have gotten bigger.

STEPHANA

What do you know? The journalist from Honfleur!

DE LONGUEFUGUE

If I'm not mistaken, Madame the Countess of Haut-Cassis.

STEPHANA

No, monsieur, you're mistaken.

DE LONGUEFUGUE

Well, that's a first.

SIR GAVESTON, *returning.*

Here is my comb!

DE LONGUEFUGUE

Thank you! (*Saluting.*) Madame la Comtesse. (*Exiting.*) I am swimming in these boots.

SIR GAVESTON

So what is it that brings you here to visit me? (*He invites her to sit on the sofa and sits down next to her.*)

STEPHANA

I just came to see if our wonderful police—the envy of all Europe—had released you and your family.

SIR GAVESTON

Oh yes, as you can see. Everything is taken care of.

STEPHANA

I'm happy to see that the *coppers* released you.

SIR GAVESTON

The *coppers*?

STEPHANA

Yes, it's a British expression. It means peacekeepers.

SIR GAVESTON

Really? I had no idea! Miss, what do you think of me?

STEPHANA

Me? I find you very nice!

SIR GAVESTON

Miss, I have to tell you that, as you say in France, I've got money to burn.

STEPHANA

That's one way to stay warm in winter!

SIR GAVESTON

In summer, too. Miss, would you consider leaving France to live in America?

STEPHANA, *excitedly.*

I love my homeland! But I'd consider leaving if someone made me a serious offer.

SIR GAVESTON

Well, what do you do in France?

STEPHANA

I operate a sewing machine when I have a moment.

SIR GAVESTON

Miss, would you like to come operate a sewing machine in America? Would you like to become the seventh mother to my daughters?

STEPHANA

Milord! What are you saying?

SIR GAVESTON

The truth. Tell me that you love me and that you will be my wife.

STEPHANA

Is that what you want? I love you!

SIR GAVESTON, *after a moment.*

Say it again?

STEPHANA

I love you!

SIR GAVESTON

No. The little jewel didn't buzz.

STEPHANA, *aside.*

Damn!

SIR GAVESTON

If you truly loved me, your heart rate would have increased, and my little machine would have sounded. I withdraw my proposition.

STEPHANA, *aside.*

Oh no!

SIR GAVESTON

I only said it because I believed that you were in love with me.

STEPHANA

But I am in love with you, milord! Your invention must just be blocked by my extreme shyness.

SIR GAVESTON

No!

STEPHANA

Then it must have a bug. It must not be working correctly.

SIR GAVESTON

My invention always works correctly. (*He distances himself from her.*)

STEPHANA, *aside.*

Dammit! (*Noticing the little bell on the table.*) Oh! . . . (*She quickly stuffs it in her pocket and goes to Gaveston.*) Milord, listen to me.

SIR GAVESTON

What do you want?

STEPHANA

My inherent shyness could have momentarily disrupted the chemistry of your tomcat detector, but I've regained my confidence, and I tell you from the bottom of my heart: Gaveston, I love you! (*She rings the bell in her pocket.*)

SIR GAVESTON

It sounded! It sounded! Oh, what joy! You are my seventh wife! And I'm in seventh heaven! Would you permit me to seal our relationship with a little kiss?

STEPHANA, *holding her cheek out to him.*

Seal away!

SCENE 12

The same, CORPULENCIA

CORPULENCIA

Excuse me! I hope I'm not interrupting anything.

SIR GAVESTON

No!

STEPHANA, *aside.*

His wife! She'll claw my eyes out!

SIR GAVESTON

Corpulencia, I present your new companion. What do you think of her?

CORPULENCIA

Very good! Very good! (*Extending a hand to Stephana.*) We'll get along great!

STEPHANA, *to herself.*

This is all so civilized!

CORPULENCIA

Come, let me introduce you to our daughters.

JULES, *entering.*

The Rubineaus are here asking for room 33.

SIR GAVESTON

Show them in!

JULES, *upstage.*

Come in!

SCENE 13

The same, AUGUSTE, RUBINEAU, MADAME RUBINEAU, CHARLOTTE, OSCAR

AUGUSTE

Here we are, Uncle! Mother and Father have come to make the request official.

SIR GAVESTON

Ah! Have they reconciled?

OSCAR

Thanks to me.

(*Stephana and Corpulencia exit to the right.*)

SIR GAVESTON, *to Oscar.*

Thanks to you?

OSCAR

Yes! Mademoiselle Charlotte said she'd kill herself if she couldn't marry me.

CHARLOTTE

And I meant it!

RUBINEAU

Calm yourself, my child!

OSCAR

So, I said to Monsieur and Madame Rubineau: "If you don't get back together, I won't marry your daughter."

MADAME RUBINEAU

So we've gotten back together to save her life.

AUGUSTE

Go on, speak for me, Papa!

RUBINEAU

I'm speaking. My dear . . .

SIR GAVESTON

Forgive me . . . where are the two witnesses?

OSCAR

I'm one.

CHARLOTTE

And I'm the other!

SIR GAVESTON

A woman?

AUGUSTE

That's all I could find: my sister.

RUBINEAU

I told him to ask a stockbroker on the street.

MADAME RUBINEAU

I didn't want to. It would have lacked dignity . . . and it would have cost fifty francs.

SIR GAVESTON

We need males to be witnesses. Our laws don't accept females. We'll have to postpone.

AUGUSTE

You should've said that before!

SCENE 14

The same, DE LONGUEFUGUE

DE LONGUEFUGUE, *entering with his face covered in soap.*

These are definitely not my boots.

SIR GAVESTON, *examining his feet.*

Why, no! Those are mine. Take them off immediately!

RUBINEAU

Forgive me, but not before serving as a witness for my son.

DE LONGUEFUGUE

Witness?

AUGUSTE

Say, that's a great idea!

DE LONGUEFUGUE

I accept, but only on condition that we do it in Belgium.[32]

OSCAR

In Belgium? It's not a duel. It's a marriage proposal. There's going to be a wedding.

DE LONGUEFUGUE

In that case, I accept. Go on, propose . . . but will I have time to change my boots during the proposal?

SIR GAVESTON

Yes. You just need to be here, that's all.

(*De Longuefugue goes to the back to change his boots.*)

AUGUSTE

Go on, Papa!

RUBINEAU

My dear cousin, it is my privilege to ask, on behalf of my son, for the hands of your six daughters, to marry in your country, one every two weeks, according to your traditions.

MADAME RUBINEAU

My poor child, don't you think this is beyond your capabilities?

AUGUSTE

I am your son, Mother!

SIR GAVESTON

My good fellow, I accept. Let me present the six fiancées. (*Going to the door at the right.*) Wives, come present the girls to their fiancé.

OSCAR

Wives? Did he bring the other five?

SCENE 15

The same, STEPHANA, CORPULENCIA, the six daughters

CORPULENCIA, *to Stephana.*

Speak up! It's the last wife who serves as mouthpiece.

STEPHANA

Yes, gladly! Mesdames and Messieurs, I present my six daughters.

OSCAR

Her six daughters!

STEPHANA

Yes, I don't know their names yet, but I will learn them in time.

MADAME RUBINEAU, *aside.*

He passed me over for this Stephana!

SIR GAVESTON, *to his daughters.*

Here is the young man I've chosen to be your husband. What do you think? Respond with modesty. (*The six girls lower their eyes and we hear buzzing from all of their pockets.*)

SCENE 16

The same, AUNT FLORA

AUNT FLORA

My niece! Where's my niece?

STEPHANA

Here I am, Auntie!

AUNT FLORA

I came to tell you that there's a young man at the house . . .

STEPHANA, *stopping her.*

Aunt Flora, let me present my husband . . .

AUNT FLORA

Your husband? You're getting married? Oh, you poor thing! She's lost forever!

SIR GAVESTON

She's coming to live with me in America!

AUNT FLORA

In America? I'll come with you. Maybe I'll marry a negro!

(*Curtain.*)

ACKNOWLEDGMENTS

FROM CORRY

Eugène Labiche (1815–1888), the most prolific and famous of the Boulevard Theater playwrights, wrote 171 of his 175 plays with a co-author. All the plays in this volume, likewise, were written by two authors. This seems to have been done systematically for French operettas and vaudevilles because it made for better, richer, and funnier scripts. The same has certainly been true in my case: working with my co-conspirator and co-translator Christopher Flood has made this a more enjoyable experience and the end product is better, richer, and funnier thanks to his collaboration. Like the protagonist of *Stephana's Jewel*, who received an academic medal as an infant, Chris deserves a medal for all his contributions, for his keen sense of humor, and for putting up with my late-night texts about the project.

This book owes a great deal to Daryl Lee and Heather Belnap. I have been working with them on a broader project on representations of Mormons in French literature, art, and anthropological writings for several years. Many ideas in this book come from that collaboration, and they deserve credit for pointing me toward many of the sources and images cited in the introduction.

FROM CHRIS

Thanks first and foremost to Corry Cropper. He has been a great friend and mentor since I began in the profession, and he continues to be one of my best examples of a dedicated, practical academic professional. I am particularly grateful to Corry for inviting me to work on this project with him. It has been a joy. I likewise express gratitude for the support of our colleagues in the French and Italian Department and the College of Humanities at Brigham Young University.

FROM CORRY AND CHRIS

A special thanks to Rachel Mesch, whose help with the introduction made all the difference, and to Bob Hudson and Steven Nördstrom, who carefully read parts of the manuscript and provided extremely useful feedback. We thank colleagues and students who participated in readings of the translations and helped us work out the orality of the plays. We express appreciation to Brigham Young University's College of Humanities and Department of French and Italian for funding research travel. We thank both Caleb Dame, our student assistant who transcribed *Les Mormons à Paris* and *Berthelier chez les Mormonnes*, and Daniela Seare, also a student, for formatting and editing several of the translations. We are very appreciative, too, of the support from Brigham Young University's Faculty Publishing Service for their helpful editing. Finally, thank you to the entire team at Bucknell University Press for their feedback, professionalism, and support.

NOTES

INTRODUCTION

1. H. Moreno, "Semaine théâtrale: Reprise de *Carmen*," *Le Ménestrel: Journal de musique* 49, no. 22 (April 29, 1883): 171. Susan McClary also mentions the 20-percent statistic and argues that the Opéra Comique expressly catered to the marriage set; see Susan McClary, *Georges Bizet: Carmen* (Cambridge: Cambridge University Press, 1992), 16. See also Lesley A. Wright, "Rewriting a Reception: Thoughts on *Carmen* in Paris, 1883," *Journal of Musicological Research* 28, no. 4 (2009): 284.
2. Pauline de Broglie confirms the importance of marriage interviews at the time in this description of her sister's 1891 engagement: "She was barely eighteen and did not know a soul. My father returned from his club one evening and announced that he had met a suitable young man who would be an acceptable son-in-law. Inquiries were made, *there were two or three interviews, and everything was arranged within a fortnight*. As usual, it was never a question of love." Quoted in Adeline Daumard, "Affaire, amour, affection: Le Mariage dans la société bourgeoise au XIXe siècle," *Romantisme* 68 (1990): 38. Emphasis added.
3. Ludovic Halévy, "La Millième représentation de *Carmen*," *Le Théâtre* 145 (January 1905): 5. Ellipses in original.
4. The Church of Jesus Christ of Latter-day Saints has recently rejected the term Mormon when referring to the church or its members. We want to respect the church's style guide. However, given that the French authors we analyze use the term Mormon as part of their fictional world, and that the word refers to characters and to a largely fictional idea of the church, we use the words Mormon and Mormonism throughout. The four plays in this volume are not the only ones to represent Mormonism in nineteenth-century France. The most notable other examples include: Louis Figuier's 1877 *Les Six parties du monde*, a "scientific" play performed at the Théâtre Cluny (where *Stephana's Jewel* would be performed in 1892) and that features a scene where a French woman marries a Mormon man only to discover she is wife number seven and responsible for raising his thirty-two children; and Philippe Gille's 1890 one-act comedy *Camille*, about a Camille Prélard, a young man who, due to a clerical error at his birth, is officially a woman and can only marry his

American Mormon fiancée when her "twenty-seventh variety Mormon" pastor decrees that she is officially a man. *Camille* was performed at the Comédie Française, France's national theater.

5. The original, handwritten scripts of two of these plays (*Mormons in Paris* and *Berthelier Meets the Mormons*) are in an extensive collection of French plays examined by government censors and now housed in France's Archives Nationales.
6. Rachel Mesch and Masha Belenky, "State of the Union: Marriage in Nineteenth-Century France," *Dix-Neuf* 11, no. 1 (2008): 1–6.
7. Jean Elisabeth Pedersen, *Legislating the French Family: Feminism, Theater, and Republican Politics, 1870–1920* (New Brunswick, NY: Rutgers University Press, 2003), 1.
8. Hippolyte Taine, *Nouveaux essais de critique et d'histoire* (Paris: Hachette, 1865), 299. Taine based his understanding of Mormonism on Jules Rémy's 1860 *Voyage au pays des Mormons.*
9. In *Rabelais and His World*, trans. Hélène Iswolsky (Bloomington: Indiana University Press, 1984), Mikhail Bakhtin writes, "One might say that carnival celebrated temporary liberation from the prevailing truth and from the established order; it marked the suspension of all hierarchies, rank, privileges, norms, and prohibitions" (10).
10. Paul Duplessis, *Les Mormons* (Paris: Alexandre Cadot, 1859), 5:329.
11. Terryl Givens, *The Viper on the Hearth: Mormons, Myths, and the Construction of Heresy* (Oxford: Oxford University Press, 1997), 143.
12. J. Spencer Fluhman, *"A Peculiar People": Anti-Mormonism and the Making of Religion in Nineteenth-Century America* (Chapel Hill: University of North Carolina Press, 2012), 9.
13. W. Paul Reeve, *Religion of a Different Color: Race and the Mormon Struggle for Whiteness* (Oxford: Oxford University Press, 2015), 7.
14. Megan Sanborn Jones, *Performing American Identity in Anti-Mormon Melodrama* (New York: Routledge, 2009), 2.
15. Jones, *Performing American Identity*, 2.
16. Marie d'Agoult, known by her pen name, Daniel Stern, offered one explanation for why the French attitude toward Mormons may have differed from that of their English and German neighbors: "In France, people don't believe in love, we laugh at it; we believe even less in conjugal fidelity. . . . In this matter, the French perspective differs entirely from the sentiment of the Germans who are outraged by us, and that of the English who hold us in contempt." Quoted in Daumard, "Affaire, amour, affection," 38.
17. Duplessis, *Les Mormons*, 3:173.
18. The Latin is from Virgil, *Georgics*, bk. 3, v. 244: "They rush into the flame for love is lord of all." See also Montesquieu's *De l'Esprit des lois* (1758), bk. 16, ch. 3, where he maintains that "in hot climates people have fewer needs; it costs

less to support a wife and children. Therefore, one can have more wives there" (our translation). Edward Said notes that in nineteenth-century France, "the association is clearly made between the Orient and the freedom of licentious sex" (*Orientalism* [New York: Vintage Books, 1994], 190).

19. Alexis de Tocqueville, *Democracy in America* (New York: Alfred A. Knopf, 1980), 2:204.
20. Tocqueville, *Democracy in America*, 2:201.
21. Tocqueville, *Democracy in America*, 1:251.
22. Tocqueville, *Democracy in America*, 1:296.
23. Elisée Reclus, "Le Mormonisme et les Etats-Unis," *Revue des deux mondes* 31 (1862): 890.
24. Victor Fournel, "Les Harems du nouveau monde: Vie des femmes chez les Mormons," *Revue contemporaine et athenaeum français* 27 (September 15, 1856): 628.
25. Fournel, "Les Harems," 629.
26. B. H. Révoil, trans., *Les Harems du nouveau monde: Vie des femmes chez les Mormons*, 2nd ed. (Paris: Michel Lévy Frères, 1869), vii.
27. Révoil, *Les Harems du nouveau monde*, viii.
28. Révoil, *Les Harems du nouveau monde*, viii.
29. Révoil, *Les Harems du nouveau monde*, vi.
30. Révoil, *Les Harems du nouveau monde*, vii.
31. Gérard de Nerval, *Voyage en Orient* (Paris: Calmann Lévy, 1884), 1:87.
32. Said, *Orientalism*, 6.
33. Alfred Naquet, "Le Mariage chez les Mormons," *Le Journal: Quotidien, littéraire, artistique et politique* (April 6, 1893): 1–2.
34. Biographic information on Naquet comes from Jean-Paul Chabaud, *Alfred Naquet: Parlementaire comtadin, père du divorce* (Mazan, France: Etudes Comtadines, 2002).
35. Assemblée nationale, *Annales du Sénat: Débats parlementaires: Session ordinaire de 1884*, 10:1122.
36. Assemblée nationale, *Débats parlementaires*, 10:1004.
37. Assemblée nationale, *Débats parlementaires*, 10:1150. Here is another notable quote from Senator Barthe: "[Naquet] thought that the most efficient way to provide room and board for children abandoned by their fathers was to allow people to live together. Here is what [Naquet wrote in 1869]: 'Can love exist simultaneously between one man and several women and vice versa?' That is polygamy!" (10:1015).
38. Jules Demolliens, "Vitriolons! Vitriolons! Echos de l'année 1880," *La Caricature* 53 (January 1, 1881): 3.
39. G. Rémi, "Le Théâtre et l'dromadaire," *Le Tintamarre* (August 1, 1886): 3.
40. Alfred Naquet, *Le Divorce* (Paris: E. Dentu, 1877), ii–iii.
41. Duplessis, *Les Mormons*, 1:6.

42. Duplessis, *Les Mormons*, 1:7.
43. In the first part of vol. 1 alone, the year 1830 is brought up on pp. 3, 23, 113, and 114. It is looked on disparagingly as the end point of legitimist rule and the beginning of a middle-class reign of mediocrity.
44. Daniel Darc, *Joyeuse vie: Polygamie parisienne* (Paris: Librairie Illustrée, 1886), 12.
45. Darc, *Joyeuse vie*, 13–14.
46. Darc, *Joyeuse vie*, 15.
47. Henri Rochefort, *Retour de la Nouvelle-Calédonie: De Nouméa en Europe* (Paris: Jeanmaire, 1877), 271.
48. Naquet, *Le Divorce*, 21.
49. Henri Second, "Le Surménage," *Le Journal Amusant* 1801 (March 7, 1891): 3. It is worth noting that Louis Leroy, co-author of *Mormons in Paris*, often published in this paper.
50. Second, "Le Surménage," 3.
51. Second, "Le Surménage," 6.
52. Quoted in Karen Offen, *Debating the Woman Question in the French Third Republic 1870–1920* (Cambridge: Cambridge University Press, 2018), 27.
53. Offen, *Debating the Woman Question*, 27.
54. Offen, *Debating the Woman Question*, 27.
55. Laurence Klejman and Florence Rochefort, *L'Egalité en marche: Le Féminisme sous la troisième république* (Paris: Des Femmes, 1989), 48.
56. Quoted in Offen, *Debating the Woman Question*, 15–16.
57. Maria Deraismes, *Oeuvres complètes de Maria Deraismes* (Paris: Félix Alcan, 1896), 327.
58. Deraismes, *Oeuvres complètes*, 328.
59. Quoted in Offen, *Debating the Woman Question*, 17.
60. V. Faneau, "L'Emancipation des femmes," *La Science Sociale: Revue bi-mensuelle du socialisme pratique et rationnel* 4, no. 1 (April 1, 1870): 109.
61. Faneau, "L'Emancipation des femmes," 109.
62. Jules Verne, *Le Tour du monde en 80 jours* (Paris: Hetzel, 1873), 159.
63. Albert Robida, *Voyages très extraordinaires de Saturnin Farandoul dans les 5 ou 6 parties du monde et dans tous les pays connus et meme inconnus de M. Jules Verne* (Paris: Librairie Illustrée, 1879), 168.
64. Robida, *Saturnin Farandoul*, 171–172.
65. Robida, *Vingtième siècle*, 326.
66. Dominique Kalifa, "L'Invention des agences matrimoniales," *L'Histoire* 365 (2011): 79.
67. Kalifa, "L'Invention des agences," 77.
68. Robida, *Saturnin Farandoul*, 173–174.
69. Alfred Maury, "Sectes religieuses au XIXe siècle: Les Irvingiens et les Saints-du-dernier-jour," *Revue des Deux Mondes* 23 (September 1, 1853): 967, 994–995.

70. Robida, *Saturnin Farandoul*, 176.
71. For a discussion of race and Mormons, see Reeve, *Religion of a Different Color.*
72. Jules Rémy, *Voyage au pays des Mormons* (Paris: E. Dentu, 1860), 2:173.
73. Rémy, *Voyage au pays des Mormons*, 2:173–174.
74. Bakhtin, *Rabelais*, 11.
75. Edward Muir, *Ritual in Early Modern Europe* (Cambridge: Cambridge University Press, 1997), 91.
76. Muir, *Ritual in Early Modern Europe*, 91.
77. Olivier Bara has written extensively on vaudeville and French theater in the nineteenth century. His edited volume on the playwright Eugène Labiche is particularly noteworthy. Olivier Bara, Violaine Heyraud, and Jean-Claude Yon, eds., *Les Mondes de Labiche* (Paris: Presses Sorbonne Nouvelle, 2017).
78. Alexandre Dumas *fils*, *Les Femmes qui tuent et les femmes qui votent* (Paris: C. Lévy, 1880), 168.
79. Dumas *fils*, *Les Femmes qui tuent*, 169.
80. M. L. Simonin, "De Washington à San Francisco à travers le continent américain," *Le Tour du monde: nouveau journal de voyages* 27 (1874): 192.
81. Rochefort, *Retour de la Nouvelle-Calédonie*, 247.
82. Rochefort, *Retour de la Nouvelle-Calédonie*, 247.
83. We have recorded some of the music and made it available online at http://MormonsInParis.byu.edu.
84. "Victor Roger," *Le Petit poucet: Journal des concerts militaires* 25, no. 75 (September 13, 1898).
85. Adrien Laroque, *Acteurs et actrices de Paris* (Paris: Aux Bureaux de l'Entr'acte, 1889), 105; Edouard Noël and Edmond Stoullig, *Annales du théâtre* (Paris: Bibliothèque Charpentier, 1892), 395. The latter describes Miss Gallayx's voice in a review of *Stephana's Jewel.*
86. See Alan Baker, *Amateur Musical Societies and Sports Clubs in Provincial France, 1848–1914* (London: Palgrave Macmillan, 2017).

MORMONS IN PARIS

1. "Foreign Affairs," *New York Times*, September 21, 1874, 5.
2. A. de Bragelonne, "Chronique théâtrale," *Le Voleur*, September 18, 1874, 607.
3. Gérôme, "Courrier de Paris," *L'Univers illustré: Journal hebdomadaire*, September 5, 1874, 563.
4. "La Semaine dramatique," *Le Journal des débats politiques et littéraires*, September 14, 1874, 1.
5. Robert Nuay, "Revue dramatique," *La Fantaisie Parisienne: Littérature, théâtre, musique et modes*, August 15, 1874, 8.
6. Louis Leroy, "L'Exposition des impressionnistes," *Le Charivari*, April 25, 1874.
7. *Eugène Labiche: Théâtre* (Paris: Robert Laffont, 1991), I:CXLV.

8. Adeline Daumard, "Affaire, amour, affection: Le mariage dans la société bourgeoise au XIXe siècle," *Romantisme* 68 (1990): 37.
9. "La journée: La mi-carême," *Figaro: Journal non-politique*, March 22, 1873, 3.
10. The cast is not listed in the manuscript; instead it can be found in press coverage. See, for example, *La Liberté*, September 7, 1874, 4.
11. Where possible, we have included first names for actors even though they are rarely listed in scripts or even in the press. We have also followed the nineteenth-century convention of listing actors and actresses separately.
12. Grenier spent nearly his entire acting career at the Théâtre des Variétés (from 1859 to 1875). He died in January 1875 at the age of forty-two, several months after creating the role of Albert in *Mormons in Paris*.
13. According to *Le Figaro*, September 5, 1874, 3, Léonce was slated to play the role of Jonathan but, due to illness, was replaced by Deltombe.
14. Baron, the stage name of Louis Bouchenez, was a fixture of the Parisian musical comedy scene. A bass, he created roles in works by Jacques Offenbach, Eugène Labiche, and Meilhac and Ludovic, among many others.
15. Aline Duval studied acting as a child before appearing in plays at the Théâtre du Palais Royal at the age of eighteen. She performed there for nearly twenty years before moving to the Théâtre des Variétés. Her obituary appeared in the newspaper *Le Temps*, July 22, 1903, 3. She died at age seventy-nine.
16. As mentioned in the introduction, the lyrics to a number of the chorus numbers are neither in the score nor in the script. We have nevertheless indicated where they were to be performed.
17. The manuscript reads, "La maison n'est pas au coin du quai." Translated literally this means "The house isn't at the corner of the quay." It was a common phrase in Parisian advertising at the time and meant that the item in question could not be found just anywhere.
18. Eva uses the English word here and it is, in fact, spelled "schoking" in the manuscript.
19. The *Veau qui tette* (Suckling Calf) restaurant was located at the place du Châtelet in the heart of Paris before being torn down during renovations in the 1850s. See Edouard Fournier, *Chroniques et légendes des rues de Paris* (Paris: E. Dentu, 1864), 160–164.
20. A royal edict of 1685, the Code Noir governed the slave trade in French colonies until slavery was abolished in 1794 and again, after Napoleon reinstated it in 1802, in 1848. In the operetta, Albert's legal expertise will be put to good use, since marriage with no possibility of divorce can be envisioned as a form of slavery.
21. The manuscript here has another line crossed out that reads: "If I have made the idea of indefinite nuptial multiplication bloom . . ."
22. This is very similar to what Joseph Smith, founder of the Church of Jesus Christ of Latter-day Saints, reportedly said as he was taken away to jail

before being killed ("I am calm as a summer's morning; I have a conscience void of offense towards God, and towards all men" [*Doctrine and Covenants* 135:4]). It is unclear how well the playwrights knew the history, but given his other satirical writings about Mormons, Leroy may have been making a conscious reference to Joseph Smith.

23. In nineteenth-century France, the National Guard was largely comprised of members of the middle class and tended to be politically conservative. They were typically mobilized for crises and to help quell public unrest.
24. Here and in several other instances in the play, Eva speaks English.
25. The word "grue" is a double entendre: it means a crane (the long-necked bird) and is slang for a prostitute.
26. A savarin is a rum-soaked cake, usually topped with whipped cream.
27. Potier (1816–1878) composed and accompanied for the Opéra Comique in Paris.
28. In nineteenth-century Paris, maids typically had a small room on the sixth floor of apartment buildings.
29. "A nous deux, maintenant," is the famous last sentence of Honoré de Balzac's novel *Le Père Goriot* (1835). Rastignac shouts it to the city of Paris and to the Parisian society he hopes to conquer.
30. Albert is referencing Beaumarchais's eighteenth-century play *The Marriage of Figaro*, in which Figaro, the servant, challenges the authority of his aristocratic master.
31. An odalisque (mispronounced here by Madame Chamboran) was a member of a Turkish seraglio. Odalisques feature in a number of well-known nineteenth-century French paintings, most notably by Ingres and Delacroix.
32. Dubouloy is attempting to allow Madame Chamboran to save face.
33. At the time it was believed that jaundice stemmed from an excess of anger or emotion. In Emile Zola's *La Fortune des Rougon* (Paris: Gallimard, 1963), we learn that "fear of insurgents" causes one character to be struck with jaundice (1:305). In Alphone Daudet's *Jack* (Paris: Dentu, 1876), the eponymous character's escapade puts another character "in such an angry state that he became jaundiced" (254). And writing to his niece in 1876, Gustave Flaubert refers to someone who was "struck with jaundice after being vexed" (*Correspondance* [Paris: La Pléiade, 2007], 5:138).
34. The lyrics for this chorus are in the conductor's musical score—not in the script.
35. Along with her previous line, Eva is speaking English in the original manuscript.
36. Argenteuil première was a bitter, acidic wine produced near Chatou. See the 1885 collection *Pierres précieuses et pierres fines* (Amsterdam: Van Hokema and Warendorf), 1:654.
37. Mabille was an open-air dance garden on Avenue Montaigne in Paris. It closed the year after *Mormons in Paris* premiered.

38. See this play's foreword for a description of mid-Lent.
39. The original actually references a character from Rossini's opera *The Thieving Magpie* who is falsely accused and condemned for theft.
40. The lines for this chorus are in the musical score—not in the script.
41. The primary court in the center of Paris.
42. The manuscript has the phrase "rue de Suresnes" crossed out here.
43. Sardanapalus is the legendary decadent king of Assyria whose death with his harem was portrayed in a well-known painting by Eugène Delacroix.
44. The manuscript refers to Jonathan as a "gilet rouge," or a "red vest."
45. Batignolles is a suburb near the Parc Monceau on the edge of Paris.
46. Throughout the operetta, Jonathan uses the phrase "water the seed" as a double entendre both for increasing faith and for drinking. In the New Testament, preachers are described as sowers, and the word of God as a seed (see Luke 8:11). The Book of Mormon, first translated into French in 1852, has several extended allegories of planting and "nurturing" seeds. However, Leroy and Delacour use the phrase *arroser le pépin* (literally, "spray the pip") instead of the more traditional *nourrir la semence*, thereby pointing to similarities between Mormon phrases and conventional French religious language while also insisting on humorous differences.

BERTHELIER MEETS THE MORMONS

1. Edouard Noël and Edmond Stoullig, *Les Annales du théâtre et de la musique 1875* (Paris: Charpentier, 1876), 279.
2. Charles de Senneville, "Bénéfice de Berthelier," *La Comédie* (July 15, 1875): 1.
3. Senneville, "Bénéfice de Berthelier," 1–2.
4. Neither the manuscript nor reviews in the press list the attribution of roles.
5. This role was likely created by Louis Bouchenez who went by the stage name Baron (1838–1920) and who played Doubouloy in *Mormons in Paris*. A regular collaborator at the Théâtre des Variétés, he is mentioned as holding the second role by Noël and Stoullig, *Annales du théâtre*, 279. Bouchenez's obituary can be found in *La Presse*, March 2, 1920, 2.
6. "As-tu du cœur?" is a clear reference to *Le Cid*, the well-known seventeenth-century play by Pierre Corneille. In *Le Cid*, Don Diègue wants revenge after suffering an insult and, too old to take up arms himself, gives the responsibility to his son via the famous question, "Rodrigue, do you have heart?" Like Rodrigue and his father, the women in this play seek revenge for affronts they have suffered at the hands of men.
7. As with *Mormons in Paris*, a number of chorus numbers are indicated but the lyrics do not appear in the script.
8. The province of Savoy was annexed by France in 1860. The term *Savoyard*, widely used in nineteenth-century France as an insult, implied a lack of education and culture.

9. The Odéon Theater was (and still is) one of the most distinguished and reputable theaters in Paris. Sarah Bernhardt debuted on its stage.
10. This is a reference to the 1874 play *Mormons in Paris* (also performed at the Variétés), in which a Mormon apostle, who turns out to be a French coachman, is also named Isidore.
11. Léonce and Aline Duval were, along with Berthelier, well-known comedians who worked with Offenbach and frequently performed at the Théâtre des Variétés. Aline Duval played the role of Madame Chamboran in *Mormons in Paris*.
12. Louis-Hyacinthe Duflost, well known for his large nose, performed in comedies at the Théâtre des Variétés and the Palais-Royal in Paris.
13. In this play, long beards become a synecdoche for Mormon men. This conception of Mormon men as long-bearded, domineering, and feckless is confirmed by Robida's caricature of a Mormon man (see the introduction) as a hirsute, if emasculated, leader of female troops. In the play *Japheth's Twelve Wives*, the playwrights insist on the similarities between Smith, a Mormon pastor, and Cassoulet, the character who runs a marriage agency, so Mormons are clean-shaven in that play, thereby reducing the difference between the French and Mormon characters.
14. The musical score indicates that a short musical passage was performed during Berthelier's "initiation."
15. The following line has been crossed out of the manuscript: "in the quiet of our dressing room, and we have all added our signatures." The use of the word "signatures"—along with the use of the word "code" that remains in the play—underscores the legal and political aspect of the wives' uprising. The musical score indicates that the code was sung by the women.
16. This list of demands, though more militant and legalistic, may have reminded theatergoers of an old French play, *La Farce du cuvier*. In this medieval farce, Jacquinot's wife and mother-in-law give him a long list of duties to perform around the house. When his wife falls into the *cuvier*, a large laundry tub, Jacquinot refuses to save her under the pretext that pulling her from a *cuvier* is not on his list of chores. Once she agrees to let him live in peace as master of the house, he saves her from drowning. Like *Berthelier Meets the Mormons*, the farce is about gender relations and roles. Unlike the farce, the women in *Berthelier* succeed in overcoming the most egregious abuses of domestic power.
17. The manuscript shows that the Italian Barbarini was initially meant to be an Alsatian named Fortunia.
18. The manuscript reads, "un rôle de huit cents," meaning a role with eight hundred verses. In other words, Berthelier would prefer a tedious rehearsal to the situation in which he finds himself.
19. Here the manuscript has the following sentence crossed out: "I have the hair, the voice, and the nose of a man."

20. Berthelier means that he is prepared to vandalize streetlights so that the rebellion can be carried out in darkness.
21. The original reads, "saxotromba," which is a low-brass instrument with an upward-pointing bell widely used in French military bands in the nineteenth century.
22. The French press covered the granting of suffrage to women in Utah in 1870. On July 6, 1870, the *Journal amusant* published a cartoon featuring an armed militia of Mormon women and an emaciated and emasculated man holding a broom (see the image in the introduction). The play takes that imagery up here, presenting a militia of armed women who resist the established male order.
23. The manuscript indicates that this is a *Tyrolienne*, or a country folk song.
24. While crinoline dresses may seem cumbersome to modern eyes, they were considered liberating for women in nineteenth-century Europe. They freed women from the heavy layers that characterized dresses from earlier decades and allowed them to walk and move with less restraint. These Mormon rebels have adopted the crinoline as their standard, a symbol of their newfound freedom.
25. The work of urban planner Georges-Eugène Haussmann was ongoing, leaving many of Paris's districts under what seemed constant construction.
26. A Parisian theater where Offenbach premiered some of his comic operas.

JAPHETH'S TWELVE WIVES

1. H. Moreno, "Semaine théâtrale," *Le Ménestrel: Journal du monde musical, musique et théâtres* 56, no. 51 (December 21, 1890): 402–403.
2. A review of the play at the Eldorado: Petitban, "La soirée d'hier," *La Justice*, no. 6279 (March 22, 1897): 2; a note about the staging in Austria: "Vienne," *Le Monde Artiste: Théâtre, musique, beaux-arts, littérature* (October 31, 1897): 699.
3. Paul-Emile Chevalier, "Semaine théâtrale," *Le Ménestrel: journal du monde musical, musique et théâtres* 63, no. 12 (March 21, 1897): 91.
4. "Lille," *Comœdia*, no. 414 (November 17, 1908): 4.
5. Richard O'Monroy, *La Soirée parisienne* (Paris: P. Arnould, 1890–1891), 2: 337–339.
6. In addition to *Japheth's Twelve Wives*, the duo wrote the following operettas together: *La Demoiselle du téléphone* (The Young Woman on the Telephone, 1891), *Le Truc de Séraphin* (Séraphin's Thing, 1896), *Mam'zelle quat'sous* (Miss Two Bits, 1897), *Le Fils à papa* (Daddy's Boy, 1906), *La Chaste Suzanne* (Chaste Suzanne, 1913),
7. Dominique Kalifa and Pierre Karila-Cohen, eds., *Le Commissaire de police au XIXe siècle* (Paris: Publications de la Sorbonne, 2008), 8.
8. Kalifa and Karila-Cohen, *Le Commissaire*, 12–13.
9. Kalifa, "L'Invention des agences," 79.

10. Kalifa, "L'Invention des agences," 76.
11. Kalifa, "L'Invention des agences," 77.
12. Kalifa, "L'Invention des agences," 77–78.
13. Kalifa, "L'Invention des agences," 76.
14. Gildès also directed the play.
15. It is worth mentioning that cast photos show Mr. Smith as beardless. In *Berthelier* the beards of Mormon men are underscored to distinguish Mormons from Berthelier. Here, the Mormon men are beardless, underscoring a conflation of the Mormons with the clean-shaven French characters.
16. A village just west of Paris also mentioned in *Stephana's Jewel.*
17. The original French here ("Après m'être trouvé dépourvu, lorsque la bise fut venue") is nearly an exact quote of Lafontaine's seventeenth-century version of the ant and the grasshopper fable. Like the grasshopper (or cicada in Lafontaine), Des Toupettes played and sang until all his money was gone and now finds himself obliged to work.
18. There were a number of "Folies," or theaters that featured variety performances, dancing, and operetta, in nineteenth-century Paris.
19. Extremely popular in the nineteenth century, cafés-concerts were halls where people could eat, drink, and smoke while watching shows that almost always featured singing. See Elisabeth Pillet, "Cafés-concerts et cabarets," *Romantisme* 75 (1992): 43–50.
20. Sean Quinlan, in his book *The Great Nation in Decline: Sex, Modernity and Health Crises in Revolutionary France, c. 1750–1850* (London: Ashgate, 2007), points to stagnating birthrates after the Franco-Prussian War and remarks that "*fin-de-siècle* activists wanted to increase fertility across the board—and by any means possible" (217). The preoccupation with birthrate and fertility, expressed in this play and in *Stephana's Jewel*, also shows up in the works of other authors from the period, notably in the stories of Guy de Maupassant (see Sara Phenix, "The Novel in a Corset: Maupassant, Monsters, and the Short Story" [*Nineteenth-Century French Studies*, 51.1–2 (Fall–Winter 2021–2022)]).
21. A character in Perrault's late seventeenth-century fairytale *La Barbe bleue*, Anne, watches from a tower for her brothers to come rescue her sister but sees nothing, repeating the well-known phrase, "Je ne vois rien que le soleil qui poudroie, et l'herbe qui verdoie" ("I see nothing but the shimmering sun and the green grass").
22. A Catholic hymn of thanksgiving that was never part of Mormon worship. Having Mormon wives sing the *Benedicite* further serves to connect them to their French audience.
23. Paris hosted the World's Fair in 1889. The Eiffel Tower was constructed especially for the event.
24. A well-known nineteenth-century eatery built around and sometimes in trees in the Parisian suburb Le Plessis-Robinson.

25. A reference to the moment Napoleon bid farewell to his troops at the Fontainebleau château in 1814.
26. Érard grand pianos were played by musical luminaries like Liszt, Chopin, Fauré, Beethoven, and others.
27. Dutch Tops is a tabletop game where contestants attempt to knock down pawns using spinning tops.
28. The artist Jean-Louis Ernest Meissonier was best known for his military paintings.
29. A neighborhood in Paris's sixteenth arrondissement.
30. Lecoq is a fictional police inspector created by French novelist Emile Gaboriau in *L'Affaire Lerouge* (1865).
31. In the French Republic, marriages were—and still are—conducted by mayors.
32. Cassoulet is a traditional stew from southern France made from white beans and pork.
33. An 1836 opera by Giacomo Meyerbeer, libretto by Eugène Scribe and Emile Deschamps.
34. The Gaîté-Lyrique Theater in Paris's third arrondissement.
35. Cassoulet describes himself as if he were Franz Liszt: fans in mid-century Paris swooned over Liszt, fought over his gloves, and tried to grab locks of his hair.
36. Lines from Meyerbeer's 1831 opera *Robert le diable*, libretto by Eugène Scribe and Germain Delavigne.
37. As mentioned in the introduction, marriage agents typically collected between 5 and 10 percent of the dowry (Kalifa, "L'Invention des agences," 77).
38. Louis-Philippe was king of the French from 1830 to 1848.
39. A horse race held at the Longchamp track since 1863.
40. The original reads, "I'll cover Saint Catherine," an expression usually reserved for women who turn twenty-five without marrying.
41. Popular nightclubs in Paris.
42. These are lines from another musical comedy, *Le Petit de la rue du Ponceau*, by Edouard Martin and Albert Monnier, performed in 1864 at the Théâtre des Variétés (act I, scene 13).
43. Since horses typically weigh about five hundred kilos, this likely reflects the handicap weight.
44. A *louis* or *Louis d'or* was a gold coin equivalent to twenty francs.

STEPHANA'S JEWEL

1. Adeline Daumard, "Affaire, amour, affection: le mariage dans la société bourgeoise au XIXe siècle," *Romantisme* 68 (1990): 37.
2. The newspaper *Le Petit parisien* ("Courrier des théâtres") announced on July 23, 1892, p. 3, that the Théâtre Cluny was considering another play to replace *Stephana's Jewel* in September.

3. "Les Théâtres," *Le Rappel*, no. 8158 (July 11, 1892): 2.
4. Willy, *Soirées perdues* (Paris: Tresse et Stock, 1894), 254.
5. Hippolyte Lemaire, "Théâtres," *Le Monde illustré* 36, no. 1842 (July 16, 1892): 42.
6. Lemaire, "Théâtres," 42.
7. Willy, *Soirées perdues*, 253.
8. Marguerite Gallayx would go on to become a regular performer at the prestigious Théâtre du Gymanse.
9. Lureau was a member of the troupe at Théâtre Cluny from 1885 until his death at age sixty-seven in 1908. See his obituary in the newspaper *Le Temps* (May 27, 1908): 3.
10. The author puns on the homophony "mal de mer," seasickness, and "mal de mère," pregnancy morning sickness.
11. The Comédie Française is the oldest state theater in France, founded in 1680.
12. *La Dame blanche* is an 1825 comic opera by François-Adrien Boieldieu based on some gothic works by Walter Scott. One of the main characters is a deceitful steward named Gaveston.
13. The Auvergne region was considered something of a foreign country in nineteenth-century France.
14. Bougival is a community near Paris that is also mentioned in *Japheth's Twelve Wives* (act I, scene 2).
15. *La Favorite* is an 1840 grand opera by Gaetano Donizetti with a French libretto by Alphonse Royer and Gustave Vaëz. It recounts the story of a love triangle involving the king of Castile.
16. *Robert le Diable* is an 1831 opera by Giacomo Meyerbeer with a French libretto by Eugène Scribe and Germain Delavigne. The line sung by Flora comes from the finale of the first act where the protagonist gambles away his love in a game of dice with fellow knights.
17. The exact nature of Oscar and Stephana's relationship is unclear. This might represent an alimony payment if they were married, which some later dialogue seems to indicate. See note 20.
18. This variant of the card game Bezique was described by Alphonse Daudet in his *Les Rois en exil* as an easy way to lose vast sums of money.
19. The original French reads "belle-mère de la main gauche." The phrase "mariage de la main gauche" is traditionally used to describe an illegitimate relationship, like that between a sovereign and a concubine. Stephana is describing her possible relationship to Oscar as the mistress of his future father-in-law.
20. The script implies that Oscar and Stephana have been previously married. Stephana complains that Oscar is attempting to marry "without my consent" and without providing "the customary notice" (I.2). She then threatens to appeal to a judge if Oscar doesn't pay her a reasonable amount (I.3). See the

section "Staging Hypocrisy" in the introduction for a discussion of divorce in this play.

21. "Avoir des cornes," to have horns, was a traditional epithet for a cuckolded husband.
22. Alcibiades was a prominent Athenian statesman and military leader. He is depicted in several of Plato's Socratic dialogues as an ambitious former student of Socrates whose accusations play a role in his teacher's trial.
23. A *louis* or *Louis d'or* was a gold coin equivalent to twenty francs.
24. In the original, Auguste suddenly switches to the familiar "tu" form rather than "vous" as he tells Stephana again that he loves her. She asks him not to use "tu" with her, conspicuously addressing him in the "tu" form to do it.
25. *Phèdre* (1677) is a French tragedy by Jean Racine based on Greek mythology in which the title character fatally falls in love with her stepson and eventually commits suicide after confessing to her husband. The Odéon, completed in 1782 and originally intended to house the Comédie-Française, is one of the six national theaters in Paris.
26. *L'Africaine* is a grand opera by Giacomo Meyerbeer; it was first performed in 1865 after the composer's death. This line comes from act 1, scene 3.
27. An 1890 operetta by Edmond Audran and Maxime Boucheron.
28. Almehs were female courtesans and performers in Egypt. The term became synonymous with belly dancers in nineteenth-century France.
29. In the late nineteenth century, the Moulin Rouge included a garden party area that featured a larger-than-life elephant statue with a stage attached to it where dancers would perform. The dancers would appear to descend from the elephant's belly onto the stage.
30. *La fille de Madame Angot* is an 1872 comic opera by Charles Lecocq, Clairville, Paul Siraudin, and Victor Koning. Madame Angot was a market woman known for her beauty, loose morals, and sharp tongue.
31. Instituted in 1808, the Ordre des Palmes Académiques recognizes scholars for their academic contributions.
32. De Longuefugue is assuming that he's being asked to witness a duel. While duels had been outlawed in France since 1626 (under the reign of Louis XIII), the nineteenth century saw an increase in such contests. A common practice to avoid prosecution was to carry them out in a neighboring country, like Belgium.

BIBLIOGRAPHY

Anonyme. *La Farce du Cuvier.* Paris: Flammarion, 2017.

Atelier Nadar. *Berthelier. Nouveautés.* 1875–1895. Albumen print, 14.5 cm × 10.5 cm. Bibliothèque nationale de France. https://gallica.bnf.fr/ark:/12148/btv1b53148469h.

———. *Mr Regnard [Groupe. Renaissance]. Les Douze Femmes de Japhet: [Photographie, Tirage de Démonstration].* 1890. Albumen print, 10.5 cm × 14.5 cm. https://gallica.bnf.fr/ark:/12148/btv1b531647871.

Audran, Edmond, and Maxime Boucheron. *Miss Helyett* (operetta), 1890.

Baker, Alan. *Amateur Musical Societies and Sports Clubs in Provincial France, 1848–1914: Harmony and Hostility.* Cham, Switzerland: Palgrave Macmillan, 2017.

Bakhtin, Mikhail. *Rabelais and His World.* Translated by Hélène Iswolsky. First Midland book edition. Bloomington: Indiana University Press, 1984.

Balzac, Honoré de. *Le père Goriot.* Paris: Gallimard, 2000.

Bara, Olivier, Violaine Heyraud, and Jean-Claude Yon, eds. *Les Mondes de Labiche.* Paris: Presses Sorbonne nouvelle, 2017.

"Baron Est Mort." *La Presse.* March 2, 1920. https://gallica.bnf.fr/ark:/12148/bpt6k5999327.

Beaumarchais, Pierre Augustin Caron de. "Le Mariage de Figaro." In *Œuvres*, edited by Pierre Henri Larthomas and Jacqueline Larthomas. Bibliothèque de la Pléiade 22. Paris: Gallimard, 1988.

Boieldieu, François-Adrien, and Eugène Scribe. *La Dame blanche* (opéra comique), 1825.

The Book of Mormon, the Doctrine and Covenants, the Pearl of Great Price. The Church of Jesus Christ of Latter-day Saints, 2012.

Bragelonne, A. de. "Chronique théâtrale." *Le Voleur illustré: Cabinet de lecture*. September 18, 1874. https://gallica.bnf.fr/ark:/12148/bpt6k6370135d.

Chabaud, Jean-Paul. *Alfred Naquet, 1834–1916: Parlementaire comtadin, père du divorce*. Mazan: Etudes comtadines, 2002.

Chevalier, Paul-Emile. "Semaine théâtrale." *Le Ménestrel: Journal du monde musical, musique et théâtres*, March 21, 1897. https://gallica.bnf.fr/ark:/12148/bpt6k5615572g.

Corneille, Pierre. "Le Cid." In *Œuvres complètes*, edited by Georges Couton. Vol. 1 of 3. Bibliothèque de la Pléiade 19. Paris: Gallimard, 2003.

"Courrier des théâtres." *Le Figaro: Journal non-politique*, September 5, 1874. https://gallica.bnf.fr/ark:/12148/bpt6k275333j.

"Courrier des théâtres." *Petit parisien*, July 23, 1892. https://gallica.bnf.fr/ark:/12148/bpt6k516428v.

Darc, Daniel. *Joyeuse vie: Polygamie parisienne*. Paris: Librairie illustrée, 1886. https://gallica.bnf.fr/ark:/12148/bpt6k96014140.

Daudet, Alphonse. "Jack." In *Oeuvres*. Vol. 2 of 2. Bibliothèque de La Pléiade 370. Paris: Gallimard, 1990.

———. "Les Rois en exil." In *Oeuvres*. Vol. 2 of 2. Bibliothèque de La Pléiade 370. Paris: Gallimard, 1990.

Daumard, Adeline. "Affaire, amour, affection: Le Mariage dans la société bourgeoise au XIXe siècle." *Romantisme* 20, no. 68 (1990): 33–47.

Delacroix, Eugène. *La Mort de Sardanapale*. 1827. Oil on canvas, 392 cm × 496 cm. Louvre.

Demolliens, Jules. "Vitriolons! Vitriolons! Echos de l'année 1880." *La Caricature*, January 1, 1881. https://gallica.bnf.fr/ark:/12148/bpt6k5700761s.

Deraismes, Maria. *Oeuvres complètes de Maria Deraismes. Nos principes et nos moeurs. L'ancien devant le nouveau*. Paris: Félix Alcan, 1896. https://gallica.bnf.fr/ark:/12148/bpt6k1657599.

Donizetti, Gaetano, Alphonse Royer, and Gustave Vaëz. *La Favorite* (grand opera), 1840.

Dumas, Alexandre *fils*. *Les Femmes qui tuent et les femmes qui votent*. Paris: Calmann Lévy, 1880. https://gallica.bnf.fr/ark:/12148/bpt6k37275q.

Duplessis, Paul. *Les Mormons*. Vol. 5 of 5. Paris: Alexandre Cadot, 1859.

Faneau, V. "L'Emancipation des femmes." *La Science sociale: Revue bi-mensuelle du socialisme pratique et rationnel* 4, no. 1 (April 1, 1870).

Figuier, Louis. *La Science au théâtre*. Paris: Stresse et Stock, 1889. https://gallica.bnf.fr/ark:/12148/bpt6k54919v

Flaubert, Gustave. *Correspondance*. Vol. 5 of 5. Paris: La Pléiade, 2007.

Fluhman, J. Spencer. *A Peculiar People*. Chapel Hill: University of North Carolina Press, 2012.

"Foreign Affairs." *New York Times*, September 21, 1874. https://timesmachine.nytimes.com/timesmachine/1874/09/21/86345512.pdf.

Fournel, Victor. "Les Harems du nouveau monde: Vie chez les Mormons." *Revue contemporaine et athenaeum français* 27 (September 15, 1856).

Fournier, Édouard. *Chroniques et légendes des rues de Paris*. Paris: E. Dentu, 1864. https://gallica.bnf.fr/ark:/12148/bpt6k2029403.

France Assemblée Nationales. *Annales du Sénat: Débats parlementaires: Session ordinaire de 1884*. Vol. 10 of 170. Paris: Imprimerie du journal officiel, 1884.

Gaboriau, Emile. *L'affaire Lerouge*. Paris: Dentu, 1865. http://www.gutenberg.org/ebooks/15579.

Gérôme. "Courrier de Paris." *L'Univers illustré: Journal hebdomadaire*, September 5, 1874. https://gallica.bnf.fr/ark:/12148/bpt6k5735622q.

Gille, Philippe. *Camille: Comédie en un acte*. Paris: Calmann Lévy, 1890. https://gallica.bnf.fr/ark:/12148/bpt6k58132084

Givens, Terryl. *The Viper on the Hearth*. New York: Oxford University Press, 2013.

Halévy, Ludovic. "La Millième représentation de Carmen." *Le Théâtre*, January 1905.

Jones, Megan Sanborn. *Performing American Identity in Anti-Mormon Melodrama*. New York: Routledge, 2009.

Kalifa, Dominique. "L'Invention des agences matrimoniales." *L'Histoire* 6, no. 365 (June 2011): 76–79. https://www.lhistoire.fr/linvention-des-agences-matrimoniales.

Kalifa, Dominique, and Pierre Karila-Cohen. *Le Commissaire de police au XIXe siècle*. Paris: Publications de la Sorbonne, 2008.

Klejman, Laurence, and Florence Rochefort. *L'Egalité en marche: Le féminisme sous la troisième république*. Paris: Des Femmes, 1989.

Labiche, Eugène. *Théâtre*. Edited by Jacques Robichez. Vol. 1 of 2. Paris: R. Laffont, 1991.

"La Journée: La mi-carême." *Le Figaro: Journal non-politique*, March 22, 1873. https://gallica.bnf.fr/ark:/12148/bpt6k2748134.

Laroque, Adrien. *Acteurs et actrices de Paris*. Paris: Aux Bureaux de l'Entr'acte, 1889.

"La Semaine dramatique." *Le Journal des débats politiques et littéraires*, September 14, 1874. https://gallica.bnf.fr/ark:/12148/bpt6k4591151.

"La Soirée d'hier." *La Justice*, March 22, 1897. https://gallica.bnf.fr/ark:/12148/bpt6k8244340.

Lecocq, Charles, Clairville, Paul Siraudin, and Victor Koning. *La Fille de Madame Angot* (opéra comique), 1872.

Lemaire, Hippolyte. "Théâtres." *Le Monde illustré*, July 16, 1892. https://gallica.bnf.fr/ark:/12148/bpt6k63831027.

Leroy, Louis. "L'Exposition des impressionnistes." *Le Charivari*, April 25, 1874. https://www.spectacles-selection.com/archives/expositions/fiche_expo_I/impression-soleil-levant-V/charivari/le-charivari.htm.

"Les Théâtres." *Le Rappel*, July 11, 1892. https://gallica.bnf.fr/ark:/12148/bpt6k7544915h.

"Lille." *Comœdia*, November 17, 1908, no. 414. https://gallica.bnf.fr/ark:/12148/bpt6k76460670.

Martin, Édouard, and Albert Monnier. *Le Petit de la rue du Ponceau*. Paris: E. Dentu, 1864.

Maury, Alfred. "Sectes religieuses au XIXe siècle: Les Irvingiens et les Saints-du-dernier-jour." *Revue des deux mondes* 23 (September 1, 1853).

McClary, Susan. *Georges Bizet, Carmen*. Cambridge: Cambridge University Press, 1992.

Mesch, Rachel, and Masha Belenky. "State of the Union: Marriage in Nineteenth-Century France." *Dix-Neuf* 11, no. 1 (November 1, 2008): 1–6.

Meyerbeer, Giacomo, and Eugène Scribe. *L'Africaine* (grand opera), 1865.

Meyerbeer, Giacomo, Eugène Scribe, and Germain Delavigne. *Robert Le Diable* (opera), 1831.

Meyerbeer, Giacomo, Eugène Scribe, and Émile Deschamps. *Les Huguenots* (opera), 1836.

Montesquieu, Charles Louis de Secondat de, and Roger Caillois. *Œuvres complètes*. Vol. 2 of 2. Nouv. éd. Bibliothèque de la Pléiade 86. Paris: Gallimard, 2008.

Moreno, H. "Semaine théâtrale." *Le Ménestrel: Journal du monde musical, musique et théâtres*, December 21, 1890. https://gallica.bnf.fr/ark:/12148/bpt6k5614488p.

———. "Semaine théâtrale: Reprise de Carmen." *Le Ménestrel: Journal du monde musical, musique et théâtres*, April 29, 1883. https://gallica.bnf.fr/ark:/12148/bpt6k5614488p.

Muir, Edward. *Ritual in Early Modern Europe*. 2nd ed. *New Approaches to European History*. Cambridge: Cambridge University Press, 2005.

Naquet, Alfred. *Le Divorce*. Paris: E. Dentu, 1877.

Nerval, Gérard de. *Voyage en Orient*. Vol. 1 of 2. Paris: Calmann Lévy, 1884.

Noël, Édouard, and Edmond Stoullig. *Les Annales du théâtre et de la musique: Première année 1875*. Paris: Charpentier et Cie., 1876. https://gallica.bnf.fr/ark:/12148/bpt6k54949s.

———. *Les Annales du théâtre et de la musique: Première année 1892*. Paris: Charpentier et Cie., 1893. https://gallica.bnf.fr/ark:/12148/bpt6k616870.

Nuay, Robert. "Revue dramatique." *La Fantaisie parisienne: Littérature, théâtre, musique et modes*, August 15, 1874. https://gallica.bnf.fr/ark:/12148/bpt6k5403633b.

Offen, Karen. *Debating the Woman Question in the French Third Republic 1870–1920*. Cambridge: Cambridge University Press, 2018.

O'Monroy, Richard. *La Soirée parisienne*. Vol. 2 of 2. Paris: Paul Arnould, 1890. https://gallica.bnf.fr/ark:/12148/bpt6k111804p.

Pedersen, Jean Elisabeth. *Legislating the French Family*. New Brunswick, NJ: Rutgers University Press, 2003.

Perrault, Charles. "La Barbe bleue." In *Les Contes de Perrault illustrés par Gustave Doré*. Paris: J. Hetzel, 1864.

Phenix, Sara. "The Novel in a Corset: Maupassant, Monsters, and the Short Story." *Nineteenth-Century French Studies* 51, nos. 1–2 (Fall–Winter 2021–2022).

Pierres précieuses et pierres fines. Amsterdam: Van Hokema and Warendorf, 1885.

Pillet, Elisabeth. "Cafés-concerts et cabarets." *Romantisme* 22, no. 75 (1992): 43–50.

"Programme des spectacles du 6 septembre 1874." *La Liberté*, September 7, 1874. https://gallica.bnf.fr/ark:/12148/bpt6k4779586f.

Quinlan, Sean M. *The Great Nation in Decline: Sex, Modernity and Health Crises in Revolutionary France c. 1750–1850*. Aldershot, UK: Ashgate, 2007.

Racine, Jean. "Phèdre." In *Œuvres Complètes*, edited by Georges Forestier. Vol. 1 of 2. Bibliothèque de La Pléiade 5. Paris: Gallimard, 1999.

Reclus, Elisée. "Le Mormonisme et les Etats-Unis." *Revue des deux mondes* 31 (1862).

Reeve, W. Paul. *Religion of a Different Color*. New York: Oxford University Press, 2015.

Rémi, G. "Le Théâtre et l'dromadaire." *Le Tintamarre*, August 1, 1886.

Rémy, Jules. *Voyage au pays des Mormons*. Vol. 2 of 2. Paris: E. Dentu, 1860.

Révoil, B. H. *Les Harems du nouveau monde: Vie des femmes chez les Mormons*. 2nd ed. Paris: Michel Lévy Frères, 1869.

Robida, Albert. *Le Vingtième siècle*. Paris: G. Decaux, 1883.

———. *Nouvelles du Grand Lac Salé*. March 16, 1870. Cartoon. https://gallica.bnf.fr/ark:/12148/bpt6k5861280m.

———. *Voyages très extraordinaires de Saturnin Farandoul dans les 5 ou 6 parties du monde et dans tous les pays connus et même inconnus de M. Jules Verne*. Paris: Librairie illustrée, 1879.

Rochefort, Henri. *Retour de la Nouvelle-Calédonie: De Nouméa en Europe*. Paris: Jeanmaire, 1877.

Rossini, Gioachinno, and Giovanni Gherardini. *La Gazza Ladra* (opera semiseria), 1817.

Said, Edward W. *Orientalism*. New York: Vintage Books, 1994.

Second, Henri. "Le Surménage." *Le Journal amusant*, March 7, 1891. https://gallica.bnf.fr/ark:/12148/bpt6k5519412v.

Simonin, M. L. "De Washington à San Francisco à travers le continent américain." *Le Tour du monde: Nouveau journal de voyages* 27 (1874).

Taine, Hippolyte. *Nouveaux essais de critique et d'histoire*. Paris: Hachette, 1865.

Th. de La Renaissance. Les Douze femmes de Japhet, musique de Victor Roger. Vaudeville-Opérette de M.M. Antony Mars et Maurice Desvallières: Paris—Au Ménestrel, 2 Bis Rue Vivienne. 1891. Poster, 80 × 60 cm. Bibliothèque nationale de France. https://gallica.bnf.fr/ark:/12148/btv1b9008821q.

"Théâtres." *Le Temps*, July 22, 1903. https://gallica.bnf.fr/ark:/12148/bpt6k2375692.

"Théâtres." *Le Temps*, May 27, 1908. https://gallica.bnf.fr/ark:/12148/bpt6k2393808.

Tocqueville, Alexis de. *Democracy in America*. 2 vols. New York: Alfred A. Knopf, 1980.

Verne, Jules. *Le Tour du monde en 80 jours*. Paris: Hetzel, 1873.

"Victor Roger." *Le Petit Poucet: Journal des concerts militaires* 25, no. 75 (September 13, 1898).

"Vienne." *Le Monde artiste: Théâtre, musique, beaux-arts, littérature*, October 31, 1897. https://gallica.bnf.fr/ark:/12148/bpt6k5454120p.

Virgil. *Georgics*. Translated by H. Rushton Fairclough. Loeb Classical Library. Cambridge, MA: Harvard University Press, 1916.

Willy. *Soirées perdues*. Paris: Tresse & Stock, 1894. https://gallica.bnf.fr/ark:/12148/bpt6k56273377.

Wright, Lesley A. "Rewriting a Reception: Thoughts on Carmen in Paris, 1883." *Journal of Musicological Research* 28, no. 4 (October 27, 2009): 282–294.

Zola, Émile. *Les Rougon-Macquart: histoire naturelle et sociale d' une famille sous le second Empire*, edited by Armand Lanoux and Henri Mitterand. Vol. 1 of 5. Bibliothèque de la Pléiade 146. Paris: Gallimard, 2018.

INDEX

ABOUT THE EDITORS

Corry Cropper is a professor of French at Brigham Young University. His book, *Playing at Monarchy: Sport as Metaphor in Nineteenth-Century France*, examines French literary representations of sports and games. He has also published on nineteenth-century Fantastic literature, and on cycling, gambling, and poaching in French fiction.

Christopher M. Flood is an assistant professor of French at Brigham Young University. His research focuses on the unique insights offered by comedies and satires into the contexts that produced them. He has previously published on medieval and early modern political and religious satires.